DATE DUE

JA 31 '97			
JE 10 '00			
MR 21 01			
AP 16 '01			
MY 8 01			
MY 2 0 '01			
MR 22 02			
DE 5 '02			
AP 21 '03			
JY 3 0 03			
JY 3 0 03			
FE 9 '05			
AP 0 10			

DEMCO 38-296

MACHIAVELLI'S
THREE ROMES

VICKIE B. SULLIVAN

MACHIAVELLI'S THREE ROMES

RELIGION, HUMAN LIBERTY, AND POLITICS REFORMED

🏛 *Northern Illinois University Press*   *DeKalb 1996*

© 1996 by Northern Illinois University Press

inois University Press,
60115

tes using acid-free paper
ı Gibson

ng-in-Publication Data
Sullivan, Vickie B.
Machiavelli's three Romes :
religion, human liberty, and politics reformed /
Vickie B. Sullivan.
p.   cm.
Includes bibliographical references and index.
ISBN 0-87580-213-3 (alk. paper)
1. Machiavelli, Niccolò, 1469–1527—Contributions in political science.
2. Machiavelli, Niccolò, 1469–1527—Views on Christianity.
3. Catholic Church—Controversial literature. 4. Liberty.
I. Title.
JC143.M4S85   1996
320.1'092—dc20   96-10830
CIP

Excerpts taken from *Machiavelli's Discourses on Livy*,
translated by Harvey C. Mansfield and Nathan Tarcov
(University of Chicago Press, copyright 1996), and *The Prince*,
translated by Harvey C. Mansfield (University of Chicago Press,
copyright 1985), are used with permission of the publisher.

TO THE MEMORY OF MY MOTHER

CONTENTS

ACKNOWLEDGMENTS

The first debt that I incurred in the preparation of this book is to Catherine and Michael Zuckert, who introduced me to Machiavelli's political works in a course devoted to his thought that they taught at Carleton College. From my seminar paper, through my dissertation, to the manuscript of this book, they have been most generous readers, helping a student to make arguments with which they have not always agreed. Only now do I feel as though I have answered to my own satisfaction the questions they raised in that undergraduate class.

Anything of value in this interpretation has been profoundly influenced by Nathan Tarcov's work on Machiavelli and by Joseph Cropsey's extraordinary example of intellectual probity and clarity of vision in the study and teaching of political philosophy.

John Scott, Carol Fiedler, and George Greene read and commented on all or portions of the manuscript at various stages. Grace Burton listened patiently to my theories and offered excellent advice. Skidmore College provided me with a sabbatical for the completion of this project, and the students at Skidmore, whose indefatigable questioning in two seminars I taught on Machiavelli, helped me to refine my arguments.

The suggestions of the two readers for Northern Illinois University Press have improved the manuscript. *Polity* allowed me to reprint material in chapters 5 and 7 that originally appeared in an article.

Finally, I thank my husband, Daniel, whose critical eye and dialectical skills aided me and whose patience and good humor sustained me.

NOTE ON TEXTS CITED

Unless otherwise referenced translations of Machiavelli cited in this book are indicated by the following abbreviations:

AW   *The Art of War,* from vol. 2 of *Machiavelli: The Chief Works and Others,* trans. Allan Gilbert, 3 vols. (Durham: Duke University Press, 1989). Book number is cited first, followed by page number.

CW   *Machiavelli: The Chief Works and Others,* trans. Allan Gilbert, 3 vols. (Durham: Duke University Press, 1989).

D   *Discourses on Livy,* trans. Harvey C. Mansfield and Nathan Tarcov (Chicago: University of Chicago Press, 1996). Book number is cited first, followed by chapter and paragraph number.

FH   *Florentine Histories,* trans. Laura Banfield and Harvey C. Mansfield, Jr. (Princeton: Princeton University Press, 1988). Book number is cited first, followed by chapter number and, sometimes, page number.

P   *The Prince,* trans. Harvey C. Mansfield, Jr. (Chicago: University of Chicago Press, 1985). Chapter is indicated first, followed by page number.

O   For Machiavelli's works in Italian, reference is to *Machiavelli: Tutte le opere,* ed. Mario Martelli (Florence: Sansoni, 1971).

MACHIAVELLI'S
THREE ROMES

INTRODUCTION

Wisdom and goodness to the vile seem vile.—Shakespeare

Three Romes are to be found in the pages of Niccolò Machiavelli's political thought. At times each distinct Rome exists in a
state of war with the others, as each, informed by its own divergent
worldview, threatens to vanquish its rivals; at other times they co-
exist in surprising harmony. The first Rome is the one familiar to the
Florentine from his experience as a secretary of his republic and
then as a disreputable, tortured, but ever astute exile from government. This is the Rome of the Christian dispensation—the one in
place immediately before the Reformation that was guided first by
the machinations of Pope Alexander VI and his son Cesare Borgia,
both of whom sought to capitalize on the invasion of the French,
then by the cry of *"Fuori i Barbari"* of impetuous Pope Julius II, and
finally by the patronage of a Medici man of the cloth, Pope Leo.

The second Rome is that which Machiavelli transfers to his own
pages from those of his beloved historian, Titus Livy. So different

from the Rome of Machiavelli's own age, it is the one in which the men of the most aggressive republic ever known competed for the worldly prizes of honor and renown as they subjected other peoples to Roman authority. By retelling in his own time the feats of heroism of these ancients, Machiavelli participates in their pagan pursuit of glory by assuring that they continue to receive the reward of perpetual remembrance to which their lives, and sometimes their deaths, were dedicated.

The third Rome is that of Machiavelli's imagination. Ultimately what motivates his search for this new land is his concern for human liberty and his recognition that neither ancient nor modern Rome can be considered an adequate guardian of it. Indeed, his new Rome will allow human liberty to flourish for the first time. Although the view that Machiavelli is the discoverer of a third Rome is unique in the scholarship, the association of Machiavelli's political thought—particularly that contained in the *Discourses*—with liberty is not. Quentin Skinner, for instance, offers the view held by many scholars that "the basic value in the *Discourses* is that of liberty."[1] While I add my voice to this chorus with the refrain that Machiavelli is engaged in a valiant attempt to free human beings from tyranny, I sound a discordant note in the very next verse: the tyrant from whose grip Machiavelli would see humanity extricated is the Christian god.[2] Machiavelli is, indeed, an advocate of a *"vivere politico,"* but because at one place he indicates that this manner of life can be established by way of either a republic or a kingship (*D* 1.25; *O* 109), I shall argue that Machiavelli finds that Christianity alone has made the practice of a true political life impossible.[3]

Although it is true, as Sebastian de Grazia reminds us, that sprinkled throughout Machiavelli's writings, "like poppies in a field of chick peas, are many references to God," I argue that it cannot be concluded that these references add up to the tidy sum of Machiavelli's firm intellectual basis in Christianity.[4] As I shall demonstrate in part 1, just behind this orthodox veneer lies a forceful criticism of not only the clergy, but also Christianity itself—a reaction to what Machiavelli sees as the deleterious effect that the Church and its doctrines have had on the practice of politics. An examination of passages drawn primarily from the *Florentine Histories, The Prince,* and the *Discourses* reveals that he regards the clergy as a particularly pernicious type of nobility, which derives its vitality from draining political actors of theirs. Machiavelli repeatedly presents his readers with the spectacle of seemingly mighty rulers humbled before the shepherds of the Christian flock.

In addition, in a more subdued manner, Machiavelli indicates that Christian doctrines themselves have enfeebled human beings. Without entering into the elaborate theological debates of the Middle Ages, Machiavelli objects categorically to the manner in which Christianity exerts a type of rule over human beings that reduces all politics to fundamental weakness. According to Machiavelli, adherence to the Christian notions of such politically important conceptions as cruelty, humility, and human virtue produces disastrous political results. Indeed, so politically enervating does he find Christian beliefs that after he describes and denounces in vehement terms the effects of the *"tiranno virtuoso"* (D 2.2; O 148), he treats in the same chapter the harmful effects that Christianity has had on political life. The effects of each are remarkably similar. The virtuous tyrant cannot bestow honor on any of his subjects for their earthly accomplishments, and neither does the Christian religion:

> Our religion has glorified humble and contemplative more than active men. It has then placed the highest good in humility, abjectness, and contempt of things human; the [ancient religion] placed it in greatness of spirit [*animo*], strength of body, and all other things capable of making men very strong. And if our religion asks that you have strength in yourself, it wishes you to be capable more of suffering than of doing something strong. (D 2.2.2; O 149)

Because the demands of the Christian religion have had such a devastating effect on political life, I argue that the form of tyranny that he endeavors to combat above all is one of a religious character. Nevertheless, the effects of this religion are political. Therefore, part 1 finds that, although Christianity weakens human beings, it is itself a tremendously powerful ruling force—the ruling force of Machiavelli's age.

Part 2 continues this theme of reevaluation: not only does it become necessary to view as strong what Machiavelli initially presents as weak but also to view as weak what he initially presents as strong. Although Machiavelli lends his eager support to both the constitution of the ancient Roman republic and the manner in which Rome's pagan religion supported the city's political enterprises, the second part of this book reveals Machiavelli's ultimate dissatisfaction with both. In examining the grounds for this dissatisfaction, the focus of the study is drawn more intently to his *Discourses,* for in this work—where he appears to praise in the strongest terms Rome and its religion—he produces his elaborate criticism of ancient Rome for its engendering of Christian Rome. Christian Rome emerged from ancient Rome in his view because it was ill equipped to thwart the designs of its ambitious men who strained for tyranny. To support their ascension to power, these clever men offered ever more appealing prizes to the Roman populace. Ultimately, civil life was transcended utterly when an appeal to the people combined with the transcendent claims of religion to produce the incomparable prizes that Christianity proffers. Ancient Rome's pagan religion furnished an environment that led to this volatile combination. Numa's introduction of religion made it possible for the patricians, in the pursuit of their own class interests, to use fraudulent appeals to the divine to manipulate a credulous people. Thus the Roman leaders accustomed their populace to look to the heavens for salvation. As a result, the claims of Christianity found a most receptive audience when clever plebeians, who came to understand the patricians' use of fraud, encouraged a belief in a doctrine that proclaims the victory of the plebeians over the nobles. The doctrine of these clever tribunes declared that to attain rewards in the Eternal City, one need not participate in the earthly city's martial causes, which had hitherto aggrandized the nobles and their country. Civil life was thus transcended when the populace contended for the prizes of paradise rather than for those of the earthly city. In this manner, Christian Rome deepened an impulse that was present in pagan Rome from the time of Numa. Therefore, although ancient Rome in many important respects offers the model for his new republic, Machiavelli must improve upon this model.

As part 3 argues, although the construction of a new Rome is necessitated by the defects of both pagan and Christian Rome, its foundation is furnished by the strengths of both. Their defects and strengths become evident because at times Machiavelli regards the unarmed Christians with contempt in light of the worldly might of their predecessors; at times he regards the unarmed Christians as possessing tremendous resourcefulness because they defeated the armed pagans; at times he castigates pagan Rome for furnishing the Christians with their foothold in Rome; and at times he regards republican Rome as hopelessly defective because its inadequate constitution led the republic inexorably to collapse. Each of these perspectives furnishes a portion of Machiavelli's final understanding. Because he accepts the strengths and discards the defects of each, he creates an amalgamation that is neither Christian nor pagan. His Rome is both ancient and modern, and it is unquestionably his own.[5] Because its construction is necessitated by the defects of a Rome that appealed to divine entities for relief, Machiavelli opens up the possibility that the better alternative for a city would be to dispense with religious appeals altogether, thereby eliminating a powerful weapon of potential tyrants and, thus, preventing their easy route to the transcendence of civil life that they seek. I contend that this is the alternative to which Machiavelli points.

When one considers the presumption of Machiavelli's plan, the question that must come to mind is the following: Is it possible that a society can thrive—even exist at all—without any appeals to transcendent beings? To find Machiavelli's answer to the question, it is necessary to consider his depiction of pagan religion's function. As Leslie Walker recognizes, Machiavelli "seems to regard it from the political standpoint as nothing more nor less than an instrument which the state can use in order to induce the masses to do what it wants them to do."[6] Religion, as Machiavelli presents it, is merely a response to temporal events. It does not give expression to spiritual longing; it does not find a way to explain the inherently mysterious unless what is considered mysterious is the outcome of a pending battle or of a political election. In these cases Machiavelli believes that political—not religious—means can better direct this concern. In Machiavelli's universe the political triumphs over the religious. The religious is not only pernicious, it is wholly superfluous. Therefore, in making this argument I challenge the almost universal view among commentators that Machiavelli regards religion—be it in the form of a Christian or of a pagan appeal to divinity—as a useful instrument of politics.

A rare divergence from this unanimity of presentation occurs when Leo Strauss notes that certain observations induce one to "wonder whether Machiavelli was convinced that religion fulfills an important function." These observations notwithstanding, Strauss curtails this investigation abruptly, claiming that it "goes too far," objecting on grounds both of practicability and of desirability to the view that religion is unnecessary to a state. Regarding practicability, Strauss offers the following objection: "Religion as reverence for the gods breeds deference to the ruling class as a group of men especially favored by the gods and reminiscent of the gods. And vice versa, unqualified unbelief will dispose the people not to believe in what they are told by venerable men."[7] In contrast to Strauss's objection, I argue that for Machiavelli the inculcation of a belief in a divine realm to which the leaders of a city have special access is quite dangerous. In fostering in the people this belief that their leaders are somehow especially blessed, or possessed of a special grace, religion arms potential tyrants with a most virulent weapon against their city. By appealing directly to the desires of the people, demagogues can upstage the city's leaders, and if they can support this appeal with the claim of their own divinity, and hence with claims to unseen benefits emanating from the divine realm, the type of tyranny that Christianity engendered is imminent. As I argue, Machiavelli's new Roman republic prevents the people—and, indeed, the city as a whole—from revering any of its leaders, or any being whatsoever.

Regarding the undesirable effects that would flow from a state's extirpation of religion, Strauss says: "Society would be in a state of perpetual unrest, or else in a state of constant and ubiquitous repression, if men were not made incorrupt by religion, i.e., if they were not both appeased by religious hopes and frightened by religious fears."[8] Although Strauss's assessment may well be correct in the larger sense, it is not accurate in its application to Machiavelli's thought. Neither unrest in a state nor repression of the people in the name of the practice of politics and the prosecution of war can be said to characterize Machiavelli's primary concerns. Indeed, in Machiavelli's view, the unrest of the Roman state conduced to its ability to expand and kept it free (D 1.4). Moreover, although Machiavelli's envisioned irreligious state allows the people enough outlet for its ambition to create unrest, the few will continue to harness the many to political enterprises, particularly the prosecution of the state's wars, from which the people will always seek liberation.[9] Therefore, if by repression Strauss means this type of dominance of the many by the few, Machiavelli's irreligious state is designed to promote such repression rather than to eliminate it.[10] On a deeper level, however, Machiavelli's proposal offers the opportunity to dispense with the most politically damaging repression—Christianity's repression of human politics. Thus an irreligious republic offers the possibility of human liberation.

Although he suggests that appeals to the divine are both pernicious and dispensable, Machiavelli does not entirely dispense with the insights of Christianity. With perverse satisfaction, he finds, in the religion that claims to proceed through the way of love, methods of punishing that will sustain the type of republic he favors by furnishing the proper measure of fear. In applying these Christian notions to his new republic, he divorces them entirely from their theological context.

The earthly application of such fear-inducing devices is required to overcome the drawbacks of ordinary republics. Republics, in his view, tend to act too slowly (D 3.6) and to regard their leading men with too much love (D 1.29). Because this is the case, such republics are particularly vulnerable to those who possess ambition enough to endeavor to strive for preeminence. By contrast, Machiavelli's republic, although it contains a multitude of "princes," will not yield to any one of them. He applies the doctrine of original sin to a republic to assure that no one leader gains preeminence, for in his new republic all of its leaders will be viewed as inherently corrupt, and hence as potential corrupters of the regime. It will have no hesitation in punishing any of its leading men most severely. Moreover, he recommends the horrifying practice of sacrificing at consistent intervals a promising youth. This resolute and arbitrary—indeed, tyrannical—act will restore the republic to health, keeping corruption at bay by restoring the republic to its origins in fear (D 3.1). On the basis of such sacrifices, Machiavelli thus holds out the promise of salvation for a republic. Unlike Christianity's promise, however, Machiavelli's redemption is of an entirely earthly character, as is his notion of sin (P 12).[11]

Therefore, Machiavelli's account of this new Rome points to the tremendous impact that he believes Christianity has had and can have on politics.[12] In order to overcome the politically deleterious consequences of Christianity and the pagan beliefs that engendered it, as well as to forestall the rise of another tyranny of its magnitude, Machiavelli appeals to certain Christian doctrines to support his vision of an earthly discipline that exercises the strength that he views as essential to sustain political life. In so doing, he creates a wholly temporal interpretation of Christianity.

Although I find Machiavelli to be a proponent of a republic, the republicanism I identify in his thought does not point to a fundamental gulf between his most prominent political writings: *The Prince,* which appears to reveal him as a ruthless advisor to princes; and the *Discourses,* which appears to indicate that he was in fact a dedicated partisan of republican government who desired to restore the ancient concern for the common good.[13] My endeavor identifies several prominent points of contact between these two seemingly contradictory works. First, of course, both works reveal the lamentable effects that the Church and Christianity have had on the practice of politics. Second, as I have suggested, Machiavelli infuses tyrannical elements into the republic so that it can oppose the forays of tyrants successfully. Thus, the ways of a tyrant, detailed in *The Prince,* are an important resource for a republic, addressed in the *Discourses.* Third, the harsh methods of a tyrant are also a necessary resource for the lone individual who founds a republic (*D* 1.9, 18, 55). Finally, Machiavelli himself has recourse to some of these same tyrannical methods in order to offer the prospect of a new epoch. He suggests that he himself must utilize some of the methods of the tyranny he opposes.

The argument that he infuses his presentation of Livy's Rome with a temporal form of Christianity that can fortify political life allows me to account for several otherwise puzzling and controversial features of Machiavelli's work. For example, it allows insight into his seemingly contradictory claims to both imitation and innovation in the *Discourses.* He is quite serious in making both claims; he imitates when he appeals to elements both of ancient Rome and of Christian Rome, and he innovates when he transforms these elements into something new—his new Rome. Moreover, his method of writing has been an issue of substantial contention. I can account for his many changes in Livy's history, as a conscious—indeed, an acknowledged—attempt to mask his innovations as a recourse to antiquity. His divergences from Livy reveal an innovation that, if successful, will establish a new epoch.

Machiavelli must so disguise his intent because it is essential that he make this project attractive to others who will finish what he himself cannot (*D* 1. and 2.pr.). He musters his necessary successors by offering the prospect of a return to the glory associated with ancient Rome (*D* 1.pr.; cf. *FH* 6.29). Glory seekers of the Renaissance were far more likely to want a return to the achievements of the pagan past than the establishment of some future of Machiavelli's imagination. He is able to make such a factitious appeal to the "partisans of past things" (*D* 2.pr.1) because the Rome he urges them to restore is capable of lodging within itself (Trojan horse-like) the Rome of his imagination. Those who are defeated in their own intentions will unwittingly establish a city that will be Machiavelli's own.

Because this new epoch, if established, would have a real political effect, it should work to Italy's happiness. Italy, like any province, can be happy only if it is united (D 1.12). Therefore, Machiavelli's project aims at a type of unification, and thus embraces Florence as well as Rome. He acknowledges that transforming Rome into a republic of the sort he envisions would be a particularly difficult undertaking (D 1.55), but precisely for that reason the task is all the more attractive to those motivated by political ambition (P 6 and D 1.9).

In seeing that Machiavelli appeals to certain elements of both paganism and Christianity to enhance his political system and mask the radical character of his undertaking, one finds it easier to grasp how his thought can continue to baffle on the subject of religion. The vexing character of this question is illustrated by the opposition between Mark Hulliung's contention that Machiavelli's thought is informed by his admiration of paganism and de Grazia's view that Machiavelli is a Christian.[14] In discerning that Machiavelli rejects one alternative, even a careful and insightful scholar is likely to conclude mistakenly, before the whole of his intention comes to light, that Machiavelli embraces the other.

Machiavelli applies his acumen to the prospect of a founding that will accord with the Epicurean intention of liberating human beings from fear of the gods,[15] but unlike Epicurean thinkers, he does not propose that philosophy provide the vehicle for such liberation. Unlike the Epicurean, who claims to lead a few from the terrors of the city and its religion in pursuit of knowledge of the whole and thus of a truly happy human life, Machiavelli shuns philosophy in the name of politics. For Machiavelli, human beings are to be liberated from fear of the gods, but not from that of human beings, for human beings are to assume the role of punisher that had been consigned to divine beings (cf. D 3.1).

This book concentrates on Machiavelli's fight against religion, rather than on his rebellion against classical political thought. The divergence of Machiavelli's thought from the form and content of ancient thought has already been investigated. Indeed, when he repudiates "imagined republics and principalities that have never been seen or known to exist in truth" in the name of "the effectual truth of the thing" (P 15), clearly he is taking aim at the view of politics that emerges from both Greek and Christian thought.[16] I do not propose to contribute to the discussion of Machiavelli's divergence from classical thought in any detailed way, although my findings do bear on his ultimate response to the problem that philosophy poses to his politics.

One finds, for example, that in Machiavelli's famous castigation of Christianity for having "glorified humble and contemplative more than active men" (*D* 2.2.2), the ancient philosopher would receive the same amount of vituperation as the Christian saint. His repudiation of both the religious and the philosophic hero arises from his rejection of the leisure that characterizes the two types of lives—a leisure that conflicts with the type of vigorous political life he endeavors to encourage. He understands Christianity to be antithetical to a vigorous politics because it fosters an *ambizioso ozio*, a form of idleness that entices human beings with the promise of rewards awaiting them in another world if they properly repudiate the rewards of their earthly city. For Machiavelli this is the height of political corruption. Nevertheless, in his view there exists another form of corruption, a philosophical form:

> it has been observed by the prudent that letters come after arms and that, in provinces and cities, captains arise before philosophers. For, as good and ordered armies give birth to victories and victories to quiet, the strength of well-armed spirits cannot be corrupted by a more honorable leisure [*onesto ozio*] than that of letters, nor can leisure enter into well-instituted cities with a greater and more dangerous deceit than this one. (*FH* 5.1.185; *O* 738)

After Cato perceived that the philosophers sent by Athens had amassed a following of Roman youth, he "recognized the evil that could result to his fatherland from this honorable leisure." The stern Roman did well when he forbade philosophers in Rome, judges Machiavelli.

Thus, to Machiavelli, both forms of idleness—the Christian and the philosophic—are deleterious to politics. Indeed, he suggests in one place that they are related. In treating the prodigies that occur before a disaster, he admits that their cause can be explained adequately only by one who possesses knowledge of "things natural and supernatural." Because he claims to lack such an understanding, he offers only the speculation that "it could be, as some philosopher would have it, that since this air is full of intelligences which foresee future things by their natural virtues, and they have compassion for men, they warn them with like signs so that they can prepare themselves for defense" (D 1.56.1). According to Machiavelli, then, some philosopher maintains that another unseen realm exists that takes care of human beings. Such a realm could easily be transformed into the religious beliefs of the masses.[17] Machiavelli maintains that "we do not have" "knowledge of things natural and supernatural" to judge whether such spirits exist (D 1.56.1). Nevertheless, he possesses enough knowledge of politics to know that the belief in such entities ultimately undermines political practice. People will not have to rely on spirits who bid them to prepare for crisis, for Machiavelli will assure that they are already so prepared.

Although he believes philosophical leisure to be truly pernicious, Machiavelli launches his greatest attack on Christian leisure. Because he devotes most of his energies to lauding ancient practice and attacking modern practice, his explicit treatments of ancient philosophy are rather rare. He appears to wish to consign most of Greek philosophy to oblivion.[18] He can wage an attack on Christianity because, if successful, his new city will banish ozio—whether philosophical or religious. In other words, his victory over religion will produce a simultaneous victory over Greek philosophy.

What then should be made of Machiavelli's own ozio? Expelled from his position in government with the return of the Medici to Florence, he was forced to exchange the practice of politics for the pleasure of books.[19] As a result, he himself was engaged in that corrupt activity of "letters." Yet he participated in this activity to redeem politics. Indeed, in the Discourses he indicates that "utility" is the reason that we "should seek knowledge of histories" (D 1.pr.2; see also 2.pr.).[20] When fortune affords the "youths men who . . . read" the opportunity to institute the new modes and orders that lie concealed in his appeal to the past, Machiavelli's writings will be of the utmost political value for they will have a most salubrious impact on politics (D 2.pr.3, 1.9).

As the passage on the corrupting influence of philosophy drawn from the Florentine Histories suggests, philosophy has always had an effect on politics through the philosopher's contact with the young. Machiavelli's contact with the young through his writings will reform rather than corrupt politics. In addition, in "A Discourse on Remodeling the Government of Florence," he suggests that previous philosophers, because they coveted the glory of founders, desired to influence politics more directly, but were unable to do so:

> And so much has this glory been esteemed by men seeking for nothing other than glory that when unable to form a republic in reality, they have done it in writing, as Aristotle, Plato, and many others, who have wished to show the world that if they have not founded a free government, as did Solon and Lycurgus, they have failed not through their ignorance but through their impotence for putting it into practice. (CW 1:114)

Machiavelli corroborates this view that ancient philosophy is ineffectual when his only mention of Plato in the *Discourses* refers to the Greek as the teacher of failed conspirators (D 3.6). Machiavelli's thought, however, teaches the effectual truth, and thus he expects that his imagined republic can come into being. If founded, the republic would proscribe *ozio*. On the one hand, philosophy can promote corruption in a state; on the other, when a state is overrun with corruption, philosophy can overcome it—if it is of the quality of Machiavelli's thought.

PART I

CHRISTIAN ROME

And one of the doctors of Italy, Nicholas Machiavel, had the confidence to put in writing, almost in plain terms, that the Christian faith had given up good men in prey to those that are tyrannical and unjust. —Francis Bacon

Machiavelli insists that the political problems of modern Italy emanate from Rome: the insidious power of the papacy keeps the region divided. Belief in the Christian religion fosters other related problems: this religion has taught people to rely on the arms of others and its morality prevents cities from dealing effectively with their political problems. Unarmed and divided, the Christians are left as prey to others. Such are the political punishments that they deserve as a result of their commission of earthly sins, according to the rhetoric of the prophet of an earthly religion.

Although the earthly punishments on which he expatiates are revelatory of Christianity's devastating political toll, they also show the religion's tremendous strength. Christianity is the heir to the Roman Empire, and it exercises a type of political rule. Because its power derives from depreciating the human capacities needed for the sustenance of political communities, this power, in Machiavelli's view, cannot be made compatible with the power of a secular prince. To make his rule secure, a prince must make his people soldiers in a temporal—not a heavenly—cause.

Understanding the tremendous import for Machiavelli of Christianity's rule will be essential for comprehending his depiction of ancient Rome, for, as part 2 will document, he introduces into his discussions of that pagan city terms that evoke his treatment of Christianity. To recognize the full significance of this evocation, it is necessary to examine in detail his criticism of Christian Rome.

❖ CHAPTER 1 ❖

THE CHURCH AND MACHIAVELLI'S DEPICTION OF ITALY'S HISTORICAL SITUATION

Machiavelli's many references to the various popes who acted on the political stage confirm that the institution whose purpose was to care for souls had become a mighty power; through means both direct and insidious it found itself arbitrating the dispensation of territory and riches on earth. Machiavelli's ultimate judgment regarding the Church's temporal influence is particularly important in assessing his intentions because he dedicates his most famous work, *The Prince*, to Lorenzo de' Medici, nephew of the then reigning pope, Leo X.[1] Florence's fortunes at this time were closely tied to Rome. The city had returned to Medicean dominance after the disastrous events of 1512. The French, whom the Florentine republic had supported, retreated after the battle of Ravenna, where they had engaged the forces of the Holy League, formed by Pope

Julius II. A few months later the Florentines were unable to repel the Spanish attack on Prato. The Florentine republic collapsed, and the Medici, who had been expelled since 1494, returned to Florence. After their return, Florence was directed by Rome because the family's leading men were clerics. The guiding influence of the family, and hence of Florence, Giovanni de' Medici, became Leo X in 1513. After Pope Leo's death in 1521, Giulio de' Medici succeeded his cousin both as familial head and as leader of the Church when he became Pope Clement VII in 1523. Thus Rome guided Florence during the time that Machiavelli, excluded from participating in government due to the suspicions of the Medici, completed his political works, *The Prince* and the *Discourses*. Later the author managed to work himself into the good graces of the Medici to the extent that he received a commission from Leo X for the composition of the *Florentine Histories*.

Machiavelli's choice of dedication of *The Prince* seems to bear not only on the fate of his native city and of his personal political ambitions, but also on that of Italy as a whole, for he appears to link the Church to the prospect that Italy can be redeemed from the twin scourges of division and foreign invasion. In the famous last chapter of *The Prince* he exhorts the Medici to expel the foreigners from Italy (*P* 26.102–3). Because Lorenzo was dominated by his much more influential uncle, if the Medici were to undertake the enterprise of forming a new state that would dominate Italy for the purpose of resisting the waves of foreign predators, that state would clearly be directed from Rome. Speculation that Machiavelli views the alliance between a secular prince and a pope as the means for Italy's redemption seems to be corroborated by his treatment in the same work of Cesare Borgia, famous for the political ambition his father, Pope Alexander VI, had nurtured. Perhaps Machiavelli's recitation of the crucial events in Cesare's rise to power in the Romagna is meant to excite similar ambitions in Lorenzo. If this is Machiavelli's intention, then papal patronage would appear to furnish the critical ingredient in the establishment of a border state that could stem the tide of foreign invasion.[2]

Despite this evident obsequiousness to both the secular and the clerical Medici in *The Prince*, Machiavelli at no time regards the Church as a mechanism with which to remedy the politics of his time. Neither his *Discourses* nor his *Florentine Histories* need be regarded with special care to determine that he regarded the Church as an obstacle—not as a means—to Italy's unification. Careful consideration of *The Prince* not only accords with this view but also completes the analysis presented in these other works. This analysis indicates that the papacy's characteristic features—its lack of arms and its politically deleterious form of nobility—produce a weakness so debilitating to Italian politics as to prevent the founding of a state resilient enough to solve Italy's very evident problems. When this analysis is properly grasped, Cesare's fate stands not as an example worthy of emulation, but as a warning to anyone who looks to the Church to assume responsibility for Italy's political fate. Machiavelli's view of this institution as irremediably troublesome induces him to contemplate the possibility of its violent extirpation. Even if these passages are to be regarded merely as devilish sport on Machiavelli's part, they still retain a chilling character that bespeaks the depth of his hatred of the Church's hierarchy.

An Invigorated Church

Certain prominent statements in *The Prince* suggest that Machiavelli hoped the Church could furnish a solution to Italy's political ills. In the dedication, for example, he expresses his wish that Lorenzo "will learn from it my extreme desire that you arrive at the greatness that fortune and your other qualities promise you" (4). In a later chapter, after recounting the way both Alexander VI and Julius II had increased the temporal power of the Church, Machiavelli adds that "one may hope" Lorenzo's uncle, the current occupant of the Holy See, "with his goodness and infinite other virtues, can make it very great and venerable" (*P* 11.47). Finally, in the last chapter, Machiavelli declares: "Nor may one see at present anyone in whom [Italy] can hope more than in your illustrious house, which with its fortune and virtue, supported by God and by the Church of which it is now prince, can put itself at the head of this redemption" (*P* 26.102–3). These statements suggest that Machiavelli regarded the power that resided in Florence and Medicean Rome as Italy's best current hope. Because the infamous duo of Pope Alexander and Cesare came close to founding a state, perhaps the combination of Leo and his nephew will succeed.[3]

It is quite possible, however, that he regarded this best current hope as ultimately futile. Indeed, rather than encouraging Leo to undertake a similar attempt to build a northern buffer state for his scion under the aegis of the Church, *The Prince*, if carefully read, should have dampened his enthusiasm for such a project. As that treatise indicates, the favor of the French King Louis and the pope produced disastrous consequences not only for Cesare but also for themselves. Machiavelli's view is that, because the benefit of the actors' deeds redounded to it, the Church was the only winner in this play for temporal power. Moreover, as a later section of this chapter will document, despite the gains that accrued to the Church from this victory, Machiavelli believes it will never be able to assume the leadership of Italy without recourse to the arms of others. Hence, if the strength of the Church were to increase, Italy's subjection to foreign powers would only intensify.

The drama of Cesare was played out during a time when much of the foreign policy of the Italian states entailed inviting outside powers to intervene in Italian affairs, a situation Pope Alexander believed offered him an opportunity to augment his own power.[4] Even before this chaotic period Machiavelli suggests that the papacy already possessed significant influence. He comments in *The Prince* that before France's Charles VIII "came into Italy, this province was under the domination [*sotto lo imperio*] of the pope, the Venetians, the king of Naples, the duke of Milan, and the Florentines" (*P* 11.45–46; *O* 274). Although France's invasion of Italy under Charles in 1494 was short-lived, it had a profound effect on Italy in general and on Florence in particular in that almost sixty years of Medicean domination ended when Piero de' Medici fled his city. Although a secular Italian prince, Lodovico Sforza of Milan, furnished the initial impetus for Charles to press his claim to Naples,[5] it was a churchman, the future Pope Julius II, who rekindled Charles's ambitions when the king had lost heart.[6]

Charles's invasion provided the precedent for the subsequent invasion of Louis XII in 1499, in which the intervention of the clergy was more direct and its effects even more harmful than those of the earlier incursion. When the new French king sought a divorce to marry the widow of Charles, the duchess of Brittany, so as to keep the realm intact, Pope Alexander saw the opportunity to promote his son, Cesare Borgia. As a result of Alexander's machinations, Louis attained his divorce and also gained papal support for his invasion of Milan and a promotion to cardinal for one of his ministers, paid for with prizes for Cesare: the dukedom of Valentinois, French troops, and a royal wife. Machiavelli writes poetically of this bald exchange:

So because by himself alone the Pope had no strength to do anything great, he set out to win the new king's favor,/ granted his divorce, and gave him Brittany; and in return the King promised him the lordship and the states of Romagna./ And since Alexander lacked a man to hold his banner aloft after Candia's death and defeat,/ he turned to his son who had a place among the great clerics and withdrew him from them, changing the cardinal's hat to the soldier's cap.[7] ("First Decennale," *CW* 3:1448–49)

Machiavelli reveals the fate of this deal through his many references to its victims in *The Prince*. In his view, the actors, who intended to aggrandize themselves, promoted only the power of the Church. These discussions constitute a parable illustrating the dangers the Church poses to secular rulers.

Already by the third chapter of *The Prince*, Machiavelli makes it obvious that the cunning Alexander had gotten the better of the French king by using Louis's own faith as an instrument by which to strangle the king's territorial hopes. In this analysis we find first that when the monarch gave "aid to Pope Alexander so that the pope might seize the Romagna," Louis broke Machiavelli's rule against increasing "the power of a power" in a subject province (14, 15). Machiavelli observes that Louis paid for this violation because the "greatness in Italy of the Church and of Spain has been caused by France, and France's ruin caused by them" (16). Moreover, Machiavelli will not accept the palliative, offered on Louis's behalf, that the king had merely kept the "faith that [he] had pledged to the pope, to undertake that enterprise for him in return for dissolving his marriage and for the hat of Rouen." Indeed, he attributes to himself the incisive reply to the cardinal of Rouen's charge that the Italians do not understand war: "the French do not understand the state, because if they understood they would not have let the Church come to such greatness" (15–16). Thus, at the same time he attributes Louis's downfall to his naïve entanglement with Pope Alexander, Machiavelli issues a general warning to states regarding the insidious power of the clergy in temporal affairs. The understanding that prompts him to issue this warning must serve to challenge any idea that he would initiate plans to promote the temporal preeminence of the Church.

It becomes apparent, moreover, that neither Cesare nor even Alexander were the winners in Louis's downfall. Even though Cesare fulfilled his own territorial ambitions with Machiavellian vigor by reclaiming the lands from the petty tyrants whom previous occupants of the papal chair had established in the Romagna and by ridding Rome of its disruptive competing noble families, the Colonna and Orsini, ultimately he was unable to free himself from his father's fortune.[8] Machiavelli reveals Cesare's inferior status even when he examines in detail Cesare's triumphs in chapter 7 of *The Prince*. Here Machiavelli's encomium to Cesare's bloody deeds comes to an abrupt end and the author's admiration turns to censure when it becomes clear that the ruthlessly calculating prince of the Romagna had misapplied his influence with the college of cardinals. As a result, Cesare was unable to sustain himself after his father's death. According to Machiavelli's last word on the subject in this chapter, the duke erred here by overestimating the power of forgiveness:

> One could only indict him in the creation of Julius as pontiff, in which he made a bad choice. . . . And he should never have accepted for the papacy those cardinals whom he had offended. . . . And whoever believes that among great personages new benefits will make old injuries be forgotten deceives himself. (*P* 7.33)

As a result, when the father succumbed to death, so too did the ambitions of the son.

Machiavelli's commentary on these events continues in subsequent chapters, where he repudiates the virtue of forgiveness through his unwillingness to forgive Cesare this misstep.[9] Machiavelli vengefully reclaims from Duke Valentino even the credit he had bestowed on him when examining his deeds in the earlier part of the seventh chapter. Now, when considering Cesare in the full flush of victory, Machiavelli does not allow him his own agency and reveals in the eleventh chapter that Cesare's deeds, spoken of with such admiration in the earlier chapter, belong not to him, but to his father, Pope Alexander:

> of all the pontiffs there have ever been he showed how far a pope could prevail with money and forces. With Duke Valentino as his instrument and with the invasion of the French as the opportunity, he did all the things I discussed above in the actions of the duke.

If Alexander was the author of his son's actions, the author was not actually the beneficiary of these deeds. The beneficiary was the Church:

And though [Alexander's] intent might not have been to make the Church great, but rather the duke, nonetheless what he did redounded to the greatness of the Church. After his death, the duke being eliminated, the Church fell heir to his labors. (*P* 11.46–47)

In this manner, Italy's disaster was not Louis's boon, nor Cesare's, nor Alexander's, but rather the Church's.

From the perspective of Machiavelli's *Florentine Histories* and *Discourses* one can assess the Church's gain alluded to in *The Prince;* the designs of Alexander, executed by Cesare, overcame a long-standing problem for the Church. In instituting a movement for independence that threw off the dominion of the emperor, Italy had divided into discreet states.[10] "[B]ecause Italy had been abandoned by the emperors, many towns became free and many were seized by tyrants" (*FH* 1.26.37). Pope Benedict XII, fearing Emperor Ludwig desired to reassert control in Italy, "decided to make friends in it of all those who had usurped the towns that used to obey the emperor, so that they would have cause to fear the Empire and draw together with him for the defense of Italy." To this end, Benedict favored these tyrants by issuing a decree declaring that they should keep their usurpation with "just titles." Not to be outdone, Ludwig "gave to all the tyrants in the towns of the Church their own towns, so that they might possess them by imperial authority." As a result of this liberality on the part of the pope and emperor, of "all the towns of the Church, few were left without a prince" (*FH* 1.30.42). Alexander, operating through the duke, overcame some of these divisions and the bad government his predecessor's deeds had engendered. Machiavelli comments that it was this division "that kept the Church weak until Alexander VI in our time, by ruining their descendants, returned its authority to it" (*FH* 1.30.42). In the *Discourses* Machiavelli pays homage to the quality of Alexander's work: "Before those lords who commanded the Romagna were eliminated in it by Pope Alexander VI, it was an example of every most criminal life, because there one saw very great slaughter and rapine occur for every slight cause" (*D* 3.29.1).[11]

Although the work of the pope's favorite was quite successful in eliminating these lords, it did not serve his own interests in the end; the duke's career ended ignominiously despite his many "successes." Machiavelli's analysis of Cesare's career in *The Prince* suggests the inherent difficulties presented to the previous pontiff's favorite by the succession of popes. Even if Cesare had not misapplied his influence with the college of cardinals, his hold on power would have been tenuous, for any new pope could not be expected to endure for long the political exaltation of his predecessor's favorite minion.[12] For this reason, far from inspiring emulation, the example of Cesare could hardly have inspired anything but unease in Lorenzo (if this Medicean sapling had read *The Prince* and given Cesare's example any consideration).

Machiavelli provides more detailed reasons for the ephemeral character of papal client states in the *Florentine Histories,* when discussing the weakness of the "principalities" that popes have "ordered." These states, he declares, "have had short lives because most times the pontiffs, by living a short time, either do not provide for planting their plants or, if they do plant them, leave them with roots so few and weak that they wither at the first wind" (*FH* 1.23.35).[13] He is so confident of their inherent weakness, that he reiterates his assessment at a time when he was actually witnessing continuity in the pontifical succession. A little more than a year separated the reigns of the Medicean popes, Leo X and Clement VII.[14] Although the analysis is more elaborate in the later *Florentine Histories,* Machiavelli already refers to the primary obstacle to a sustained policy in *The Prince:* the lack of longevity of the popes, hence a frequent change in policies. He says here that on average the pope lives only ten years (*P* 11.46). Moreover, the pope is chosen from the factious college of cardinals (*P* 11.47); the elections of this body reflect the shifting fortunes of its competing factions. As a result, from the evidence Machiavelli provides in *The Prince,* no guarantee existed that Leo's successor would continue an alliance with Medicean Florence or its newly created client state. Although at first *The Prince* offers such a hopeful depiction of the political prospects of the pope and his nephew, Machiavelli's analysis does not differ from the one in the *Florentine Histories,* which deems any pope's temporal "plantings" fundamentally weak. Thus, the favor of a pope can bring some initial success, but such success is fleeting. Machiavelli's own analysis in *The Prince* suggests that anyone who followed Cesare's example, without endeavoring to break his dependence on the papacy, would offer himself up as a sacrificial victim to the ambitions of the succeeding pope.

Foreign Arms and the Weakness of the Church

In addition to these considerations pointing to the feebleness of papal "plantings," the argument that Machiavelli looks to the papacy as the solution to Italy's ills must confront his declaration in 1.12 of the *Discourses* that the papacy is their very cause:

> [T]he Church has kept and keeps this province divided. And truly no province has ever been united or happy unless it has all come under obedience to one republic or to one prince. . . . The cause that Italy . . . does not also have one republic or one prince to govern it, is solely the Church. For although it has inhabited and held a temporal empire there it has not been so powerful nor of such virtue as to be able to seize the tyranny of Italy and make itself prince of it [*occupare la tirranide d'Italia e farsene principe*].[15] (D 1.12.2; O 96)

Machiavelli then proceeds to answer anyone who would doubt his analysis of the source of Italy's ills to "send the Roman court, with all the influence it has in Italy, to live in the cities of the Swiss." He concludes in advance of this experiment that such largesse on the part of the Italians would cause great disorder even among the Swiss, the only modern people who live in a manner akin to the ancients with regard to military and religious orders.

This consideration need not be decisive, of course. The source of Machiavelli's complaint in *Discourses* 1.12 is that the papal state, while strong enough to assert itself into politics, is incapable of uniting Italy. Perhaps if the Church were somehow strong enough so as not to rely on foreign powers, then Machiavelli would no longer have grounds for objection. He is obviously impressed with the power that has accrued to Pope Leo, who has benefited from the accomplishments of both Alexander and his successor, Julius II.[16] Thus, at the time Machiavelli was writing *The Prince,* Leo, the inheritor of the efforts of both Alexander and Julius, "found this pontificate most powerful" (P 11.47).

If the fundamental obstacle to Italy's happiness is its disunion, as Machiavelli writes in the *Discourses,* then all the papal efforts to overcome the division within its own territory appear to be steps in overcoming Italy's fundamental problem. Perhaps in writing *The Prince* Machiavelli envisions not a papal client state with a nephew as figurehead, but the papacy itself as the vehicle for Italian unity. Perhaps he viewed the papacy as being well on its way to achieving hegemony—to occupying *"la tirranide"* of Italy and making "itself prince" (cf. D 1.12; O 96). Indeed, *"Fuori i Barbari,"* Julius's battle cry against the French in Italy, would appear to be emblematic of such an effort.

Yet in *The Prince* Machiavelli provides strategic considerations, indicating that he does not believe the leadership of the papacy can provide the long-term solution to Italy's problems.[17] He explains here that the papacy simply cannot be fortified in a manner that would allow it to be the bulwark against foreign arms, precisely because its strength resides in such arms. In this manner, *The Prince* actually provides analysis that supports those conclusions in the *Discourses* and in the *Florentine Histories* that reveal the detrimental role the papacy has played in Italian politics.

In considering that the accomplishments of Alexander and Julius suggest to Machiavelli the possible basis for Italy's future unity, one should not overlook that Machiavelli laments the consequences for Italy of Alexander's dalliance with Louis, and Louis's subsequent involvement with the Spanish on Italian territory. Machiavelli obviously believes that this series of events was a disaster for the province.[18] Even those who read Machiavelli as a bloodless tactician of statecraft cannot ignore the emotion his concluding chapter of *The Prince* exudes. Italy has suffered "barbarous cruelties and insults," he declares there (102). In the "First Decennale," written in 1504—a time still painfully close to these events—he laments that "discordant Italy opened into herself a passage for the Gauls and suffered barbarian peoples to trample her down" (CW 3:1445).[19]

Although evidence from the *Florentine Histories* cannot settle the question of Machiavelli's intentions in *The Prince*, it should not be overlooked that, in this later work, he indeed finds far in the past the origin of the type of papal politics that engendered the French invasion. He pinpoints the pivotal time as that of Theodoric, king of the Ostrogoths, a time that coincides with the fall of the Roman Empire in the West. Zeno, the Roman emperor in the East, encouraged Theodoric to invade Italy to expel Odoacer. Odoacer was the chieftain of the Heruli, the mercenaries in the service of the Romans who had rebelled and deposed the last Roman Emperor in the West before Charlemagne. Theodoric vanquished Odoacer and made himself governor of the Romans (thereby alleviating for Zeno the threat of the Ostrogoths in the East).[20] Machiavelli comments that when Theodoric moved his headquarters to Ravenna, he left Rome ungoverned, and as a result "the Romans for their own safety had cause to give greater obedience to the pope" (*FH* 1.9.19).

Later, when the "Lombards came and divided Italy into more

parts, they gave the pope cause to be more active. Because [the pope] was now almost the head of Rome, the emperor of Constantinople and the Lombards respected him." After the downfall of the Eastern empire, the power of the Lombards grew, and the pope "decided he needed to seek new support, and he had recourse to those kings in France" (*FH* 1.9.19–20). In the *Discourses,* Machiavelli also finds cause to comment on these events: "by means of Charlemagne, [the Church] expelled the Longobards, who were then almost king of all Italy . . ." (*D* 1.12.2). Consideration of this papal appeal to a foreign force compels Machiavelli in the *Florentine Histories* to echo the charge he levels against the papacy in *Discourses* 1.12:

> So henceforward, all the wars waged by the barbarians in Italy were for the most part caused by the pontiffs, and all the barbarians who invaded it were most often called in by them. This mode of proceeding continues still in our times; it is this that has kept and keeps Italy disunited and infirm. (*FH* 1.9.20; cf. *FH* 1.23.34)

Examination of the subject of mercenary arms in *The Prince* suggests why the papacy played this role in Italian politics: the ascendancy of Christianity, and hence of the papacy, engendered military weakness in Italy—a weakness so fundamental as to raise the question of whether Machiavelli could have intended in this same text for this institution to serve as the vehicle for Italy's redemption from the circumstances of which it is itself the cause.[21] Machiavelli's analysis first finds a target among the modern secular rulers. He advises that, "if one keeps his state founded on mercenary arms, one will never be firm or secure" and explains that this is because "they have no love nor cause to keep them in the field other than a small stipend which is not sufficient to make them want to die for you" (*P* 12.48–49). The consequences extend beyond the insecurity of any individual state, however, for he declares that "the present ruin of Italy is caused by nothing other than its having relied for a period of many years on mercenary arms." In his best parody of the rhetoric of the Dominican friar Savonarola, Machiavelli avers that the invasion of the French was a result "of our sins" (the sins of being unarmed, that is) and the princes who committed them "have suffered the punishment for them" (*P* 12.49). Machiavelli's military sins have earthly punishments.[22]

In discoursing in chapter 12 on the princes' sins of hiring mercenaries, Machiavelli finds it necessary to treat these arms in more depth "so that, when their origin and progress have been seen, one can correct them better." This deeper examination reveals that although secular princes have committed grievous wrongs in employing these arms, the Church is actually responsible for planting them and for providing the environment in which they so flourished. He states that in "recent times" when Italy began to throw off the authority of the empire, "the pope gained much reputation in temporal affairs." Because "the priests and the other citizens did not have knowledge of arms, they began to hire foreigners" (*P* 12.52). From this initial hiring of foreigners the discipline of the *condottieri* was born.[23] "And the result of their virtue has been that Italy has been overrun by Charles, taken as booty by Louis, violated by Ferdinand, and insulted by the Swiss." The Church is directly responsible for the lack of native arms and hence for Italy's "slavery and disgrace" (*P* 12.53). Even papal efforts directed at remedying this political situation end in a deepening dependence on foreigners: Julius, the warrior-pope, whose undertakings resulted in a papacy even stronger than he had found it, succeeded in expelling the French from the peninsula only by recourse to auxiliary arms, a move that established the Spanish more firmly.

Machiavelli further corroborates the devastating character of mercenary arms—as if further corroboration were required—in chapter 13 when he locates the Roman Empire's fall as the time when it had recourse to such arms. "And if one considers the first cause of the ruin of the Roman Empire, one will find it to have begun only with the hiring of Goths, because from that beginning the forces of the Roman Empire began to weaken, and all the virtue that was taken from it was given to them" (*P* 13.57). Although Machiavelli does not supply the name of the emperor responsible for such devastating decline here, it is not difficult to find. Theodosius was the one culpable.[24] He is remembered also for making paganism illegal and Christianity the official religion of the empire. Therefore, in *The Prince* Machiavelli associates these hirelings with two periods of Italian weakness: the fall of the Roman Empire and modern Italy. During the earlier time Christianity gained its ascendancy, while in the later it ruled with the influence it had attained. Both periods are dominated by mercenaries and the Church in Machiavelli's treatment.[25]

In modern times the conflict between the Church and empire had other political effects as well. Aside from engendering bloody disputes between the Guelf and Ghibilline parties, it contributed to

Italy's lack of arms. At least initially the strife was contained within the party of the nobles. It had the politically harmful effect of devastating this party, which was composed of those who were schooled in warfare. Moreover, as the Guelf party gained preeminence "many of the large cities took up arms against their nobles, who formerly, supported by the emperor, had kept them under oppression; and the Church supported the cities to give herself reputation in temporal affairs" (*P* 12.52). These events affected Machiavelli's own city as well. "[H]aving eliminated their nobility by frequent divisions, [Florence] was left in the hands of men nurtured in trade and thus continued in the orders and fortune of the others" (*FH* 1.39.50).[26] In this way the cities were left in the hands of "citizens [who] did not have knowledge of arms" (*P* 12.50). These unarmed citizens, along with the unarmed priests, composed a helpless lot.

Because Machiavelli analyzes the manner in which the Church is associated with and, indeed, engendered Italy's military weakness in the pages of *The Prince,* it is simply no longer possible to presume that in this work he entertains the notion that the Church could be the means with which to remedy the weakness. Its only weapon—that of the strategy of depredation by invitation—cannot hold the key to Italian unity.

The Parasitic Nobility of the Church

In narrating this process that enfeebled Italy, Machiavelli makes it clear that the clergy attained a new status in temporal affairs after the old nobility, which had made war its pursuit, had been eliminated. His further comments on the clergy indicate he believes this new status actually elevated the clergy to a new type of nobility. In 1.12 of the *Discourses,* for example, Machiavelli refers to the clergy of Rome as a court—"the *corte romana.*" Unlike the nobility of old, however, this one is useless. He lodges his general complaints against "*geniluomini*" in 1.55 of the *Discourses,* and realizes he needs to explain his idiosyncratic use of the term:

> To clarify this name of gentleman such as it may be, I say that those are called gentlemen who live idly [*oziosi*] in abundance from the returns of their possessions without having any care either for cultivation or for other necessary trouble in living. Such as these are pernicious in every republic and in every province, but more pernicious are those who beyond the aforesaid fortunes command from a castle and have subjects who obey them.[27] (*D* 1.55.4; *O* 137–38)

There is no reason to suppose that Machiavelli did not intend for
this excoriation to apply to the nobility as conventionally understood;[28] however, there are reasons to suppose that he also intended it to apply to the clergy.[29] Both definitions apply quite readily to certain members of the clergy of his day. Typical members of
the higher monastic orders would appear to fit the first description
of gentlemen who lead an easy but ultimately useless life on rich estates.[30] In addition, the prominent members of the more worldly
clergy had both obedient subjects and lavish castles under their
command.[31] In one place, in fact, he describes the possessions of
the cardinals as "delights" [*delizie*] (D 1.27.1; O 109). Moreover,
because the clergy were by definition unarmed, they were particularly gentle, and in listing the Italian cities where these gentle folk
can be found in abundance, he names suggestively the "town of
Rome" (D 1.55.4).[32]

Elsewhere in the *Discourses* Machiavelli is more forthright in his
contempt for the clergy's manner of living. In delineating in 1.12
the disunion caused by the Church, he also takes a swipe at their
corruption, declaring that "the bad customs of that court would
make more disorder than any other accident that could arise there
at any time" and that such bad examples would destroy the good
order of the Swiss if this people had the misfortune to be exposed
to them (D 1.12.2). Later he notes that the Church's corruption almost resulted in the ruin of the religion, had not Saint Francis and
Saint Dominick interceded. Francis and Dominick "with poverty
and with the example of the life of Christ . . . brought back into the
minds of men what had already been eliminated there. Their new
orders were so powerful that they are the cause that the dishonesty
of the prelates and of the heads of the religion do not ruin it."
These new orders also taught that "it is evil to say evil of evil, and
that it is well to live under obedience to them, and that if they make
an error, to leave them for God to punish" (D 3.1.4; see also *FH*
1.20). In this way Machiavelli suggests that although people notice
the wrongdoing of the clergy, Francis and Dominick promoted resignation in the face of it. Perhaps this resignation helps to explain
the cause for the characteristic stability of ecclesiastical principalities Machiavelli observes: such principalities "are sustained by orders that have grown old with religion, which have been so powerful and of such a kind that they keep their princes in the state
however they proceed and live" (P 11.45).[33] Thus, in Machiavelli's
view the ultimate result of the good examples set by these rigorous

orders is that other priests apparently can practice their corruption with impunity.[34]

If certain members of the clergy live idly but command castles, hold rich possessions, and have subjects under their obedience, one may legitimately wonder whether Machiavelli intimates that this peculiar sort of nobility has oppressed modern people in order to attain these privileges. In *The Prince,* for example, after noting that the Turk and Sultan are the only princes of modern times whose continued rule does not depend on the satisfaction of their people because each depends on an army, Machiavelli draws a comparison between the "sultan's state" and that of the "Christian pontificate" (*P* 19.81–82). Given the context of this discussion, some very unflattering connotations redound to the manner in which the papacy is administered. The basis of this comparison is that both the pope and Sultan are elected: "For it is not the sons of the old prince who are the heirs and become the lords, but the one who is elected to that rank by those who have the authority for it."[35] Machiavelli comments that such a state "cannot be called either a hereditary principality or a new principality" (*P* 19.82). Thus Machiavelli points to a similarity between an Eastern despotism and the Holy See.[36]

Whereas he says here that the Sultan's state is unlike any other because of its feature of election, it is similar to a past state that had this same feature—the Roman Empire. Thus, the Roman Empire, the Sultan's state, and the Christian pontificate all share this attribute. Although he does not explicitly draw this connection between the Roman Empire and the pontificate, the example is ready at hand as he has devoted a great part of this long chapter on conspiracies to a discussion of the Roman emperors. He draws from this discussion the lesson that the emperors were under a peculiar necessity to oppress the people because they dealt not only with the normal humors in a state, those of the people and the nobles, but also with an additional one—a most formidable one—the soldiers. This armed party, according to Machiavelli, was avaricious and cruel, and its members "loved a prince with a military spirit who was insolent, cruel, and rapacious," who would allow them "to practice these things on the people so that they could double their pay and give vent to their avarice and cruelty" (*P* 19.76). "And so those emperors who because they were new [who did not receive this position through inheritance] had need of extraordinary support stuck to the soldiers rather than the people" (ibid.).

This feature of election thus imposed a special necessity on the emperors because they held, according to Machiavelli's analysis, new positions within an old state and hence were in need of extraordinary support. The comparison Machiavelli does not make, but certainly suggests, concerns the necessities facing the Roman emperors and the popes. He actually goes quite far down the road when he states the papacy "cannot be called either a hereditary principality or a new principality" (P 19.82). Because the pontificate shares this characteristic with the Roman Empire, do the popes, like the emperors, have a special need for support?

Whatever answer this question demands, another evident similarity exists between the popes and the emperors: the popes certainly have to contend with a third humor. In addition to the people and the great, popes have to deal with the members of the clergy, to whom they owe their election. The picture Machiavelli paints of these gentlemen of the Church is very different from his portrait of the brutal Roman soldiers. Therefore, if Machiavelli intends by these comparisons to imply that the popes are constrained by the form of their state to satisfy the clergy rather than the people,[37] it would be a form of oppression very different from that practiced by the soldiers of Rome. Nevertheless, it would still constitute oppression according to Machiavelli's declaration that "when that community of which you judge you have need to maintain yourself is corrupt, whether they are the people or the soldiers or the great, you must follow their humor to satisfy them, and then good deeds are your enemy" (P 19.77). Therefore, the satisfaction of yet another group—the clergy—would also result in evil deeds because, as Machiavelli suggests in the Discourses, that group is corrupt.

At the very least the people can be oppressed not only by a single ruler, but also by a nobility that arrogates to itself unreasonable power. In 2.2 of the Discourses, for example, he relates how during the Peloponnesian War in the city of Corcyra the nobles had gotten the upper hand over the popular party. The people of the city were so vengeful after the loss of their liberty that, when the intervention of the Athenians afforded them an opportunity, they killed their former oppressors.

Because Francis and Dominick had convinced the generality to leave the members of the clergy to God for punishment, such an uprising on the part of the people against the privileged class of the Church was not to be expected. Nonetheless, Machiavelli himself takes an obvious delight in contemplating the prospect of an individual undertaking to murder the pope and his cardinals. In the *Discourses*, for example, he criticizes one, who, when presented with such an opportunity, did not act. He reports that when Pope Julius II undertook to expel the tyrants who had seized the land of the Church, he entered Perugia to remove Giovampagolo Baglioni. Machiavelli first comments on the recklessness of the pope (cf. *P* 25.100–1), who entered the city entirely unarmed while his enemy maintained troops there, but the tyrant Baglioni receives Machiavelli's harshest criticism. Baglioni's cowardice permits the unarmed pope to leave Perugia with his prey. "The rashness of the pope and the vileness of Giovampagolo were noted by the prudent men who were with the pope, and they were unable to guess whence it came that [Baglioni] did not, to his perpetual fame, crush his enemy with one stroke and enrich himself with booty, since with the pope were all the cardinals with all their delights" (*D* 1.27.1). Machiavelli is shocked at his uncharacteristic restraint:

> So Giovampagolo, who did not mind being incestuous and a public parricide, did not know how, or to say better, did not dare, when he had just the opportunity [*occasione*] for it, to do an enterprise in which everyone would have admired his spirit, and which would have left an eternal memory [*perpetua fama*] of himself as being the first who had shown the prelates how little is to be esteemed whoever lives and rules as they do; and he would have done a thing whose greatness would have surpassed all infamy, every peril, that could have proceeded from it. (*D* 1.27.2; *O* 109–10; *see also P* 13.54)

Moreover, Machiavelli also contemplates the possibility of bodily harm coming to Pope Leo, the one on whom he seemingly pins his hopes in *The Prince*.[38] In 1514 Leo was caught between two opposing forces contending for Milan: Francis, Louis's successor, wished to recover the province from the Swiss, who were defending it. At this time Machiavelli considers the dangers of the pope's predicament:

> If somebody answers that the Pope, through the reverence felt for his person and through the authority of the Church, is in another situation, and will always have a refuge in which to save himself, I answer that such a reply deserves some consideration, and that then building on some foundation is possible. Nevertheless it is a foundation not to be relied on; on the contrary I believe that if the Pope

is well advised, he will not think of it, that such a thought will not
cause him to make a bad choice. Because all the things that have
been I believe can be again; and I know that pontiffs have fled, gone
into exile, been pursued, suffered to the utmost, like temporal rulers,
and in times when the Church in spiritual matters was more revered
than she is today. (Letter to Francesco Vettori, 20 December 1514,
CW 2:957–58)

Such macabre reflections could, of course, come from a deep concern
for the pope's welfare; no such concern is evident, however, in this
correspondence or in his later analysis of Leo's actions, where he
comes close to criticizing a secular ruler's reverence for this pope's
person in a manner similar to his criticism of Baglioni's cowardice
when confronted by Pope Julius. In the *Discourses* he proffers as an
example of a false opinion Leo's mistaken decision to remain neutral
until after a victor was decided in the battle between the French and
the Swiss. The victorious French were not debilitated by their exer-
tions, as Leo had speculated the winners would be. Because the triumphant French king possessed a store of energy, Machiavelli chides
him for not seeking a "second victory" over the Church, a victory
which, if Francis had sought it, certainly could have harmed Pope
Leo. Machiavelli comments that Francis's hesitancy was due either to
his "coldness"—the unflattering possibility—or to his "humanity"—
the complimentary alternative (*D* 2.22.1).

The greatness of the reward that would come from an attack on
the pope—the deed from which not only King Francis but even
Baglioni, the unrepentant criminal, shrank—reveals, perhaps, the
significance of the elimination of the papacy for Machiavelli. Yet his
characterization of the potential reward as "eternal memory" (*D*
1.27.2) does not appear to accord with an earlier remark in the *Discourses*. He explains that whereas "heads and orderers of religions"
are "most praised" of all human beings, those "are infamous and de-
testable who are destroyers of religions, squanderers of kingdoms
and republics, enemies of the virtues" (1.10.1). The murderer of a
pope and his entourage would seem to merit infamy rather than
"eternal memory"—unless, of course, as must be true of the destruction of the papacy, the act were not only to destroy but also to
found.

Machiavelli corroborates that such an act of destruction could
possibly be considered one of founding when he discusses the plot
Stefano Porcari contrived against the pope during the 1450s. Machiavelli describes Porcari as a Roman citizen "noble by blood and by

learning, but much more so by the excellence of his spirit,"[39] and comments that this man

> desired, according to the custom of men who relish glory, to do or at least to try something worthy of memory; and he judged he could do nothing else than try to see if he could take his fatherland from the hands of prelates and restore it to its ancient way of life, hoping by this, should he succeed, to be called the new founder and second father of that city.[40] (*FH* 6.29.263)

Porcari's attempt failed, but by the very attempt he wins fame in the pages of Machiavelli's history. "And truly, the intention of this man could be praised by anyone, but his judgment will always be blamed by everyone because such undertakings, if there is some shadow of glory in thinking of them, have almost always very certain loss in their execution," concludes Machiavelli (264). In so taking leave of this story, he gives the reader the impression that the only blame to which this would-be murderer can be subject is in the poor execution of his conspiracy.[41]

The person who removes the religious blight from Italy would provide the possibility for the growth of healthier political institutions.[42] As Machiavelli repeatedly emphasizes in many contexts, the very act of founding or reforming requires horrifying deeds. He highlights just such deeds when speaking in the *Discourses* of an initiate into the circle of great founders contained in *The Prince*: "And whoever reads the Bible judiciously [*sensatamente*] will see that if he wished his laws and his orders to go forward, Moses was forced to kill infinite men who, moved by nothing other than envy, were opposed to his plans" (*D* 3.30.1; *O* 237; cf. *P* 6).[43] In addition, Romulus, another such initiate, committed the crime of murder but must be forgiven because his object was to found *"un vivere civile"* (*D* 1.9; *O* 90; see *D* 1.18, 3.1).[44] Rome's "new founder and second father" would similarly merit forgiveness for his criminal deed (cf. *FH* 6.29).

The *Florentine Histories* and the *Discourses*, as well as *The Prince*, reveal the extent to which the Church was a parasitic institution, depriving Italian politics of its vigor. As with any parasite, the institution cannot be expected to return to health by furnishing the parasite with greater sustenance, but only by undertaking to eradicate it. If anticlericalism was common during the Renaissance, the particular solution to Italy's ills that Machiavelli contemplates certainly was not.[45]

❖ CHAPTER 2 ❖

THE RAVAGES OF CHRISTIANITY

According to Machiavelli, the Church has had a disastrous effect on Italian politics. Does his disdain for the clergy extend beyond the ministers of the Christian religion to reach the religion itself? Is the religious doctrine of Christianity as fatal to politics as are the machinations of its clergy? Hulliung answers these questions in the affirmative, declaring that "anticlericalism . . . marks only the first layer of his condemnation of Christianity" and that "Christian values per se are attacked as corrupt and contrasted with the virtuous values enshrined by pagan religion."[1]

Hulliung's conclusion is supported by the manner in which Machiavelli opens the *Discourses*.[2] The reader witnesses Machiavelli's sacrifice of Christian piety on the altar of ancient Roman military virtue as he laments that, although the methods of antiquity hold authority in certain disciplines, in the military and political arts the moderns do not recur to the examples of their forebears. In ascertaining the reasons for this neglect, he claims such a state of affairs

> arises . . . not so much from the weakness into which the present religion has led the world, or from the evil that an ambitious idleness [*uno ambizioso ozio*] has done to many Christian provinces and cities, as from not having a true knowledge of histories, through not getting from reading them that sense nor tasting that flavor that they have in themselves. (*D* 1.pr.2; *O* 76)

In this odd statement that marries caution with boldness, he hesitates to state directly that Christianity is responsible for the failure to appreciate ancient history, but forthrightly associates Christianity with the world's weakness; Christian states are characterized by *ambizioso ozio*. Such weakness and idleness seem evident when people judge that the imitation of the ancients "is not only difficult but impossible: as if heaven, sun, elements, men had varied in motion, order, and power from what they were in antiquity" (*D* 1.pr.2).[3]

Upon consideration it becomes evident that Christianity is responsible for both the moderns' view of ancient deeds and their belief in a transformation of heaven, both of which result in the political weakness Machiavelli finds so distressing. Christians are to renounce the prize of earthly glory so as to win heaven's glory. This Christian view of the meaning of ancient deeds and its relation to heaven is illustrated by Augustine's comment on Roman history: "see how much love is due to the heavenly city for the sake of eternal life, if the earthly city was so much loved by its citizens for its gift of human glory."[4] Because Christianity has taught human beings to renounce the goods of the earth and to pursue those of heaven, the misplaced efforts of the ancient Romans instruct Christians only to undergo even greater travail for the Eternal City. Even in this capacity the power of ancient history to instruct must be limited, for the deeds that won earthly glory are different from those that garner eternal rewards in heaven.

An understanding of this transformation helps explicate Machiavelli's formulation, *ambizioso ozio*, for modern men still covet rewards—albeit heavenly ones—and as a result are still ambitious. Unlike their ancestors, however, they no longer need undertake glorious earthly enterprises to gain their rewards, and as a result they can afford to be idle.[5] To combat this understanding of history,

Machiavelli offers a commentary on "all those books of Titus Livy that have not been intercepted by the malignity of the times." Machiavelli will compare ancient examples to modern ones, so those who read his work "will more easily be found to possess the utility for which one should seek knowledge of histories" (*D* 1.pr.2). By proffering examples of the ancients for the very purpose of imitation, Machiavelli simultaneously offers a challenge to the Christian view.

Despite this early and forthright repudiation of the Christian understanding of history in the name of the imitation of pagan politics, Machiavelli infuses his additional explicit criticisms of the religion in the *Discourses* with a measure of ambiguity. Both when he offers his most stinging condemnation of the Church's role as spoiler in Italian politics (1.12) and when he censures Christianity as such (2.2), he tempers his criticism by appealing from the Christianity of the vilely corrupt prelates to a purer version of the religion. Before one concurs with Hulliung's verdict that Machiavelli repudiates Christian values per se, it is necessary to examine these statements as well as additional discussions in which Christianity is less explicit the subject. I argue that Machiavelli finds that Christianity exerts a type of tyrannical rule over human beings, one that deprives them of their honor, dignity, and power. It is this domination from which Machiavelli endeavors to liberate them.

Machiavelli's Ambiguous Condemnations of Christianity

The ambiguity of Machiavelli's criticism of Christianity in the *Discourses* is evident in 1.12, for example, when, after describing admiringly how Camillus and the other "princes [*principi*] of the city" "favored and magnified" the credulity of the Roman people in matters divine, Machiavelli declares that, if "such religion [*la quale religione*] had been maintained by the princes of the Christian republic as was ordered by its giver [*datore*], the Christian states and republics would be more united, much more happy than they are" (*D* 1.12.1; *O* 95). Although it is quite clear that Machiavelli's criticism is directed at the current interpretation of Christianity, the standard to which he appeals remains obscure, because the antecedent of "such religion" is unclear. Anthony Parel resolves this difficulty by concluding that the antecedent is the pagan religion, as Machiavelli discusses this ancient religion immediately before the phrase in question. On this basis Parel asserts, "Machiavelli is saying that while Christ allegedly founded a naturalistic religion, His followers turned it into an otherworldly, supernatural religion. Presumably, Christ intended it to be . . . an instrument of politics."[6]

If this is Machiavelli's view of Christ's lessons, he diverges significantly from the only available knowledge of Christ's teachings—the one provided in the New Testament. Christ is not portrayed there as a likely redeemer of earthly kingdoms and republics from division and unhappiness, which is the standard by which Machiavelli will judge a religious doctrine, for he tells us he seeks provinces that are "more united" and "more happy." Surely, Christ's Sermon on the Mount does not offer satisfactory ammunition for the institution of a vigorous Machiavellian politics: "Blessed are those who are persecuted for righteousness' sake, for theirs is the kingdom of heaven" and "if any one strikes you on the right cheek, turn to him the other also."[7] Thus, whereas Parel assumes that the *datore* of whom Machiavelli speaks is Christ,[8] the teachings of Christ do not seem to meet the criteria Machiavelli holds out in this chapter of the attainment and the maintenance of temporal goods. Machiavelli at once expresses an impious admiration for the pagan understanding and clothes this impiety in the wholly inappropriate vestment of an appeal to early Christianity.[9]

Machiavelli challenges his reader with a similar contradiction in *Discourses* 2.2: on one hand, he reiterates the view posited in the preface to the first book that Christian education has undermined the ability of human beings to defend themselves; on the other, he mutes this forthright criticism by appealing to a Christianity unsullied by the corruption of the clergy. The trenchant character of his indictment of Christianity is unmistakable:

> [T]he ancient religion did not beatify men if they were not full of worldly glory, as were captains of armies and princes of republics. Our religion has glorified humble and contemplative more than active men. It has then placed the highest good in humility, abjectness, and contempt of things human; the other placed it in greatness of spirit, strength of body, and all other things capable of making men very strong. And if our religion asks that you have strength in yourself, it wishes you to be capable more of suffering than of doing something strong. (*D* 2.2.2)

Machiavelli thus corroborates his seemingly offhanded statement in the preface to the first book that Christianity itself has rendered human beings weak. It appears the religion of the modern world has provided an education entirely different from that which nurtured the glory-loving Romans. Moreover, "[t]his mode of living thus seems to have rendered the world weak and given it in prey to wicked [*scelerati*] men, who can manage it securely, seeing that the collectivity of men, so as to go to paradise, think more of enduring their beatings than of avenging them" (*D* 2.2.2; *O* 149). Christianity, in other words, has altered in a most politically deleterious manner the way in which people live and regard their world: they live now so as to attain entrance to heaven.

Despite the clarity of his rejection of Christianity because it has turned the gaze of human beings from the earthly realm to the heavenly, Machiavelli claims to hold not Christianity but merely "false interpretations" of the religion responsible for these negative political consequences:

> And although the world appears to be made effeminate and heaven disarmed, it arises without doubt more from the cowardice of the men who have interpreted our religion according to idleness [*ozio*] and not according to virtue. For if they considered how it allows us the exaltation and defense of the fatherland, they would see that it wishes us to love and honor it and to prepare ourselves to be such that we can defend it. (*D* 2.2.2; *O* 150)

This passage establishes that religious belief, in Machiavelli's view—whether truly or falsely interpreted—has a direct and critical effect on political life. Still, his claim that unworldly Christianity is merely a false interpretation appears incredible. Again, as in *Discourses* 1.12, his interest in his temporal homeland suggests that his intention conflicts with the teachings of original Christianity as conveyed in the New Testament. Machiavelli in this very chapter has already acknowledged his understanding that the Christian religion itself—not merely a fallacious interpretation of it—is resistant to the type of wholehearted exaltation of the homeland he seeks: "our religion having shown the truth and the true way, it makes us esteem less the honor of the world" (*D* 2.2.2). If, as he states, Christianity's "truth and . . . true way" devalues honor, then he must concede that his proposed "interpretation" of Christianity, which would overturn the "mode of living" that has "rendered the world weak" in order to exalt the *patria* and its defenders, simply cannot accord with Christianity's "truth and . . . true way."[10] Later I argue that Machiavelli is himself the *datore* (cf. *D* 1.12) of an entirely earthly interpretation of a Christianity that will serve the earthly homeland. In this manner his clumsy attempts to maintain that early Christianity or a correct interpretation of the religion can serve his political purposes prefigure his own positing of a new temporal interpretation of Christianity.

The Control of the World

Machiavelli indicates in *Discourses* 2.2 that Christianity has had a profound effect on the manner in which the people live by making them attached less to the rewards of this life and more to those of the next. By so transforming the goals of the people, moreover, Christian education has had a deleterious effect on politics by allowing the wicked to so flourish that they can actually be said to control the world. Because most of the political leaders who populate his writings cannot be numbered among those who eschew earthly delights so as to attain the rewards of paradise, it would appear that they instead number among the wicked who control the world. The actions of such leaders as Cesare, Louis, Francis, and Baglioni—those dedicated lovers of the temporal—do indicate, however, that the doctrines of Christianity have infected their souls as well. They are thus dominated by the Church and the result, Machiavelli suggests, is that their political ambitions come to naught. In his view, therefore, Christianity has had a politically deleterious effect not only on the people but also on their leaders.

It need not follow from this that Machiavelli regards such feeble political leadership as a necessary consequence of Christianity's rule. The power that Christianity exerts on the people emanates from the faith that the many have in it, whether that faith is engendered by Paul's missions or by the example of Saints Dominick and Francis, who rekindled that original faith when it had flagged. If this religion excites the hopes and fears of people to such a degree, then perhaps a political leader could extricate himself from both the constraints of the religion's moral dictates and the control of the religion's ministers so as to benefit directly from the depth of the people's belief. In this case, such a clever leader—not the duplicitous clergy—would control the world in security. A secular ruler of this type must necessarily be distinguished from the likes of Cesare, Louis, Francis, and even Baglioni, who were dominated in their enterprises by both the hierarchy of the Church and elements of Christian belief. If a secular leader were able to utilize the otherworldly religion as a vehicle by which to promote his earthly enterprises (cf. D 2.2), then perhaps Machiavelli would grant that this religion is not merely an instrument of political weakness but also potentially one of political strength. There exists in Machiavelli's political writings a leader whose example appears to hold such promise: Ferdinand of Aragon furnishes a prominent exception to the general domination of secular leaders by religious ones. Yet Machiavelli indicates that his example must be rejected in the name of effective rule, notwithstanding that Ferdinand was able to free himself from the domination of the churchmen, and thereby suggests that any political rule in the name of the otherworldly religion is ultimately disabling.

The influence of Christian doctrines is pervasive in Machiavelli's treatment of contemporary political events. As the examination of *The Prince* in the previous chapter showed, the ruthless Cesare was ultimately unsuccessful in his worldly undertakings because he relied upon forgiveness, which manifested itself most inconveniently when he permitted Julius, one whom the duke had previously injured, to ascend to the pontificate. Such a belief in forgiveness appears to be an unfortunate and unexpected manifestation of the enfeebling Christian education. Cesare moreover succumbed to the hierarchy of the religion when the rewards of his enterprises redounded to the Church. According to Machiavelli's analysis the Church ruled in a very real sense over the actions of the duke.

Christianity's influence can also be discerned in the failures of other modern leaders as well. Machiavelli ascribes the failure of King Louis of France to his maintaining the "faith" he had given to Pope Alexander. In addition his successor, King Francis, displayed reverence for the person of Pope Leo and, as a result, did not seek a second victory over the Church. Even the audacious criminal Baglioni displayed the same hesitancy when confronted by the person of Julius II. Such capitulations by secular leaders to the ruler of the Church illustrate that although these secular leaders are not so enthralled with the promises of Christianity that they renounce the goods of this world—as does the generality—their decisions nevertheless are informed to some degree by Christianity's dictates, and thus they allow the prelates to control them in some fashion. The difference between ancient and modern times emanates from the changes Christianity has exerted on human beings, and these changes have elevated the princes of that religion; the wicked who rule the world, therefore, appear to be in large measure those who rule the Church. To compound these problems, these wicked ones do not believe in God's punishment (*D* 3.1).

Despite what appears to be a consistent domination of political leaders by religious ones, Ferdinand emerges as a secular leader capable of bending the hierarchy of the Church to his will to promote his earthly enterprises. The Spanish king furnishes a contemporary example of armed and crusading Christianity, for he undertook the pious enterprise of forcibly driving the Moors from their outpost in Granada. He is famous, moreover, for instituting the Spanish Inquisition and expelling the Jews from Spain. In undertaking these deeds in the name of Christianity, he dominated the churchmen of his age.[11] Machiavelli's treatment of the Spanish king helps to reveal his own view of Christianity when it becomes a tool of statecraft.

Machiavelli, however, appears reluctant to express himself on this subject because he appears reticent about discussing the king forthrightly. When discussing the extent to which a prince must be a breaker of faith, Machiavelli apparently refers to this king, who had entered the battlefield of Italy, but refuses to name him. The author coyly adduces a "certain prince of present times, whom it is not well to name, [who] never preaches anything but peace and faith, and is very hostile to both."[12] Machiavelli here furnishes the important information that although this prince, whoever he may be, operates in Christianity's name, he is not himself constrained by the religion's dictates. These particular methods have been most useful to him, for Machiavelli notes that, "[i]f he had observed both [peace and faith], he would have had either his reputation or his state taken from him many times" (*P* 18.71).

Three chapters later Machiavelli is willing to name Ferdinand and to describe his successes. This discussion occurs in the chapter entitled "What a prince should do to be held in esteem," which begins with Machiavelli's exhortation to a prince "to carry on great enterprises and to give rare examples of himself." The first example he offers is of Ferdinand: "from being a weak king he has become by fame and by glory the first king among the Christians" (*P* 21.88–89).[13] As the discussion continues, Machiavelli offers Ferdinand as a model to be imitated, yet appears to recoil from his methods, which a comparison to those of Hannibal suggests are an ultimately ineffective type of cruelty.[14]

Machiavelli's ambivalence toward Ferdinand is evident in that, although he calls the Spanish king's deed of expelling the Marranos *"miserabile,"* his attitude—in the discussion and its context—is more one of praise than of blame. In Machiavelli's estimation Ferdinand is admirably devious:

> in order to undertake greater enterprises, always making use of religion, he turned to an act of pious cruelty, expelling the Marranos from his kingdom and despoiling them; nor could there be an example more wretched [*miserabile*] and rarer than this. He attacked Africa under this same cloak, made his campaign in Italy, and has lately attacked France; and so he has always done and ordered great things, which have always kept the minds of his subjects in suspense and admiration, and occupied with their outcome. (*P* 21.88; *O* 291)

The Spanish king employs a form of Christian cruelty that awes his subjects but is not condoned by Machiavelli.[15]

That a ruler utilizes cruelty does not in itself preclude Machiavelli's admiration, however. Machiavelli distinguishes between cruelties well used and those badly used: "Those can be called well used (if it be permissible to speak well of evil) that are done at a stroke, out of necessity to secure oneself, and then are not persisted in but are turned to as much utility for the subjects as one can" (*P* 8.37–38). In discussing the infamous tyrant Agathocles, he offers the conventional view that his "savage cruelty and inhumanity, together with his infinite crimes, do not allow him to be celebrated among the most excellent men," yet he condones these offenses of Agathocles: "Those who observe the first mode [of cruelty well used] can have some remedy for their state with God and with men, as had Agathocles" (*P* 8.35 and 38).

The question thus arises whether Machiavelli regards Ferdinand's cruelty as well used. In order to derive Machiavelli's judgment, it is necessary to contrast Ferdinand's "pious cruelty" with Hannibal's "inhuman cruelty." Machiavelli clearly regards Hannibal's cruelty as conducive to his political well-being:

> Among the admirable actions of Hannibal is numbered this one: that when he had a very large army, mixed with infinite kinds of men, and had led it to fight in alien lands, no dissension ever arose in it, neither among themselves nor against the prince, in bad as well as in his good fortune. (*P* 17.67; see also *D* 3.21)

Hannibal's success in this endeavor "could not have arisen from anything other than his inhuman cruelty which together with his infinite virtues, always made him venerable and terrible in the sight of his soldiers; and without it, his other virtues would not have sufficed to bring about this effect." The writers who admire the effects of his rule but condemn his cruelty engage in self-contradiction, Machiavelli suggests (*P* 17.67). Cruelty is sometimes necessary, and when necessary Machiavelli readily condones it. Hannibal's cruelty was necessary.

Ferdinand's use of cruelty differs strikingly from Hannibal's. Hannibal's cruelty was employed to hold together an army containing different races of men, whereas Ferdinand's was utilized in expelling people of differing creeds from his kingdom. Therefore, Hannibal's related to an act of unification that increased the numbers of men at his command, whereas Ferdinand's served to deplete his population.[16] Because Ferdinand's cruelty did not serve his military exploits, it was not well used. One can readily envision Machiavelli chastising Ferdinand for expelling these people rather than arming them.[17] As long as the ostensible purpose of Ferdinand's army was to exalt the Christian religion, naturally people of differing creeds had no place there. Moreover, Machiavelli suggests in several contexts that useless cruelty will result in a leader's ruin rather than in his preservation (e.g., *D* 2.24 and 3.6).[18]

Because they were committed in the name of a god whose rule enfeebles human beings, the pious exploits Ferdinand employed must ultimately be injurious to any sort of human rule, as the next section will illustrate. Machiavelli's ultimate dissatisfaction with Ferdinand's methods can be reconciled with his apparent praise of the king in *The Prince* if Machiavelli's intention is that a prince who understands Machiavelli's lesson will retain Ferdinand's lack of faith but apply such faithlessness to the subversion of both the Church and the otherworldly understanding of Christianity.[19]

The Modern Education

Further insight into Machiavelli's view of the debilitating character of the Christian education and its relation to politically unsalutary cruelty emerges from reconsideration of Machiavelli's treatment of Baglioni in the *Discourses*. After chastising Bologna's tyrant for his cowardice in failing to attack the pope and his cardinals, Machiavelli appears to absolve him from blame. Baglioni failed only in the impossible; Machiavelli notes with resignation that men do not know "how to be honorably wicked [*cattivi*] or perfectly good; and when malice has greatness in itself or is generous in some part, they do not know how to enter into it" (*D* 1.27.1; *O* 110). Because one cannot expect any human being to be altogether bad, Machiavelli apparently concludes that such badness—badness that "would have surpassed all infamy" (*D* 1.27.2)—cannot reasonably be expected even from Baglioni, who had been so notably bold in the commission of other crimes.

Two books later (*D* 3.27), however, Machiavelli blames not the universal character of human beings but modern education for the tendency of individuals to recoil from the commission of the horrible deeds he deems generous. In speaking of the remedy for a city divided by faction, he recommends that the leaders of such factions be killed, just as the Romans did when quieting a dispute in a city subject to their rule. Rather than following this Roman example, he finds instead that the moderns generally do as the Florentines did when confronted with the same problem in Pistoia: the Florentines demanded that each side lay down its arms and come to an agreement. From the Florentines' conscientious effort on behalf of peace "always greater tumults and greater scandals arose" (*D* 3.27.2). In censuring the moderns for not following the example of the ancient Romans, he refers to his preface to the first book of the *Discourses:* "[t]hese are among the errors I told of at the beginning that the princes of our times make who have to judge great things." "[B]ecause like executions have in them the great and the generous," Machiavelli declares, "a weak republic does not know how to do them." This unwillingness of the moderns to emulate the ancients, he again insists, arises from "their weak education and their slight knowledge of things." As a result, they "judge ancient judgments in part inhuman, in part impossible" (*D* 3.27.2). He again indicts the modern education—and thus the Christian education—for the inability of modern people to imitate the deeds of the ancients.[20] If this inability to countenance spectacularly violent deeds arises from the enfeebling modern education, perhaps Baglioni's cowardice is not ultimately a manifestation of the failure of human beings everywhere and always to be either thoroughly bad or completely good, but rather of this same devitalizing education. Whether or not such a speculation represents Machiavelli's ultimate conclusion in the case of Baglioni's cowardice, clearly Machiavelli blames modern leaders for their obtuseness in not discerning the benevolence of some violent acts. Rather than correctly deeming such actions generous, they reject what they believe to be inhuman and take measures that serve only to perpetuate the very disturbances they endeavor to quell.

In *The Prince* Machiavelli links such misplaced kindness—kindness that actually results in cruelty—even more explicitly to the Christian teaching. He enters this analysis by way of the same example he gives in the *Discourses*—that of the misguided attempts of the Florentines to quiet the division in Pistoia. He immediately offers a Christian context for this discussion by placing it in the chapter he entitles "Of cruelty and mercy [*pietate*],[21] and whether it is better to be loved than feared, or the contrary" (*P* 17.65). As Clifford Orwin notes, the *pietà* of which Machiavelli here speaks corresponds to the Christian virtue of love or charity; the Christian doctrine proclaims that the person who loves God is to replicate God's love of human beings in acts of charity.[22] Christ commands: "'A new commandment I give to you, that you love one another; even as I have loved you, that you also love one another.'"[23] Machiavelli offers the actions of the Florentines with regard to Pistoia as an exemplification of *pietà* conventionally understood and Cesare's actions in the Romagna as exemplifying cruelty conventionally understood. He begins this discussion by asserting that "each prince should desire to be held merciful [*pietoso*] and not cruel" but immediately notes that, although "Cesare Borgia was held to be cruel," "his cruelty restored the Romagna, united it, and reduced it to peace and to faith" (*P* 17.65; *O* 281).[24] Conversely, the Florentines who desired "to escape a name for cruelty, allowed Pistoia to be destroyed." Machiavelli defends his view that the acts conventionally considered merciful are actually cruel, by asserting that misplaced kindness "allows disorders to continue, from which come killings or robberies," which "customarily harm a whole community" (65–66). Hence, Cesare was actually "much more merciful [*pietoso*] than the Florentine people" (*P* 17.65; *O* 282).[25]

Christians have so misunderstood mercy that in order to avoid cruelty they take half-measures that produce greater acts of political cruelty than those they sought originally to avoid. In offering this analysis Machiavelli takes the part of the community as a whole—of the people who demand only a government that maintains order and does not despoil those subjected to its power (see *D* 1.16 and *P* 9). The popular perspective he offers here complements his criticism, discussed in the previous chapter, of the Church hierarchy for oppressing the people.

Despite Machiavelli's tendency to highlight the bloody and the spectacular in the name of mercy correctly understood, he also suggests that the avoidance of half-measures need not always result in carnage, as it can also result in *generosi* acts that actually "caress" a subject people. As Machiavelli declares in *The Prince*, "men should either be caressed or eliminated" (*P* 3.10). He examines in detail the former strategy in 2.23 of the *Discourses*, entitled "How much the Romans, in judging subjects for some accident that necessitated such judgment, fled from the middle way." In this chapter Machiavelli reports that when the Romans had forced the Latins to such a pass that they could no longer maintain the struggle against their Roman adversaries, Camillus addressed the Senate to declare that it must decide whether Rome is to destroy Latium or to embrace its people by making the conquered Latins citizens of Rome. If it chose the latter alternative, Camillus offered, Rome would enlarge its fighting force "'with material for rising to the greatest glory'" (*D* 2.23.2).[26] Machiavelli reports that after Camillus's speech the Senate decided to benefit Rome by embracing the subjugated Latins, and comments that the Romans either benefited their vanquished foes or extinguished them. In this manner, Machiavelli shows that generous acts do not always require the violence he advocates elsewhere; rather, a state can avoid the middle way and the cruelty it entails through the "generosity" of embracing its enemy.

Such mercy, when properly applied, produces temporal advantages. In this particular case the result is an increase of population necessary for territorial acquisition. He makes the rewards of implementation of this doctrine evident in the chapter entitled "Rome became a great city through ruining the surrounding cities and easily admitting foreigners to its honors" (*D* 2.3). He claims here that a city that endeavors to be a great power must increase the number of its inhabitants. This end, he says, can be reached in two modes, "by love and by force." He explains: "By love through keeping the ways open and secure for foreigners who plan to come to inhabit it so that everyone may inhabit it willingly; by force through undoing the neighboring cities and sending their inhabitants to inhabit your city" (*D* 2.3.1). Again, the effects of Ferdinand's pious cruelty stand in stark contrast to the military ends and methods Machiavelli recommends.

In advocating this particular species of generous act, Machiavelli himself appears to embrace the Christian exhortation to love one's enemy. The correspondence of his recommendation with Christianity's command should not be overestimated, however. Because Machiavelli's purpose is so different from the Christian one, his version is but a perverse parody of it. In the case of the Christian injunction, if human beings were able to fulfill its command, human relations would be remade: concord and harmony would reign. In contrast Machiavelli asks that states love others only to the extent that these others can provide soldiers for the continuing prosecution of war. The love Machiavelli preaches is for the sake of armed conflict.

The moderns do not follow the example of such loving deeds of the Romans, however, because they do not endeavor to make their earthly cities great. As a result, they neither arm their people nor cherish the attendant rewards of earthly conflict; they do not consider the virtues of the soldier to be human virtues. The product of their misunderstanding is, as Machiavelli repeatedly claims, that their states are weak and overrun. Christianity enfeebles human beings.

The Character of Christian Rule

Machiavelli's hostile engagement with Christianity, however, extends far beyond this accusation that the religion's promulgation of the doctrine of mercy actually produces cruelty. Machiavelli defends human beings in general against tyrannical rulers who depreciate their dignity and power. In denouncing this type of subjugation he finds that the Christian god poses the most acute threat to human liberty, and so his most principled challenge to Christianity comes from his concern for human dignity. In challenging Christianity, then, Machiavelli defends human liberty against the tyrannical ruler of his age.

Machiavelli's opposition to the Christian conception of virtue is encapsulated by his bold assertion in the chapter title of *Discourses* 2.14—that "Often men deceive themselves believing that through humility [*umiltà*] they will conquer pride [*superbia*]" (O 164). The chapter treats the manner in which the Romans' dispute with the Latins eventuated in war, and this story seems particularly ill chosen to illustrate the maxim of the chapter heading. Machiavelli uses the term *"umilità"* only once, and does not use the term *"superbia"* at all, in the body of the chapter. Instead, he speaks of the *"pazienza"* of the Romans and the *"arroganza"* of the Latins (O 164).

Perhaps the inappropriateness of this ancient Roman story for his purpose derives from the terms of his chapter's heading, *superbia* and *umilità*, cognates of the Latin *superbia* and *humilitas*, which are suited more to the modern era because they are strikingly evocative of prominent Christian doctrine. For the Christian, humility is a virtue and pride a sin. The Latin *humilitas* originally carried a derogative sense, signifying the indignity of low birth or submissiveness.[27] In regarding humility as a virtue, the Christians exalt this meaning: "'God opposes the proud, but gives grace to the humble.'"[28] Christians follow the example of their Savior in cultivating this virtue: "the humility of the God-man was praiseworthy in the extreme when . . . to change the spirits of men over from love of worldly glory to love of divine glory He willed to bear . . . a death abject in the extreme."[29]

Machiavelli appears here to reject the belief in humility by noting that in holding it people often deceive themselves. His opposition to Christian humility is unmistakable, however, in *Discourses* 2.2. Recall that he categorically rejects it when he asserts that by exalting "humble and contemplative" men rather than men of action, Christianity has made the "world weak" (*D* 2.2.2). He favors an understanding that would consign men to the battlefield rather than to the presbytery or to the pew. Indeed, as chapter 1 showed, the hesitancy of modern people to undertake their own defense—and hence to eschew Christian humility—has resulted in their political and military subjugation.

This hesitancy of modern people to undertake their own defense may derive, in Machiavelli's view, not only from Christian humility but from a type of Christian pride. Humility itself eventuates in pride, for the humility that renounces arms is proud in assuming divine protection. Christians tend not to see to their own defense because in their pride they do not think such efforts necessary. The effects of their negligence can be disastrous: "To believe that without effort on your part God fights for you, while you are idle [*ozioso*] and on your knees, has ruined many kingdoms and many states," muses the protagonist of the *Golden Ass* (*CW* 2:764; *O* 967). The ruination of kingdom and states reveals for Machiavelli the pernicious character of the self-deception that occurs when one believes humility can vanquish pride.

Machiavelli prefers both a humility different from that which the Christians profess and a pride different from that into which they unwittingly fall. He assumes that human beings have to fight for themselves and that recognizing this need is the type of humility that could render men soldiers. In making men active, he renounces the Christian beatification of humble men and would instead bestow glory on men for their worldly exploits.

He acknowledges that their virtue resides in their activity as fighters, and hence their ability to control their military and political fates. He promotes this pride and believes such a transformation is far from unattainable: "It is more true than any other truth that if where there are men there are no soldiers, it arises through a defect of the prince" (D 1.21.1).

His opposition to the Christian humility that withholds honor from human beings for their earthly undertakings, and renders them complacent as a result, is evident elsewhere as well. The belief that all of one's attainments ultimately derive from God's grace has undesirable consequences, because, as a result, people believe that they do not have to exert themselves:

> It is not unknown to me that many have held and hold the opinion that worldly things are so governed by fortune and by God, that men cannot correct them with their prudence, indeed that they have no remedy at all; and on account of this they might judge that one need not sweat much over things but let oneself be governed by chance. (P 25.98)

Machiavelli diverges from this common view, but he is modest in estimating the extent of that divergence: "in order that our free will not be eliminated, I judge that it might be true that fortune is arbiter of half of our actions, but also that she leaves the other half, or close to it, for us to govern" (ibid.). Although reticent in estimating the ability of human power to oppose God or fortune, at the end of the chapter he leaves the reader with the immoderate image of a young man who has beaten an extrahuman force into submission.[30]

Machiavelli dissents most stridently regarding the role of extrahuman forces in human affairs when discussing the earthly accomplishment that surpassed all others, undertaken by men who were spurred on by the love of worldly glory, that of the acquisition of the Roman Empire. "Many have had the opinion, and among them Plutarch, a very grave writer, that the Roman people in acquiring the empire was favored more by fortune than by virtue." An extrahuman force, the goddess Fortuna, was, in Plutarch's view, responsible for the Romans' accomplishment. "I do not wish to confess this thing in any mode, nor do I believe even that it can be sustained," asserts Machiavelli against the likes of Plutarch and of Livy as well (D 2.1.1).[31] In contrast, Machiavelli finds that human ingenuity and virtue were the cause of this accomplishment.[32]

In giving credit to the human endeavors of the Romans, Machiavelli diverges also from Christian writers who view the Roman Empire as the result of Divine Providence.[33] Augustine, for example, sees the hand of the Christian god in the pagan Romans' accomplishment: "Without any doubt, it is by divine providence that human kingdoms are set up."[34] Dante too declares the expanse of the Roman Empire to be the work of God: "I see the most evident sign of divine Providence behind . . . the way the Roman people made itself pre-eminent throughout the world."[35]

Although Machiavelli does not explicitly draw attention to his disagreement with such Christian writers on the role of a transcendent force in this human accomplishment (as he does with pagan writers), he interposes a term evocative of Christianity into his discussion. He says that he does "not wish to confess . . . in any mode [*confessare in alcuno modo*]" that fortune is responsible for the Roman acquisitions (O 146). In declaring that he is unwilling to confess such a thing, he brings his dispute with Plutarch regarding the role of human capacity in human accomplishment onto the ground of the Christians. The Christian practice of confession brings with it the notion of human sin, and although Christians ultimately attribute to God's providence any human achievement, they maintain that their errors are their sole responsibility.[36] Christians must acknowledge their responsibility for those deeds that are willful divergences from God's grace before taking the sacrament of penance. Christianity allows human beings their faults, but it will not allow them their accomplishments.[37] Machiavelli, by contrast, maintains against staunch and most reputable authority that their accomplishments should belong to them as well.[38]

To be sure, the Christian understanding that ascribes human virtue to God's grace does not consider the qualities that won the territory of the Roman empire to be virtues correctly understood. Although Augustine, for example, acknowledges that in the pursuit of glory the Romans checked their other appetites and as a result were less depraved than they would have been otherwise, he still maintains that these qualities are not themselves virtues because they are cultivated for the glory of men rather than of God.[39] Such self-abnegating men who died for the sake of the glory of their homeland and of their name are declared to be blameworthy rather than virtuous in the eyes of the Christian god.

The depth of Machiavelli's opposition to this Christian understanding of the world cannot be appreciated fully until one recognizes that his description of the effects of this understanding replicates those of the type of tyranny he most vehemently denounces. Machiavelli likens the effects of Christianity to those of a tyranny. Although it was quite common for Christians to refer to God or Christ as a king or as a prince, a denunciation of the character of divine rule implied by such a comparison was quite dangerous at the time.[40] Given this danger, the similarities he draws between Christianity and tyranny are all the more bold. The equation of the two is based in the very chapter in which Machiavelli laments that Christianity has beatified "humble and contemplative" men rather than "men full of worldly glory." He explains that "a virtuous tyrant . . . , who by spirit and by virtue of arms expands his dominion, the result is of no utility to that republic [*republica*],[41] but is his own. For he cannot honor any of the citizens he tyrannizes over who are able and good since he does not wish to have to suspect them" (*D* 2.2.1; *O* 148). The debilitating effects of such a tyranny are precisely those Machiavelli finds emanating from the Christian education: both rob human beings of the honor to which they are entitled; neither this virtuous tyrant nor Christianity will permit individuals possession of any good, for in either case all accrues ultimately to the benefit of the ruler. The effects on political life are devastating.

Despite the manner in which Machiavelli's two analyses mirror each other, it at first appears that his description of this type of tyrant must be distinguished from Christianity's rule in one important respect: the very definition of a *tiranno virtuoso* demands that he acquire territory through *animo* and the virtue of arms. Christianity did not spread in this manner; nevertheless, it certainly did spread. The expanse of Christendom exceeds the expanse of the Roman Empire. An acquisition of this magnitude surely merits the adjective *spirited*. Moreover, although the followers of Christ did not employ conventional arms, they did see their enterprise as a type of war—a war that demanded a new sort of arms. Witness Paul's declaration:

> For though we live in the world we are not carrying on a worldly war, for the weapons of our warfare are not worldly but have divine power to destroy strongholds. We destroy arguments and every proud obstacle to the knowledge of God, and take every thought captive to obey Christ, being ready to punish every disobedience, when your obedience is complete.[42]

Paul, who undertook to convert diverse peoples to Christianity, understood his enterprise to be a new type of war fought for the glory of God. Christianity engages in this warfare for the promulgation of belief and, in a manner of speaking, in an effort at territorial acquisition. This recognition that both the energetic tyrant and Christianity undertake to make territorial gains leads us to additional shared characteristics. Machiavelli continues, for instance, that the tyrant derives benefit from maintaining "the state disjoined and have each town and each province acknowledge him" (D 2.2.1). In 3.27 of the *Discourses* Machiavelli stridently attacks the failure of the moderns to employ the tough-minded methods that would overcome the debilitating division of their cities. Their refusal arises from their moral compunctions, which themselves originate from their Christian belief. Because these cities recognize the rule of Christianity, they remain divided. Thus, according to Machiavelli the political effects of Christianity's imperium *are* those of a *tiranno virtuoso*. Further, because Machiavelli does not offer any historical examples of such an enterprising tyrant[43] but does offer intimations enough to draw an equation between this despotism and his other discussions of the effects of the Christian religion, it appears he presents the Christian god as the example par excellence of such a dominating ruler.

Because Machiavelli provides sufficient clues to link his criticism of Christianity (in this chapter and elsewhere) with his denunciation of tyranny here, his most zealous encomium to the free way of life takes on additional meaning. As the chapter is coming to a close, he contrasts the order of the past with the disorder of the present and concludes that it arises "from the free way of life then and the servile way of life now" (20). He describes the goods of freedom as follows:

> For all towns and provinces that live freely in every part (as was said above) make very great profits. For larger peoples are seen there, because marriages are freer and more desirable to men since each willingly procreates those children he believes he can nourish. He does not fear that his patrimony will be taken away, and he knows not only that they are born free and not slaves, but that they can through their virtue become princes [*principi*]. (D 2.2.3)

He alerts us to his rather unconventional understanding of freedom when he says that children, in this free state, can grow up to be princes. According to Machiavelli, a free life need not be lived in a republic conventionally understood;[44] however, a free life must be lived apart from the devastation that Christianity exacts on political life.

Until the above consideration of Machiavelli's discussion of *Discourses* 2.2, this chapter had explored only the manner in which Machiavelli declares or intimates that Christianity has weakened human beings by depriving them of the resources necessary to defend themselves. This original criticism is not actually vitiated for, as Machiavelli declares, it is possible for a ruler to be strengthened through his subjects' weakness: the tyrant "alone and not his fatherland profits from his acquisitions" (*D* 2.2.1). Machiavelli's discussion enumerates the hurtful effects of tyrannical rule, and any comparison of it to Christianity's rule still offers a biting criticism of the religion. This discussion nevertheless furnishes a new dimension to Machiavelli's evaluation of Christianity, for it highlights the degree to which he is willing to acknowledge the strength and vigor of Christianity; it is itself a formidable power. Therefore, although in his view human beings have not profited from the ascendancy of the Christian god, Machiavelli can now be seen to acknowledge the power that effected this transformation of the world. After all, the results of its rule clearly merit that the term *virtuoso* be applied to the character of its domination.

PART II

PAGAN ROME

But Christ, as his scribe Luke testifies, willed to be born of the Virgin Mary under an edict of Roman authority in order that he, the Son of God made man, might register in that extraordinary register of mankind as a man. —Dante

The *Discourses* begins with an explicit appeal from the political weakness of the moderns to the political strength of the ancients— from the feeble inhabitants of Christian Rome to the awe-inspiring power of those of pagan Rome. Machiavelli's admiration for this lost vigor impels him to present the marvels of antiquity to his dispirited compatriots with the hope that these examples will stir the idle moderns to emulation (*D* 1.pr.). In so glorifying the pagan world, he appears to put himself at odds with the Christians, who must reject the pagan worldview in favor of the new dispensation that guides Rome.

Despite his apparently categorical rejection of his own age on the basis of its thorough weakness, Machiavelli has grudgingly acknowledged Christianity's strength. After all, Christianity successfully subverted the mighty Roman Empire to exercise with extraordinary vigor a type of tyrannical rule over a large portion of humanity. He appears to suggest, then, that Rome—albeit Christian rather than pagan—still furnishes the seat for a powerful government. Careful consideration of Machiavelli's treatment of Christianity shows that he considers the modern religion to be a more powerful force than his most explicit statements indicate.

In like manner he ultimately understands pagan Rome to be a weaker power than his explicit judgments on the character of that city would appear to indicate. The following three chapters consider in detail his presentation of pagan Rome in the *Discourses* in order to argue that he discerns fundamental weaknesses in his exemplary ancient city. Ancient Rome must be viewed in a new light because Machiavelli judges that its defective constitution not only allowed Caesar to overturn the republic, but also allowed Christianity to impose its form of tyranny on Rome; the modern tyranny exercised by the modern religion grew out of ancient Rome's inability to deal effectively with its ambitious men, who sought preeminence in the state by promising the people increasingly irresistible benefits.

Further, in Machiavelli's view, paganism actually engendered Christianity. His criticism of Numa, for example, reveals that the pagan religion introduced into Rome the problem that would devastate politics in the modern era—that of the division between the demands of religion and those of politics. Although present from Numa's reign, this virus of divisiveness would remain dormant until the promises of potential tyrants combined with the transcendent claims of religion to produce a noxious mix. Armed with this mix, a potential tyrant could prey on the religious beliefs of the people by appealing to invisible powers that could be said to offer invisible goods, invisible lands, indeed, an invisible city.

This recognition of a certain decisive continuity between ancient Rome and modern Rome is intended to deny neither that paganism warred with Christianity nor that in some ways paganism is the very opposite of Christianity. Nevertheless, the weakness of ancient Rome allowed Christian rule a firm foothold on its way to the successful imposition of a new type of rule that saps the political strength of human beings. As Machiavelli suggests to his careful readers, the beginnings of modern weakness are actually to be discovered in Rome's very beginnings. Part 2 is devoted to uncovering the defects of ancient Rome, with a view to Machiavelli's enterprise of improving on that city. Indeed, as part 3 elaborates, Machiavelli undertakes to construct a new Rome—one that corrects both ancient and modern weaknesses by marrying the strength to be found in antiquity with that evident in his own times.

❖ CHAPTER 3 ❖

THE FOUNDATION FOR TYRANNY IN ROME

Early in the *Discourses* Machiavelli undertakes to justify his presentation of ancient Rome as the exemplary republic. In so doing, he defends Rome against its critics and adduces grounds for rejecting the examples of Sparta and Venice, Rome's competitors for this honor. Although he does offer principled reasons for preferring Rome over its competitors, even in his early promotion he indicates the grounds for his ultimate dissatisfaction with the city: it did not fulfill that full measure of its life that its principles should have afforded it—Rome fell too early under the influence of a tyrant. According to Machiavelli's presentation of its downfall, the city succumbed to the ever more ingenious appeals of ambitious men who sought the favor of the people.

In treating the appeals of these aspiring tyrants, Machiavelli infuses his discussions of pre-Christian Rome with terms decidedly evocative of the Christian religion. By anticipating the coming of Christianity in this manner, he suggests that its attraction was merely a deepening of the appeals made with increasing and regrettable success during the period of Rome's decline. He states that Caesar was Rome's first tyrant and goes on to suggest that Caesar was actually outdone by Christ, in the same way that Caesar outdid the Gracchi. Caesar's efforts to gain the loyalty of the people were predicated on the efforts of his predecessors, the Gracchi, who acquired the people's partisanship through their promise of the favorable distribution of Rome's conquered land. Although Caesar's promises met with considerable success, they were surpassed by Christ's claim to transcendence—a claim that attracted adherents by promising the people they would receive riches far surpassing any to be found in an earthly city. Although Christ's appeal was deeper than Caesar's, they can be compared: each supplicated the people and the martyrdom of each allowed others to rule in the martyr's name.

Although the Roman people so readily accepted Christ's alluring appeal, Machiavelli will not censure them. He places the blame for the success of Christianity in Rome instead on the constitution of that city which was unnecessarily vulnerable to the machinations of these aspiring tyrants; ancient Rome, in his view, was itself responsible for the favorable reception Christianity received there.

Machiavelli's Unsatisfactory Case for the Roman Republic

Machiavelli begins his examination of the ancient Roman republic in the *Discourses* as an outspoken supporter of that republic's distinctive—but often derided—characteristic: its tumult.[1] He readily acknowledges that his position, which maintains that the dissension between the nobles in Rome was beneficial rather than harmful to the liberty of that state, is controversial and judiciously turns the floor over to an advocate for the opposing view:

> And if anyone said: the modes were extraordinary and almost ferocious, to see the people together shouting against the Senate, the Senate against the people, running tumultuously through the streets, closing shops, all the plebs leaving Rome—all which things frighten whoever does no other than read of them.

In responding to this critic's argument Machiavelli comes to the defense of the people of Rome, arguing that any republic that endeavors to "make use of the people in important things" must have "modes with which the people can vent its ambition" (*D* 1.4.1). Of course, the Roman republic used its people as its soldiery and furnished them with the tribunate as an outlet for their ambition.

With this claim in favor of Rome's tumultuous confusion, he explicitly confronts the claims made on behalf of Sparta and Venice, two polities that, because they did not fall victim to domestic discord in the manner of the ancient Roman republic, could be proposed as alternatives by those still disdainful of Roman tumult. The deciding factor between the stability of Sparta and Venice on the one hand and the strife of Rome on the other is the additional determination of whether a given state pursues empire:

> either you are reasoning about a republic that wishes to make an empire, like Rome, or of one for whom it is enough to maintain itself. In the first case it is necessary for it to do everything like Rome; in the second, it can imitate Venice and Sparta, for the causes that will be told in the following chapter. (*D* 1.5.3)

In the next chapter, however, he does not fulfill this promise, because the analysis that occurs there ultimately leads to the conclusion that the pursuit of empire cannot be repudiated and thus that the examples of Sparta and Venice do not, in fact, represent a viable choice; they must themselves be rejected as untenable alternatives to tumult and empire.

Despite what will be his ultimate rejection of the examples of Sparta and Venice, he begins 1.6 by detailing the institutions of Rome's competitors, as if their examples were worthy not only of consideration, but also of imitation. The Venetian republic, he reports, barred newcomers from participating in its government. Since those excluded were not utilized in matters that would cause them to demand authority, such as their employment in the prosecution of Venice's wars, they did not make disturbances. As a result, Venice attained its famous tranquillity. The Spartan regime established by Lycurgus achieved its noted harmony by decreeing that poverty be shared by all alike, thus assuring that the plebeians were not ambitious. Machiavelli points out that Rome could have done two things in order to remain "quiet" like these other republics: "either not employ the plebs in war, like the Venetians, or not open the way to foreigners, like the Spartans." Rome rejected both alternatives and as a consequence gave to the plebeians "strength and increase, and infinite occasions for tumult" (*D* 1.6.3). If Rome had instituted measures to promote domestic peace, it would have negated its ability to expand. In the early portion of 1.6, as in 1.5, the choice continues to rest on whether empire is the objective: "If someone wished, therefore, to order a republic anew, he would have to examine whether he wished it to expand like Rome in dominion and in power, or truly to remain within narrow limits" (D 1.6.4).

He next cautions that if a republic is to acquire an empire it must be constituted properly so as to be capable of maintaining its acquisitions: empire demands "a great number of men, and well armed" (D 1.6.4). Although neither Sparta nor Venice was organized as an imperial state, each found itself later in a position that demanded it rule the empire it had acquired.[2] Indeed, so pernicious does Machiavelli find the addition of empire to their type of internal organization, he declares that both the Spartan and Venetian states met their ruin when they were unable to manage the empires of which they found themselves in control.

Ultimately, the manner in which these states were ruined mitigates the force that the recognition of their longevity carries for Machiavelli. His support for Sparta and Venice takes on a provisional tone by the end of 1.6. He broaches the consideration that will provide the grounds for his rejection of Sparta and Venice when he treats the question of the requisite size of a republic: "I would well believe that to make a republic that would last a long time the mode would be to order it within like Sparta or like Venice; to settle it in a strong place of such power that nobody would believe he could crush it at once" (D 1.6.4). Machiavelli specifies an intermediate size because he identifies two causes for war: either others wish to govern your state or others fear your desire to govern their state; the intermediate size discourages offensive forays and does not provoke defensive attacks.

Such an arrangement, Machiavelli grants, "would be the true political way of life and the true quiet of a city"; however, he immediately questions whether this "true quiet" for a city is, in fact, possible. In offering the reflection that "all things of men are in motion and cannot stay steady, they must either rise or fall," he reneges on the promise of the "true quiet of a city" that Sparta and Venice appear to hold out for political life. The stability such states require cannot be found; eventually "necessity" will require that a state go to war (D 1.6.4). Successfully waged war brings enlargement, and the principles that allow this republic to enjoy domestic concord do not permit such increase. Thus when the increase occurs—as it must if the republic is victorious in the wars that will arise—the republic confronts its own ruin.

The pursuit of empire must dictate the internal arrangements of a city, for war that is to be waged successfully requires an armed, and hence a tumultuously demanding, populace. Machiavelli thus challenges the view that a city's highest purposes accord with tranquillity, which in turn dictates that laws should be established with a view ultimately toward peace and friendship rather than toward war and enmity.[3] By contrast, the principles that guide Machiavelli as he legislates for his city do not take peace as their touchstone. For Machiavelli war is not merely an unavoidable evil; it should, in fact, be cultivated.[4]

The promotion of war benefits the state. An armed state repels foreign incursions, and war keeps internal disputes under control: "if heaven were so kind that [the state] did not have to make war, from that would arise the idleness [*ozio*] to make it either effeminate or divided; these two things together, or each by itself, would be the cause of its ruin" (*D* 1.6.4; *O* 86). Later in the *Discourses* Machiavelli states explicitly that discord in a republic is due to "idleness [*ozio*] and peace" and unity to "fear and war" (2.25.1; *O* 185). Thus he suggests that states whose principles are intended to promote internal stability, and which are able to avoid war by some seemingly fortunate constellation of events, would in actuality promote the very instability that they seek to avoid, which would, in turn, threaten their very existences. He denies that the "middle way" seemingly offered by such republics can be a refuge for human beings (*D* 1.6.4).

To recapitulate, a state organized with a view to its internal stability will in all likelihood be forced to go to war. If it maintains its independence in war for any length of time, the burden of its resulting empire, which it cannot manage given its internal organization, will result in its downfall, as illustrated by the fates of Sparta and Venice. Moreover, even if such a state could avoid war entirely—a possibility Machiavelli posits as more dream than reality—such peace would engender faction, resulting ultimately in the same lamentable outcome as war successfully prosecuted for the state ill prepared for empire. He therefore seeks in the tumult of an acquisitive republic modeled on the example of Rome the only haven available to human beings.[5] According to Machiavelli, therefore, when the human situation is correctly apprehended the choice is unmistakable: "the true political way of life and the true quiet of a city" as expressed either in Venetian tranquillity or in Spartan harmony must be sacrificed in the name of Roman tumult, for it is impossible for a state not to seek expansion.

Further reflection on the grounds for Machiavelli's embrace of Rome, however, actually points to his ultimate dissatisfaction with this Roman model. Despite his insistence that states seeking tranquillity are doomed, the actual endurance of Sparta and Venice for a longer period of time than Rome flies in the face of his musings. Indeed, his tenacity in maintaining his position is itself rather remarkable, inasmuch as he acknowledges that "the liberty of Sparta and Venice had a longer life than that of Rome" (D 1.5.2). Because Machiavelli is at once fully cognizant of this fact and embraces Rome's example on the basis of longevity anyway, he suggests that Rome did not live out the full measure of its potential longevity. Despite the model's obvious usefulness in demonstrating that the people should be given a voice in the state so as to be deployed in the prosecution of an acquisitive foreign policy, the ancient Roman republic is an insufficient model because it fell into decay too early. Ancient Rome requires improvement.

The Passions of the City and the Innovation of the Gracchi

Offering his own prescription for longevity requires that Machiavelli first offer an explanation for ancient Rome's premature collapse. Although he insists that the controversies between the people and the Senate are indicative of health rather than of disease, he does concede that these controversies eventuated in the "ruin of a free way of life" during the time of the Gracchi (D 1.6.1). He insists however that the disorder the Gracchi introduced into Rome is by no means to be viewed as a typical manifestation of the ordinary and salutary contention between the few and the many. The Gracchi introduced a virulent innovation that allowed their successors to effect the republic's collapse.

Machiavelli discusses the way the Gracchi's efforts contributed to "the destruction of the republic" at the beginning of *Discourses* 1.37.[6] These brothers endeavored to resurrect the agrarian law, which forbade anyone from owning more than a certain amount of land, and demanded that land conquered from the enemy be divided among the Roman people. Because the plebeians were not particularly eager to acquire land far from Rome, the law had actually lain dormant for a time while the Romans led their armies to the frontiers of Italy and beyond. Despite the remoteness of Rome's conquests, the Gracchi succeeded in piquing plebeian interest in this law. The endeavor of the Gracchi to enforce this law with renewed vigor "altogether ruined Roman liberty. For it found the power of its adversaries redoubled, and because of this it ignited so much hatred between the plebs and the Senate that they came to arms and to bloodshed, beyond every civil mode and custom." The "humors" this controversy engendered "were revived at the time of Caesar and Pompey; for after Caesar had made himself head of Marius's party, and Pompey that of Sulla, in coming to grips Caesar was left on top. He was the first tyrant in Rome such that never again was that city free" (D 1.37.2).

The achievement of the Gracchi was truly remarkable, in Machiavelli's estimation, for the brothers succeeded in engaging the interest of the plebeians in property so remote from their lives in Rome. Indeed, consideration of their achievement in light of Machiavelli's other discussions of the passions indicates that the brothers' appeal to unseen lands furnished the essential groundwork not only for Caesar's effective appeal but also for Christianity's appeal to an unseen and transcendent land. Thus his discussion of the role the Gracchi played in Rome's collapse reveals his own intention to explore the city's ultimate degradation through its submission to Christianity's rule.

The analysis of the passions necessary to an appreciation of the Gracchi's innovation begins with a consideration of the question Machiavelli poses in the chapter heading of *Discourses* 1.5: "Where may the guard of liberty be settled more securely, in the people or in the great; and which has greater cause for tumult, he who wishes to acquire or he who wishes to maintain." In distinguishing between gaining and keeping he appears to presume the existence of a pacific desire to maintain. In other words, the nobles who already possess are apparently less troublesome to a state than the people who must scramble to possess. He does not attempt to defend this distinction in the text of this chapter but, rather, rejects it entirely. A noble's fear that he may lose what he already possesses gives rise to the same type of actions as taken by those motivated to acquire, "because the fear of losing generates in him the same wishes that are in those who desire to acquire; for it does not appear to men that they possess securely what a man has unless he acquires something else new" (D 1.5.4). Indeed, the nobles behave in the same manner as the plebeians, whose "restless spirits" (D 1.5.2) impel them to create disturbances as they seek to satisfy their appetites. Thus the heading of 1.5 offers a distinction between the desires of the haves and the have-nots, but Machiavelli's analysis offers a similar depiction of both parties: both endeavoring to acquire, one so as to possess, the other so as to maintain. Consequently, neither class is portrayed as so complacent that it wishes only to maintain in a manner that does not necessitate further acquisition.[7]

Thus, despite the heading, the chapter itself illustrates a fundamental similarity: both maintenance and acquisition must produce the same effects. In this chapter he does offer a distinction however between the passions of the nobles and those of the people:

> Without doubt, if one considers the end of the nobles and of the ignobles one will see great desire to dominate in the former, and in the latter only desire not to be dominated; and, in consequence, a greater will to live free, being less able to hope to usurp it than are the great. (D 1.5.2)

While both classes pursue unlimited acquisition, and hence are both responsible for political upheaval, the nobles pursue rule, whereas the people merely wish to avoid the imposition of the yoke the rulers long to impose (see also *FH* 2.12 and *P* 9).[8]

Later, in *Discourses* 1.16, Machiavelli confirms this distinction between the two classes as to the manner in which the passion for acquisition is manifested. He treats here the reasons people desire freedom, and in the process he enumerates two distinct parties: "a small part of them desires to be free so as to command, but all the others, who are infinite, desire liberty so as to live secure" (*D* 1.16.5). Thus this passion for acquisition manifests itself differently in the rewards different people seek. Some desire to command; as commanders, their power to acquire material goods may increase, but there are other rewards to be attained from their positions of authority such as honor and glory (*D* 2.2). Because the number of those who seek the rewards of command is small, it appears that the desire to live securely in possession of one's life and one's property cuts across class lines—that the desires of many nobles do not extend beyond property.[9]

In *Discourses* 1.37, when speaking of the agrarian law, Machiavelli confirms this very supposition, while forcefully asserting the power over human hearts of the desire for acquisition. He begins this discussion:

It is the sense of the ancient writers that men are wont to worry in evil and to become bored with good, and that from both of these two passions the same effects arise. For whenever fighting through necessity is taken from men they fight through ambition, which is so powerful in human breasts that it never abandons them at whatever rank they rise to. The cause is that nature has created men so that they are able to desire everything and are unable to attain everything. So, since the desire is always greater than the power of acquiring, the result is discontent with what one possesses and a lack of satisfaction with it. From this arises the variability of their fortune; for since some men desire to have more, some fear to lose what has been acquired, they come to enmities and to war, from which arise the ruin of one province and the exaltation of another. (D 1.37.1)

He proceeds to give an instance in which "the restless spirits" of the plebs became manifest: after the institution of the tribunes made the people secure against the domineering patricians, the populace "began at once to fight through ambition, and to wish to share honors and property with the nobility as the thing esteemed most by men" (D 1.37.1; see also 1.5). Eventually the plebeians demanded to share with the patricians the claim to the conquered lands, but the nobles would not submit to this other demand. Because the nobles took such a resolute stand on this issue, Machiavelli renders a decision on what people value more:

one also sees through this how much men esteem property more than honors. For the Roman nobility always yielded honors to the plebs without extraordinary scandals, but when it came to property, so great was its obstinacy in defending it that the plebs had recourse to the extraordinary . . . to vent its appetite. (D 1.37.3)

In the events surrounding the controversy over the agrarian law, Machiavelli discerns the operation of a universal principle: property is the end more often than honor or glory in that perpetual and strife-producing human drive for acquisition;[10] the nobles, the class that most often produces the individuals who contend for honor, more readily conceded honor than property to the people. Of course, as Machiavelli cautions, the end—whether understood as that of property or of honor—cannot itself really be an end, for people can never have enough of either good.

Having thus considered Machiavelli's lessons regarding the

ubiquitousness of the desire for acquisition and the more common manifestation of it as the desire for the acquisition of property, we are in a better position to grasp Machiavelli's understanding of the significance of the Gracchi's achievement. The proposal of the Gracchi for a more rigorous application of the agrarian law met with vehement opposition from the patricians, precisely because the majority of the nobles cared more for property than for honor. Because one part of this proposal provided for the redistribution of land when an individual's holding exceeded the established limit, many nobles would see land taken from them if the law were to be vigorously enforced. Conversely, the people's rabid enthusiasm for the application of the law is less understandable, judging from Machiavelli's presentation of the controversy in 1.37. Of course, if the plebeians stood to gain the portion the patricians' land that exceeded the limit, then the plebeians could well come to possess some desirable allotments. But Machiavelli's discussion of the controversy does not highlight land so favorably situated, but instead concentrates on land that was very far from Rome. The land in question was so remote from Rome that those "restless spirits" of the plebeians, always in search of greater gains, remained unmoved by this potential source of lucre for a long period of time. Machiavelli explains:

> This came about because the fields the enemies of Rome possessed came to be less desired by the plebs, being distant from their eyes and in places where it was not easy to cultivate them. . . . So for such causes this law lay as though asleep up till the Gracchi; when it was aroused by them, it altogether ruined Roman liberty. (*D* 1.37.2)

The innovation of the Gracchi consists, then, in their ability to ignite a hitherto unrecognized desire of the people for such apparently undesirable land. So successful were they in overcoming the plebeians' indifference to this unseen land that the brothers brought Rome to a fever pitch over its distribution.

According then to Machiavelli's analysis of these controversies, the people, when their pervasive and extreme passion for property is properly piqued, can be lured by riches far from their eyes. Individuals can indeed be lured by riches they have not seen but of which they have only heard reports; they can be attracted to lands that exist so far from where they live their daily lives as to be practically useless to them. Human beings can be so covetous of unseen goods that the desire to acquire them actually furnishes their principle of action.

In so presenting the lesson derived from the people's zealous support of the Gracchi on the basis of the brothers' appeal to these far-flung lands, Machiavelli causes one to recall Christianity's achievement in the modern era of establishing as the object of human desire a paradise in the next life.[11] As Machiavelli explicitly observes elsewhere in the *Discourses,* in order to attain paradise, that unearthly city, people have changed their mode of living from what it was previously (*D* 2.2). Although the type of goods the people covet are different from what was pursued in former times, people still covet and are still ambitious. In Machiavelli's view, however, the people can be idle to win their rewards, as he claims that *"ambizioso ozio"* characterizes the Christian era (1.pr.). Consideration of the people's actions in modern times reveals to Machiavelli that transcendent goods can be a motivating principle. Therefore, arguments in *Discourses* 1.37 confirm the powerful lure of unseen goods, for this power had a powerful and deleterious effect even on the Roman republic.

The passions that fueled the controversy over the agrarian law were a nascent form of the passions that Christianity would arouse in the people. Machiavelli's discussion of the law begins his examination of the progressive deterioration in Rome's dealings with the passions of the people. This progression eventuated in Christianity, and the appeal of the Gracchi to unseen lands was an important step in that descent.[12] Or, to put the matter another way, because the Gracchi taught the people to covet unseen earthly goods that existed far from their homes, their efforts helped to make possible Christianity's triumphant reception in Rome.

In considering the relation between Christianity and the agrarian law, and hence the criticism of the Roman republic that such a comparison would imply, it is important not to overlook Machiavelli's explicit censure of Rome for this controversy. Machiavelli is forthright in his criticism—a criticism confirming how he regards as deficient the orders of his exemplary republic. In the chapter's heading and conclusion he points to the manner in which the law was too retrospective (*D* 1.37).[13] Also in the text he implies that because these controversies occurred in Rome, the republic cannot be considered well ordered: "Because well ordered republics have to keep the public rich and their citizens poor, it must be that in the city of Rome there was a defect in this law" (*D* 1.37.1). Whether this law was defective for looking too far back or for causing the people to focus their hopes and desires too far from Rome, he forsees the ruin of Rome: the "contention over the agrarian law . . . in the end was the cause of the destruction of the republic" (D 1.37.1).

The Machinations of Leaders and Rome's First Tyrant

Machiavelli delineates in *Discourses* 1.37 how the seam that the agrarian law opened ultimately caused the whole to unravel:

> So, since the public magistrates could not remedy it, and none of the factions could put hope in them, they had recourse to private remedies, and each one of the parties was thinking of how to make itself a head to defend it. In this scandal and disorder the plebs came first, and it gave reputation to Marius, so that it made him consul four times; and he continued in his consulate, with a few intervals, so long that he was able to make himself three other times. As the nobility had no remedy against such a plague, it turned to favoring Sulla; and when he had been made head of its party, they came to civil wars. After much bloodshed and changing of fortune, the nobility was left on top. Later these humors were revived at the time of Caesar and Pompey; for after Caesar had made himself head of Marius' party, and Pompey that of Sulla, in coming to grips Caesar was left on top. He was the first tyrant in Rome such that never again was that city free. (D 1.37.2)

Machiavelli again concedes much ground to those who despise Rome for the tumult that resulted from the prominent place the people attained there; he acknowledges here that the vigorous opposition the plebeians were able to muster as a consequence of the republic's peculiar organization did result in the collapse of that state. He even notes here how his concession may be thought to vitiate his earlier argument in favor of Rome: "And although we have shown elsewhere that the enmities in Rome between the Senate and the plebs kept Rome free by giving rise to laws in favor of liberty, and although the end of this agrarian law appears not to conform to such a conclusion, I say that I do not, because of this, abandon such an opinion." Instead he maintains that if the people had not achieved a prominent place in the regime so as to oppose successfully "the ambition of the great," the state's liberty would have been lost earlier (D 1.37.3). Much later in the work he affirms this point: "the power of the tribunes of the plebs in the city of Rome was great, and it was necessary, . . . because otherwise one would not have been able to place a check on the ambition of the nobility, which would have corrupted that republic a long time before it did corrupt itself" (*D* 3.11.1).

Notwithstanding Machiavelli's continued defense of Rome, he acknowledges in 1.37 that the passions of the people did play a role in the republic's collapse. Elsewhere, Machiavelli describes the process by which the passions of the people can pose a mortal threat to a republic. These passions come into play when an individual undertakes to become the people's leader. Machiavelli indicates that popular esteem can itself furnish the basis for the beginning of a tyranny. The threat harbored by the propensity of the plebeians to look to an ambitious man who promises to satisfy their appetite with such private favors as "helping with money or by defending them from the powerful" is a great theme of the *Discourses* (*D* 1.46.1; see also 1.5, 7, 40, 46; 3.28). The ulterior motive of the man who offers such favors, of course, is to make partisans of his beneficiaries. In the chapter entitled "That one should be mindful of the works of citizens, because many times under a merciful work a beginning of tyranny is hidden," Machiavelli provides the example of Spurius Maelius, who when Rome was suffering from a famine distributed wheat "privately" to the plebeians. Recognizing the "inconvenience" that might arise from such "liberality," the Senate appointed a dictator to deal with the matter, who in turn sentenced the people's benefactor to death (*D* 3.28.1).

Later in this chapter Machiavelli draws a distinction between two methods by which an individual can acquire a reputation in a state: through public or private means. The public means are those through which an "individual by counseling well, by working better in the common benefit, acquires reputation," whereas the nefarious means of gaining a reputation are such acts as "doing benefit to this and to that other private individual, by lending him money, marrying his daughters for him, defending him from the magistrates," in addition to other unnamed "private favors" (*D* 3.28.1). From his terse discussion of these two distinct methods of gaining renown in a state, one concludes that an apparent benefactor who bestows favors in a manner that bypasses the normal channels for legislation is endeavoring to avoid the scrutiny that measures actually intended to benefit the public can sustain. In the case of Spurius Maelius, the dictator did well in sentencing this apparent benefactor to death, for his benevolent act obscured his tyrannical desire. "One of these things that may be left unpunished is capable of ruining a republic," admonishes Machiavelli, "for with that example it is only with difficulty later brought back on the true way" (D 3.28.1).

Machiavelli discerns just such recourse to private favors in the downfall of the Roman republic, a period which stretches from the time of the Gracchi's support for the reinvigoration of the agrarian law to that of the emergence of Julius Caesar. In his discussion of the agrarian law treated above, for instance, he notes that the intense controversy over the law resulted in the "recourse to private remedies," when both the plebeians and the patricians decided to enlist leaders, Marius and Sulla respectively, to defend their interests.

Similarly, Machiavelli detects such a recourse to private remedies in Caesar's endeavor to gain for himself the adherence of the people. Noting in *The Prince* that "Caesar was one of those who wanted to attain the principate of Rome," Machiavelli recognizes that Caesar, in attempting to satiate his own covetousness for preeminence in the state, utilized the covetousness of the many for property. Although Caesar's liberality was a reasonable means of attaining the exalted position he desired, Machiavelli warns that "if after he had arrived there, had he remained alive and not been temperate with his expenses, he would have destroyed that empire" (P 16.64).[14]

Although Caesar's status as "the first tyrant in Rome" was secured in this rather conventional manner, one discerns in the continued reign of his tyranny an innovation (D 1.37.2), for after his death, others "rul[ed] under that name" (D 1.10.3). Brutus failed to restore liberty to Rome when he executed its tyrant. Machiavelli attributes Brutus's failure to "the corruption that the Marian parties had put in the people; Caesar, as their head, could so blind the multitude that it did not recognize the yoke it was putting on its own neck" (D 1.17.1). Because of this corruption, therefore, Caesar's martyrdom was devastating to the republic.

In the *Florentine Histories* Machiavelli also treats these two ways by which a citizen can acquire a reputation in a state, but in this account he explicitly links this discussion to the origins of sects. After delineating these two modes and the deeds that accord with the private method, such as "ingratiating oneself with games and public gifts," he asserts from these deeds "sects and partisans arise, and the reputation thus earned offends as much as reputation helps when it is not mixed with sects, because that reputation is founded on a common good, not on a private good" (*FH* 7.1, 276–77). The private method engenders both partisans and sects. We know from Machiavelli's analyses elsewhere that partisans often give rise to tyranny (e.g., *D* 1.37 and 3.28). Sects and tyrannies, therefore, share the same origin.

Furthermore, in the *Discourses* he makes it evident that he considers Christianity to be a sect, referring to it as *"la setta Cristiana"* (*D* 2.5.1). Because Christianity is a sect, and sects begin, as do tyrannies, with the promise of private benefits, Christianity, it would appear, rose to power with the promise of such benefits. According to Machiavelli's analysis, the beginnings of Christianity were the same as the beginnings of a tyranny, but, of course, for Machiavelli Christianity is a type of tyranny.

This explicit equation of the rise of tyranny with the origin of sects in the later *Florentine Histories* confirms the connection between the rise of tyranny in Rome and the rise of Christianity, a connection that appears to be operating more tacitly in the *Discourses,* where Machiavelli analyzes the Roman republic's decline. Christ's manner of establishing a sect appears conventional in that it consisted in an appeal to the masses, but Christ and his successors also appear to have availed themselves of the innovations of the Gracchi and of Caesar. Christianity thus combined the innovation of the Gracchi in making unseen benefits appealing to the masses and that of Caesar in utilizing martyrdom to sustain political rule. Nevertheless, Christ's appeal to a realm that utterly transcended the earthly one was unique.

Machiavelli appears to broach Christ's achievement tacitly in making a successful appeal to this transcendent realm when he opposes this world to the next, the earthly homeland to the heavenly one. When he observes that the generality does not avenge wrongs in order "to go to paradise," and thereby allows "wicked men" to rule the world, he simultaneously observes that the heaven of the Christians interferes with the effective management of the political world (*D* 2.2.2). In the *Florentine Histories* as well he draws attention to this opposition when he tells the story of Messer Rinaldo, who, having been exiled from his native Florence, made a pilgrimage to the Sepulchre of Christ "to earn a celestial fatherland for himself since he had lost his earthly one" (*FH* 5.34.228).[15] In true Augustinian fashion Machiavelli understands that human beings in the Christian era have two fatherlands—that they belong to two cities—which make opposing claims on their allegiance. In contrast to Augustine, however, Machiavelli promotes the claims of his earthly city. At the end of his life he wrote to his friend Francesco Vettori that "I love my *patria* more than my soul."[16]

Understanding the manner in which Machiavelli sees these two homelands to be in conflict helps one to recognize the metaphorical significance of his discussions in the *Discourses* that quietly introduce the triumph of Christianity n Rome. He discusses, for example, how the class strife became so intense that, after the Romans had captured the Etruscan city of Veii, the plebeians desired to leave Rome and move there, unable to resist the allure of the captured city's fine buildings and fertile land (1.53).[17] In commenting upon the foolishness of this proposal, Machiavelli says that it illustrates that "many times, deceived by a false image of good, the people desires its own ruin." In support of this assertion he cites the authority of Dante, who maintains that "many times the people cries: Life to its death! and Death to its life" (*D* 1.53.1).[18] If one were to put a Machiavellian twist on Dante's words, one could say that inhabitants of Christian states, who exist so as to garner entrance to paradise, actually live the words Dante says that they shout: in living so as to gain paradise, they repudiate their earthly existences because they expect to find life in death.[19]

To return to the ancient Roman story that generated Machiavelli's reflections on this propensity of the people, the patricians were able to stem the plebeians' desire to occupy Veii, but after the Gracchi had taught the Roman plebeians to covet unseen goods, the patricians were unable to stem the desire of the people to occupy another city—that of God. Of course, this city had advantages over those of Veii, for it promised greater riches and eternal life in another world.[20]

Machiavelli also apparently wishes in *Discourses* 1.13 to draw the reader's attention to Christianity's advent when he recognizes in Livy's history another occurrence that could stand as a metaphor for the later events destined to mark a cataclysmic change in the way people would henceforth view their world (cf. *D* 1.pr). In contrast to the controversy over the habitation of Veii, here Machiavelli introduces a third party into the persistent class conflict of Rome, "a multitude of exiles [*sbanditi*] and slaves [*servi*]" who occupied the Capitol, the home of the Roman gods (*D* 1.13.2; *O* 97). The patricians feared that despite this crisis, and the threat of attack from the Aequi and Volsci that it might precipitate, the plebeians would continue to force their demands by refusing military service. Machiavelli's retelling of this incident evokes the presage of Christianity, for like those who hold the Capitol, the triumphant Christians are themselves exiles[21]—exiles from the earth itself—because they repudiate the earthly rewards in pursuing those of the city of God. In Machiavelli's words, "the collectivity of men, so as to go to paradise, think more of enduring their beatings than of avenging them" (2.2.2). Again, although unsuccessful in the incident Machiavelli relates, the slaves and exiles eventually succeeded in winning the allegiance of the Roman people to a religion that exalts the weak and the poor.

The metaphorical meanings of these stories are of course not themselves symbols of Christianity; rather they suggest that Machiavelli regards the impulses leading to Christianity's advent as existing in Rome much earlier. Rome did not control these impulses and ultimately succumbed to them; yet in pointing to them as the cause of Rome's downfall, Machiavelli must show, if he is to remain a champion of the people, that the fault lies not with the Roman people but with the constitution that allowed the ambitious ones to make such an effective appeal.

Machiavelli's Partial Agreement with Rome's Critics

In furnishing his explanation of Rome's collapse, Machiavelli extends his analysis of Rome's susceptibility to tyranny beyond the ascendancy of Julius Caesar to offer an explanation of Christianity's establishment there. In considering the charges of those critics of Rome who appear early in the *Discourses* in light of Machiavelli's extended analysis of Rome's collapse, one finds that the critics share his interest in the causes of Rome's vulnerability to Christianity's appeal. The charges of these critics can also be read as containing metaphorical meanings that evoke images of Christianity's ascent there. Because much of Machiavelli's own criticism of Rome relates to the manner in which Rome allowed Christianity to flourish in that city, it is necessary to study the bases for both his agreement and his disagreement with these critics.

These critics suggest by their use of such images that the prominent place of the people—and of the people's passions—in the republic allowed Christianity its foothold in the city. Thus for these critics the appearance of the people's propensity to look to leaders who promise rich rewards, a propensity that would eventually give rise to Christianity, signals the final stage of the Roman republic's disease. In the face of such criticism Machiavelli persists in the role of the people's stalwart defender even though he himself offers an analysis that links Rome's decline to Christianity's ascendancy.

In first proposing Rome as a model republic in 1.4 of the *Discourses,* he offers the arguments of a single critic of that republic who derides it for the prominent place the lower class attained in the state. In 1.5 he brings forth a number of critics to blame this class directly for the role it played in bringing down the republic. Machiavelli reports:

> They give as an example of this the same Rome, where because the tribunes of the plebs had this authority in their hands it was not enough for them to have one plebeian consul, but they wished to have both. From this, they wished the censorship, the praetor, and all the other ranks of empire of the city: nor was this enough for them since, taken by the same fury, they later began to adore [*adorare*] those men who they saw were apt to beat down the nobility, from which came the power of Marius and the ruin of Rome. (*D* 1.5.2; *O* 83–84)

By choosing the word *adorare*—which means to worship, as in the Italian phrase *"adorare Dio"*—to report the judgment of Rome's critics, Machiavelli infuses his criticism of Rome with a religious meaning. He thus suggests that the critics in 1.5 claim the people were all too willing to regard as gods those who desired to be their protectors. Certainly Jesus Christ must be considered the example par excellence of one who sacrificed himself for the cause of the people and who, as a result, garnered their adoration for himself and his successors. Those who offer this criticism regard the deepening impulse of the people to worship their benefactors as extending beyond the ascendancy and martyrdom of Julius Caesar, who effected the republic's downfall; in the view of these critics this impulse actually eventuates in the power and influence of Christianity, which is founded on the people's adoration of a divine benefactor.

In reconsidering Machiavelli's report of the single critic's claims in *Discourses* 1.4, after having noted the religious meaning that Machiavelli infuses into his relation of the critics' charges in 1.5, one finds that this criticism also tacitly links Rome's downfall to the ascendancy of Christianity. The critic of 1.4 maintains that the tumults of Rome led to the horrifying spectacle of the people "leaving Rome" (*D* 1.4.1). With the introduction of Christianity into that city, the people of Rome could be said to have left their city to a degree never seen during the early tumults between the plebeians and patricians; in preference to the more alluring heavenly city that Christianity promises, the people no longer give allegiance to any earthly city.

When the objections of Rome's critics are read in this manner, they replicate much of the deepest level of Machiavelli's own criticism. Although Machiavelli explicitly disagrees with the charge of his chosen opponents in *Discourses* 1.4 and 5 on the issue of the harm rendered to the republic by the people's intemperate impulses, and hence with the critics' utter rejection of the Roman example, his later discussion reveals his own agreement with much of what the critics charge regarding Rome's defects in light of the Roman people's later adoration of Christ. Even in supporting the Roman republic against the critic who would condemn its domestic turmoil, he yields much ground. In his discussion of the critical political problem of a "man who with his audacity and spiritedness wish[es] to pass beyond [*transcendere*] a civil way of life" (*D* 1.7.3; *O* 88), he defends Rome by making the extreme claim that the republic never had recourse to any "extraordinary modes" such as calling in "external forces" to quell the squabbles between the people and the nobles. In taking this extreme position he reveals its weakness, for his own analysis suggests that the plebeians did eventually prevail in the class conflict precisely by calling in "external forces" in the form of a god that promised the plebs the ultimate victory and its attendant riches in an unearthly city. Christianity achieved transcendence of civil life. But, as in all tyrannies that come to power with the support of the people, the people's victory was short-lived. After consolidating power such a tyranny will oppress the people (*D* 1.40).

Despite this similarity between the critics' position and Machiavelli's own, it is important to remember that Machiavelli takes issue with the critics' analysis; he does not conclude from these shared insights that the people are to be blamed for the loss of Roman liberty but continues to maintain that the demanding voice of the people is a critical ingredient of freedom. If the people had not had such a prominent place from which to battle the nobles, he claims, the republic would have lost its liberty earlier (*D* 1.37 and 3.11). Not so concerned with the excessive demands of a people, he wants to prevent those who seek to command from endeavoring to satisfy the desires of the people in an extraordinary manner that harms the state. His defense of the Roman republic in giving such a prominent place to the people culminates in a criticism different from that of the critics to whom he gives voice: the republic's constitution should have had mechanisms for preventing such extraordinary appeals. Caesar should not have been allowed the firm foothold he attained.

To prevent an aspirant to the principate from attaining such a foothold, a state must stave off the corruption that Machiavelli identifies as having permeated Rome by Caesar's time—the corruption that nullified Brutus's attempt to free Rome from the tyrant's grasp. My next chapter examines the difficulty a state faces in thwarting an appealing youth's rise to preeminence, as well as the character of that corruption that prevented Brutus from liberating Rome.

❖ CHAPTER 4 ❖

CORRUPTION, YOUTH, AND
FOREIGN INFLUENCES

Rather than lamenting Rome's ultimate fall, Machiavelli at the opening of the *Discourses* marvels that ancient Rome persevered so long in the face of the threat of corruption: "the fertility of the site, the convenience of the sea, the frequent victories, and the greatness of its empire could not corrupt it for many centuries" (*D* 1.1.5). As his examination of the republic intensifies, however, he confronts its collapse with candor and shows its increasing susceptibility to the machinations of aspiring tyrants.

After Caesar had achieved preeminence, it was corruption, Machiavelli maintains, that prevented his assassination from reinvigorating the republic. The complicated issue of corruption is so central to Machiavelli's view of the Roman republic and of republicanism generally that it will be treated in detail here. He turns his focus from the control of the people's passions to those of that re-public's leaders. He thus remains steadfast in his defense of the people against those who charge that they played the decisive role in Rome's collapse.

In turning to these ambitious leaders, he pays particularly concerned attention to those young men who attain prominent positions in a state. A state must manage such youths properly because their defining characteristics can be so useful:

> When a youth is of so much virtue [*virtù*] that he makes himself known in some notable thing, it would be a very harmful thing that the city not be able to take advantage of him too and that it have to wait until, that vigor of spirit and that readiness grow old with him. ... (*D* 1.60.1; *O* 144)

Despite the evident usefulness of youthful vitality to a state, particularly a militaristic one, Machiavelli insists that such *virtù* can result in a state's ruin, if it is foolish enough to permit a young man's *virtù* to attract partisans to his cause. As evidence of the weightiness of this particular threat, Machiavelli offers Caesar as an example of just such a young man whose *virtù* was not properly handled by his state.

The defects of the city's constitution that permitted the Gracchi, Marius, and Caesar to gain such prominence also allowed Christianity, a foreign religion, to find a hospitable environment in this most mighty of ancient cities. Even as Machiavelli's gratified assessment of Rome's maintenance in *Discourses* 1.1 recognizes, corruption threatens both from within and from beyond a city's borders. Machiavelli insists that Rome's conquests of increasingly far-flung places brought the city in contact with the most insalubrious customs, including the corrupting influence of *ozio* and subversive religious practices. In the importation of Christianity into Rome one finds the source of all the elements of corruption Machiavelli had previously identified: the danger of a particularly appealing young man who gathers followers and the corrupting influences of foreign *ozio* and of foreign religious practices. Ultimately Rome was felled by a conspiracy with origins in the city's foreign conquests.

The Problem of Corruption

Machiavelli observes that by the time of Marius, Rome had begun its precipitous decline to the ruin that led to Caesar's tyranny.

At various points in the *Discourses* he indicates that corruption was the decisive factor in this descent. We already know, for example, that Rome's corruption prevented Brutus's action against Caesar from restoring the republic to its former vigor (*D* 1.17). Machiavelli also notes it was corruption that allowed Sulla and Marius to make headway in Rome, for he claims that they "would have been crushed" in their first undertakings, if they had lived at an earlier time when the "material" was not yet corrupt (*D* 3.8.2). Conversely, if Spurius Cassius, "an ambitious man" who "wished to take up extraordinary authority in Rome and to gain the plebs for himself by doing it many benefits," had lived at a later period, when the people had been corrupt, his nefarious scheming would have opened the door to tyranny. As it was, the Senators needed only to bring his ambition under suspicion in the incorrupt Roman republic so that when he offered the plebeians the money from the sale of grain, they refused this questionable private benefit (*D* 3.8.1). Statements such as these support Pocock's conclusion that for Machiavelli corruption is a refusal on the part of the citizen body as a whole to put the common good before private benefits. Pocock claims that for Machiavelli an incorrupt "republic or polity was . . . a structure of virtue: it was a structure in which every citizen's ability to place the common good before his own was the precondition of every other's, so that every man's virtue saved every other's from . . . corruption."[1] When such self-abnegating virtue was no longer operative, according to this view, the republic confronted its ruin.

Despite the suggestion in these passages that corruption and decay occur when a republic's citizens turn from the pursuit of the common good to that of private benefits, we cannot leave Machiavelli's treatment of corruption at this. Most obviously, the self-abnegating virtue that would have to be operative in an incorrupt Machiavellian republic does not appear to cohere with Machiavelli's analysis of human nature. As the previous chapter demonstrates, he regards the passions—either for property or for rule—as invariably the impetus for human action; thus he cannot flatly demand that they be repudiated, and indeed, he does not.[2] He defends the Roman people against those critics who denounce popular passions for driving the republic to its demise. Despite his increasingly trenchant criticisms of Rome, he contemplates the conflicts between the many and the few of that city—conflicts that derived from the selfish desires of the members of both parties—with unabating relish. In his defense of the Roman people he specifically praises their tenacity in making vociferous demands that derive from selfish passions.

Moreover, Machiavelli explicitly acknowledges that when the city was still incorrupt the people acted on the basis of their own interests. Additional statements in *Discourses* 3.8, the very chapter that points to corruption as the decisive reason for Rome's falling under the sway of a tyrant, frustrate the easy conclusion that corruption in a state derives from its citizens' refusal to renounce their private ambitions. When describing the manner in which the Roman republic condemned Manlius Capitolinus, he notes that the people—in this incorrupt state—was "very desirous of its own utility and a lover of things that went against the nobility" (D 3.8.1). In incorrupt Rome the people operated on the principle of their own good. He praises the "goodness" of the Roman people, for example, in refusing to relinquish a tithe of the plunder from the capture of Veii in order to satisfy Camillus's vow to Apollo (D 1.55.1). This incident occurred, again according to Machiavelli's specification, before the city was corrupt, and the people's selfish interest in keeping the booty that had already come into their possession alone impelled the demand that the oath be abrogated.

Further, by explicitly praising the people's desire for property in this instance, he indicates not only that the people's willingness to act on its self-interested desire for property is not to be taken as a sign of the republic's corruption, but also that their ability and willingness to act on this desire may make a contribution to maintaining a healthy republic. Indeed, in another context in the *Discourses,* Machiavelli suggests that the selfish passions of the people—yet again, when the republic was incorrupt—kept the republic in equilibrium. He observes that when the power of the tribunes threatened to overbalance that of the nobility, the patricians would find a tribune "who was either fearful or corruptible or a lover of the common good, so that they disposed him to oppose the will of the others" (D 3.11.1). In other words, the selfish passions served the interests of the republic by impelling some tribunes to accept the bribes the nobility offered. Machiavelli's weapon of choice in the fight against corruption cannot be the demand that the citizens as a whole repudiate their selfish passions, for at least in some instances a successful fight against the nemesis of corruption demands precisely the opposite tactic.

He offers this suggestion not only in such specific cases but also in discussing the general issue of the difficulties a newly freed people are likely to confront. Such a "people," he claims, "is nothing other than a brute animal which, although a ferocious and wild nature, has always been nourished in prison and in servitude." Because this people is unaccustomed "to feed[ing] itself"—to satisfying its own interests—it easily "becomes the prey of the first who seeks to rechain it" (D 1.16.1). Thus he suggests that such a people would be ready fodder for an individual possessed of tyrannical ambitions and properly armed with the requisite promises of easy acquisitions. Conversely, if the people were accustomed to providing for themselves, the offerings of their potential captor would not be so alluring and, thus, the threat to their newfound liberty not so acute. In Machiavelli's view a populace capable of acting on its self-interested passions is the very prerequisite for a free state.

The problem Machiavelli identifies for a republic regarding the people's passions is, therefore, not that they exist at all, or that they are not fully repudiated; rather, he is most interested in the way these passions are satisfied. Problems arise for a republic when its people look to an ambitious individual who offers easy satisfaction of their desires.

In considering corruption Machiavelli's ultimate interest lies not with the mass of people but with the ambitious few in a state.[3] These few must not be permitted to gather adherents with the promise of private benefits. If such a following comes together around an individual, that individual elevates himself over his rivals, and the type of inequality Machiavelli finds so pernicious ensues. Machiavelli confirms the critical role such a following plays in his understanding of corruption when he maintains that the creation of the office of dictator was beneficial to the Roman republic. In making a case for the necessity of such an office, he reveals his objection to a specific type of inequality among the leading men of a state. Machiavelli explains that for harm to result to a city from the elevation of a single person to sole authority, that person must have many attributes that would be impossible to attain "in a noncorrupt republic." "For he needs to be very rich and to have very many adherents and partisans, which he cannot have where the laws are observed" (D 1.34.2). Elsewhere he declares that "such corruption and little aptitude for free life arise from an inequality that is in that city" (D 1.17.3). He suggests that the inequality he finds indicative of corruption is to be found in the manner in which a single individual is able to garner wealth and attract supporters and thereby is permitted to solidify his own personal power in a way that bodes ill for the free life in a state.

Corruption resides among the leaders of a state, rather than among the people. The people should not to be blamed if they look to someone who promises them relief and rewards, for naturally the people will respond to such promises. To remain free of corruption a state must concentrate on its leaders and ensure that a certain parity is maintained among them.

It would appear, therefore, that in descending into corruption, Rome did not deal appropriately with its ambitious men. In *Discourses* 1.18 Machiavelli furnishes two examples of Rome's insufficient response to its corruption, and, indeed, both examples relate directly to the difficulty the city faced in handling those individuals bent on preeminence. The first example pertains to Rome's method of electing citizens to office. Initially the Romans gave the high offices of the city only to those who requested them. This method was wholly satisfactory in the beginning because only worthies would put themselves forward for office; when the city had become complacent due to its many military victories, however, such a procedure was most dangerous because the populace was no longer concerned with the *virtù* but with the *grazia* of its leaders (*D* 1.18.3; *O* 103). In other words, office seekers sought popularity with the people and were elected to high office on this basis. As a result, the good were excluded from rule.

The second example relates to the manner in which laws were proposed. During the early times of the republic the provision that any citizen could propose a law was salutary. This order became destructive when corruption permeated the city, because now "only the powerful propose[d] laws, not for the common liberty but for their power; and for fear of them nobody can speak against them. So the people came to be either deceived or compelled to decide its own ruin" (*D* 1.18.3). Both examples provide further illustration of the process, examined in the previous chapter, by which ambitious men became resourceful in circumventing the orders of Rome as they endeavored to satisfy their desire to rule.

Machiavelli concludes from these two examples that if Rome were to maintain its liberty in corruption, it needed not only new laws but new orders, "[f]or one should order different orders and modes of life in a bad subject than in a good one" (*D* 1.18.4). Interestingly, Machiavelli proposes here not that corruption be rooted out, but rather that it be managed. Thus, it was necessary for Rome to yield to corruption by instituting new orders so that human wickedness could be thwarted rather than overcome.[4] Indeed, he does not demand that the ambitious few renounce their desire to rule. To do so would be to renounce his preference for an acquisitive republic, for their ambition, when properly channeled, provides the engine for the state's territorial expansion. Nevertheless, institutions have to be configured so as to remain invulnerable to the increasingly resourceful machinations of such men.

One also sees Machiavelli's propensity to emphasize the institutional side in a discussion of the mistakes Rome committed in establishing the authority of the decemvirate without the counterpoise of the consuls, the tribunes, or the appeal of the people. He declares: "Nor does it help, in this case, that the material not be corrupt; for an absolute authority corrupts the material in a very short time, and makes friends and partisans for itself" (D 1.35.1). In such an instance, what is critical is that an individual possess the type of authority that permits the aggregation of partisans; the condition of the matter is simply irrelevant. It is irrelevant because "men are [easily] corrupted and make themselves assume a contrary nature, however good and well brought up" (D 1.42.1).

Thus it is necessary for "legislators of republics and kingdoms" to be "more ready to check human appetites and to take away from them all hope of being able to err with impunity" (D 1.42.1). Part 3 will illuminate Machiavelli's own plans for thwarting the harmful effects of ambition as he undertakes to legislate for a new Rome. Before turning to them, however, it is necessary to continue with the reasons for Rome's decline, and thereby assess the character of the problems that his own legislation is designed to overcome. A particularly formidable set, in his view, arises from a state's youth. Both youth that is degenerate and youth with excellent capabilities have always threatened ruin to states; Rome was no exception.

The Inveterate Problem of Youth

So dangerous for a state is the appearance of an especially gifted youth that Machiavelli, who often recommends impetuous or extreme action (P 25 and D 3.44), implores that no action whatsoever be taken. Any measures taken against such an individual are sure to accelerate the collapse of the state. Temporization is the only strategy Machiavelli will countenance in 1.33 of the Discourses.[5]

Although the title of this chapter, "When an inconvenience has grown either in a state or against a state, the more salutary policy is to temporize with it rather than strike at it," suggests that a broad range of problems warrant such a circumspect response, the problem to which he devotes much of the chapter is considerably more specific. He initially offers the counterproductive measures taken by Rome's neighboring states when they realized too late the menace of their burgeoning neighbor as an example of the disastrous results that can occur when the monitory advice of the heading is ignored. Nevertheless, he shunts this example aside with the reflection that "accidents like these arise in a republic more often through an intrinsic than an extrinsic cause" (*D* 1.33.2).

Continuing to narrow the scope of his consideration, he limits those internal threats to cases that occur when "a citizen is allowed to gather more strength than is reasonable, or one begins to corrupt a law which is the nerve and the life of a free way of life [*del vivere libero*]" (*D* 1.33.2; *O* 115). In considering the characteristics of such a dangerous citizen, he focuses particularly on youth:

> It is so much the more difficult to recognize these inconveniences when they arise as it appears more natural to men always to favor [*favorire*] the beginnings of things; and more than for anything else, such favor can be for deeds that appear to have some virtue in them and have been performed by youths. For if in a republic one sees a noble youth arise who has an extraordinary virtue in him, all eyes of the citizens begin to turn toward him and agree in honoring him without any hesitation, so that if there is a bit of ambition in him, mixed with the favor that nature gives him and this accident, he comes at once to a place where the citizens, when they become aware of their error, have few remedies to avoid it. If they try to work as many as they have, they do nothing but accelerate his power. (*D* 1.33.2; *O* 115)

He names Caesar and Cosimo de' Medici as examples of such menacing youth. By furnishing Caesar as example, Machiavelli makes this discussion ominous, as four chapters later he will declare that Caesar successfully overturned the republic to become Rome's first tyrant.[6] In light of Machiavelli's recommendation of temporization, he apparently regards Brutus's action against Caesar as ill advised, because Caesar had already amassed such a following that his assassination resulted in martyrdom and the opportunity for others to rule in his name.

According to Machiavelli the appealing veneer of Caesar and Cosimo masked for a time their true intent. During this interval of disguise afforded them by their pleasing appearance, they acquired so much influence that any action taken against them was harmful to the continued existence of free life. Both Rome and Florence were wrong in taking just such action, judges Machiavelli. In the case of Rome "the remedies [Caesar's opponents] made accelerated the ruin of their republic" (D 1.33.4). So formidable is this situation that Machiavelli suggests even nature itself conspires to subjugate the state to this youth who has received nature's gifts in abundance.

To confront such a dire circumstance he recommends a highly uncertain strategy:

> I say, thus, that since it is difficult to recognize these evils when they arise—the difficulty being caused by the fact that things are apt to deceive you in beginning—it is a wiser policy to temporize with them after they are recognized than to oppose them; for if one temporizes with them, either they are eliminated by themselves or at least the evil is deferred for a longer time. (D 1.33.5)

This solution is far from comforting: Machiavelli readily concedes that this remedy may be no remedy at all; the downfall of the republic will be delayed, but not necessarily circumvented.

The extent to which the issue of youth occupies Machiavelli's mind is revealed by the domination of the problem of youth in the second chapter of the *Discourses*, where he considers the theory of the cycle of regimes. The youths who figure in this early discussion are to be distinguished from the likes of the captivating Caesar and Cosimo of 1.33. As complacent inheritors of rule in unmixed regimes, the youths of 1.2, unlike the enterprising seekers after rule in 1.33, do not know how to color their deeds as they strive to satisfy their desires. Thus 1.2 presents another perspective on the problem of youth and, unlike the example of Caesar in 1.33, reveals what Rome did well in Machiavelli's view. Rome's mixed regime had overcome the problems that arose from complacent inheritors of rule, but in so doing, the city engendered the much more insidious problem of guileful youth.

Machiavelli's discussion of the cycle—and of the degenerate youths who drive it—begins when he offers a résumé of what "some who have written on republics say." He reports that although some writers have maintained the existence of three types

of states—princedom, aristocracy, and popular government—
others, whom many deem "wiser," point to six varieties, "of
which three are the worst; that three others are good in themselves but so easy to be corrupted that they too come to be pernicious" (*D* 1.2.2). According to this latter view, so unstable are
these good forms that princedom easily transforms itself into
tyranny, aristocracy into government by the few, and popular
government into license.

Although he announces here that he merely acts as the conduit
for the opinions of other writers, he appears to resume his own
voice in the next paragraph, declaring authoritatively that "[t]hese
variations of government arise by chance among men. For since the
inhabitants were sparse in the beginning of the world they lived dispersed for a time like beasts" (*D* 1.2.3). Despite the seeming authority with which he propounds this view, many commentators
have noticed that he still is dependent on the view of others; the discussion that follows is borrowed from Polybius's treatment of the
cycle of regimes. Others have carefully compared Machiavelli's version to that of Polybius to find that he makes significant changes in
his source. These scholars conclude that Machiavelli's apparent
borrowing from Polybius becomes the vehicle for his own distinctive view of politics.[7] In the comparison that follows, we see Machiavelli emphasizing the manner in which nature, in the producing of
deficient inheritors to rule, operates only to threaten the existence
of a regime, when he does not argue—as does Polybius—that nature also operates positively for the city by assuring a foundation
for the city's justice.

In Polybius's account, nature is the very touchstone for his ex-
planatory theory of the growth and decay of the regime. Polybius
calls the theory the "natural [*kata physin*] transformation of polities," which he attributes to "Plato and certain other philosophers," but which he claims to have simplified because only a few
can understand these other accounts.[8] Polybius hypothesizes that
those people who remain after the occurrence of natural disasters
that periodically devastate the human race herd together in the
manner of other animals because of "their natural weakness."[9]
While human beings exist in this pre-political herd they will be led
by one who surpasses the others "with respect to the strength of
body and the courage of soul."[10]

Polybius attributes this submission to the strongest to a "most
genuine work of nature" because he sees it also in animals that are

driven purely by instinct. He calls this stage monarchy, and claims that it arises unaided and in accord with nature, and that its more developed form, kingship, arises from a reformation of this primitive condition.[11] When this reformation occurs, feelings of sociability and companionship develop, and so too do notions of justice and injustice. These notions arise first in familial relations, and hence nature furnishes a foundation for the incipient conception of justice. Polybius explains that human beings are inclined "by nature" to sexual intercourse, and if the children of these pairings, who have derived sustenance from their parents, reach maturity only to neglect or to abuse their parents, observers conclude that the children's ingratitude is unjust. The observers are able to draw such a conclusion because human beings are distinguished from the other animals in possessing reason, Polybius notes; this faculty permits them to look to the future and to conclude that they too may be treated in a similar fashion, and so do not like such incidents of unjust behavior.[12]

Polybius allows the indignation aroused by such a violation of obligation to inform judgments regarding other instances of ungrateful behavior occurring outside the family's natural web of relationships. For instance, when one seeks to harm rather than honor someone who has saved one's life, one acts unjustly. Further, certain actions warrant certain reactions from the community as a whole; when through bravery one saves companions from an attack of wild animals, one merits public commendation, and when one acts in a contrary fashion, one deserves public censure.[13] Once these notions of justice and injustice arise, so too does kingship, for the people will no longer follow out of fear the strongest among them, but will obey out of respect the one who dispenses rewards and punishments in accordance with these notions of justice.

Although he generally follows Polybius's account, Machiavelli alters much. Machiavelli attributes the changes in regime to chance [*caso*], for example, rather than to nature, as does Polybius. Nowhere in this chapter does Machiavelli employ the word *natura,* which he uses frequently elsewhere in the *Discourses.*[14] And while Polybius speaks of the origins of various epochs when humans lived in herds in a manner akin to the beasts, Machiavelli appears to speak simply of the beginning of the world, and specifies that humans lived apart like the beasts (cf. *D* 2.5). Moreover, although in a manner reminiscent of his source, Machiavelli speaks of the strength and courage of the man whom these primitive human beings follow, he does not specify, as does Polybius, that this man's courage resides in his soul.[15]

Most striking is that when speaking of the origins of the understanding of justice, Machiavelli neglects to speak of the family. According to Polybius, familial relations are unambiguously natural relationships. Because of their naturalness, when grown children do not reciprocate in kind the care their parents bestowed on them when young, the notion of injustice is particularly pronounced in Polybius's account; the children's conduct is especially unjust because they ignore their natural obligations.

Machiavelli condenses Polybius's intricate account of the origin of the understanding of justice to the following statement:

> From this arose the knowledge of things honest and good, differing from the pernicious and bad. For, seeing that if one individual harmed his benefactor, hatred and compassion among men came from it, as they blame the ungrateful and honored those who were grateful, and thought too that those same injuries could be done to them, to escape like evil they were reduced to making laws and ordering punishments for whoever acted against them: hence came the knowledge of justice. (D 1.2.3)

Machiavelli retains from Polybius's treatment the censure of the ingrate and the compassion for the one offended. According to both accounts this compassion appears to come from the observers' realization that the same type of ingratitude could one day afflict them. Machiavelli appears to locate the origin of justice in calculation alone, as opposed to Polybius, who finds its origin in a calculation that is buttressed by nature.

Whereas Machiavelli neglects the role of familial relations in considering the origin of justice, he does not overlook their place in the transformation of regimes. The problem of succession from one generation to the next is prominent in both Polybius's and Machiavelli's version of the transformation of regimes. Both posit six types of regimes: three are good regimes, each carrying the seeds of its degeneration.

According to Machiavelli's account, for example, when princes no longer derived their rule from election but from inheritance, the ruling principality becomes a tyranny because "the heirs began to degenerate from their ancestors; and leaving virtuous works, they thought that princes have nothing else to do but surpass others in sumptuousness and lasciviousness and every other kind of license."

Against this tyranny "plots and conspiracies" arose, and "those who were in advance of others in generosity, greatness of spirit, riches and nobility" led the multitude in arms against the prince. When the degenerate prince was vanquished, the multitude obeyed these good men, considering them liberators. The men who constituted this aristocracy, "in the beginning, with respect to the past tyranny, . . . governed themselves according to the laws ordered by them, placing the common utility before their own convenience." Machiavelli is ambiguous about whether the men who comprise this aristocracy were guided in their good administration by the thought of the horrible rule of the tyrants—not wishing to subject others to such an ordeal—or by that of the horrible downfall of the tyrant—not wishing to incur a similar fate. Whatever the cause for good government, Machiavelli makes it clear that it dissipates when the "sons" of the rulers assume the administration. Because "not knowing the variations of fortune, never having experienced evil," these inheritors of rule revert "to avarice, to ambition, [and] to usurpation of women." This government by the few is also overthrown, and is replaced by a democracy. The democratic regime for a time produces good government, but "once the generation that had ordered it was eliminated," it too degenerates in the same fashion (D 1.2.3).

For both Polybius and Machiavelli the mixed regime, composed of elements of monarchy, aristocracy, and democracy, offers a remedy for the vices to which any one regime is susceptible. Machiavelli explains its usefulness: "one watches the other, since in one same city there are the principality, the aristocrats, and the popular government" (D 1.2.5). The notion that the presence of the other orders produces a restraint on each order points to the salutary effect of the fear of immediate retribution for wrongdoing. Machiavelli's account highlights this one feature, whereas Polybius's recommends the mixed regime also for the manner in which it includes citizens who will be sure to be on the side of justice.[16] Machiavelli's depiction of the mixed regime seems to offer the ingredient so sorely lacking in each of the simple forms of government. The sons of each simple regime, perceiving no immediate restraints on their conduct, merely take what they desire. Although their superior position in the state allows them to proceed unchallenged for a time, ultimately their conduct becomes so unbearable that a rebellious populace will furnish the needed constraint. The long-awaited reaction is itself so severe that it transforms the character of the state. Constraint that comes from the knowledge that misconduct will be punished forthwith appears to be the necessary ingredient to moderate the excesses of the successors.

From what Machiavelli has chosen to accept and to reject from Polybius's teaching regarding the city and its natural transformation, he seems to view nature, in the form of the family, as only confounding politics by producing dissolute sons—sons who eventually cause the regime to collapse—rather than aiding it by assuring that the idea of justice is founded in natural relationships. This description of his intent violates the spirit of Machiavelli's presentation, however, for, to reiterate, he refuses to ascribe the family to nature or even to use the word in this chapter.

Machiavelli's statement that this cycle of regimes derives not from nature but from chance is quite a divergence from Polybius. Polybius's ascription of the cycle to nature implies that human exertion cannot subdue its inexorable effects. Moreover, although the Greek historian maintains that nature manifestly provides for political life, he also assumes it circumscribes politics by prescribing the eventual collapse of regimes. While the human contrivance of the mixed regime can keep the ravages of nature in abeyance for a time, a regime cannot escape entirely its decaying effects; Polybius anticipates the collapse of all regimes—even a mixed regime that has undertaken to subdue its corrupting effects.[17] Machiavelli, by contrast, ascribes the cycle to chance, implying thereby that the decay the cycle portends need not be inevitable.

Further, Machiavelli seems to question the very existence of this cycle in a manner entirely alien from his source. "But rarely do they return to the same governments, for almost no republic can have so long life as to be able to pass many times through those changes and remain on its feet," he comments (D 1.2.4). If a state cannot return to the same government, a cycle certainly cannot be said to hold sway over it. Instead, according to Machiavelli, it is vulnerable to a more vigorous state. The vigor of this state suggests perhaps that it is not impaired by the cycle's enervating effects. Here Machiavelli does not seem resigned to decay as he forces his readers to consider the vision of a conquering state.[18] This vision will gain clarity as Machiavelli progressively details an acquisitive republic vulnerable to neither complacently degenerate heirs to rule nor increasingly guileful pursuers of it.

As we already know, Machiavelli maintains that for such a ravenous state to digest its acquisitions without damage to itself, it cannot be a mixed regime merely; it must be a specific type of mixed regime as exemplified by Rome. The mixed regime that Lycurgus legislated for Sparta, for instance, could not acquire territory successfully because it did not contain provisions for increasing its population (D 1.6 and 2.3). The republic that allows its population to grow and furnishes that population a forum by which to express its *ambizione* will be tumultuous (D 1.4; O 83). Its internal politics, dominated by the clashes of the many who desire property and the few who desire glory, will produce a formidable foreign policy as this republic, impelled by these acquisitive passions, seeks ever more outlets for the appetites of its population.

Although ambition is given so free a reign in this state, it appears to produce good government. Because this regime is mixed, the ambitious sons of the republic know that others are watching their conduct. Owing to the way this republic unleashes the passions, these others would appear particularly vigilant, as they are concerned with satisfying themselves, an end that seems to entail ensuring that others do not acquire so much property or power as to deprive them of their share (see also D 1.30).[19] This readily perceptible constraint checks the youth of the mixed regime, who as a result will be incapable of satisfying their desires as readily as the sons of the unmixed regimes. In a mixed regime, its youth will not be able to satisfy their every desire with impunity.

Although the mixed regime offers oversight of the way the passions of the prominent young men are satisfied, the youth of the mixed regime will seek new methods by which to satisfy their passions, as the fate of the Roman republic illustrates. Here the increasing success of these new methods, which were particularly artful, brought down the republic. Given that the easy avenues to satisfaction are closed due to the attentive presence of other orders in the state, artfulness is of the utmost importance in the attempt to satisfy overweening ambition in Machiavelli's tumultuous mixed regime. As his tales of the Gracchi and of Caesar reveal, in such a regime corruption is practiced with ever increasing guile and ingenuity. The question then becomes, What can a regime do to prevent such sons from practicing their own highly developed arts of corruption? As commentators have recognized, in the remainder of the *Discourses* Machiavelli casts aside the Polybian analysis of the cycle of regimes.[20] The dissolute sons of the unmixed regime give way to the appealing sons of the mixed. Nevertheless, this problem too is susceptible to human ingenuity—that is, Machiavelli's ingenuity.

Corruption from Expansion and Foreign Influences

Machiavelli indicates that the threat of corruption and collapse emanates not only from within the state—as in the case of either the appealing youth whom the people so adore or degenerate youth utterly lacking in circumspection—but also from beyond the state's borders. A state's health may be imperiled by contact with foreigners. Machiavelli notes for example that because Lycurgus had proscribed such contact, Sparta did not have an "opportunity . . . to be corrupted" (D 1.6.2). Because Rome pursued an aggressive foreign policy, the city could not avoid the corrupting influence of foreigners. So far was Rome from Spartan caution regarding the influence of foreigners that it readily admitted foreigners to its honors. Although Machiavelli is quite liberal in his praise of Rome's policy (D 2.3), it still bore serious inconveniences for the state.

He suggests the possibility that the acquisition of foreign territory can harm the conquering state in *Discourses* 2.19. By using the Roman example as a touchstone, the heading of this chapter, "That acquisitions by republics that are not well ordered and that do not proceed according to Roman virtue are for their ruin not their exaltation," appears to announce that vigorous Rome was immune from the dangers to which weak republics are vulnerable. In the chapter itself, however, he clearly indicates that the conquests even of virtuous Rome were harmful to their conqueror. He appears to exonerate Rome from blame because even a "well ordered republic" is susceptible to damage "when it acquires a city or a province full of delights, whereby it can take their customs through the intercourse it has with them." To establish the existence of such influence in Rome's case, Machiavelli offers Livy's opinion: "'Even then least wholesome for military discipline, Capua, with its means for every pleasure, diverted the charmed spirits of the soldiers from the memory of their fatherland'" (D 2.19.2).[21] With these words Machiavelli appears to approve of Livy's diagnosis of the problem of Capua: that its delights weakened the Roman soldiers' concern for their homeland.

Like Livy, who points to the pernicious character of conquests subsequent to the subjugation of Capua, Machiavelli expresses an interest in later conquests when he notes that success in conquest "was thus about to be pernicious for the Romans in the times when they proceeded with so much prudence and so much virtue."

Although he does not here identify any later conquests that occurred when Rome was less resilient, he is in a better position than was Livy, who lived from 59 B.C. to 17 A.D., to understand the way Rome was transformed by its conquests. Of course, Pompey's conquest of Jerusalem in 63 B.C. and the events that were to occur in this territory during Rome's rule were to have a monumental effect on Rome and the course of the Roman Empire.[22] The existence of Christianity came to the attention of Roman authorities in Palestine around 30 A.D., long after Livy's death, and its effects were seen in Rome itself during the next generation.[23] By then Caesar had overturned the republic and others were ruling in his name. Of course, these events had occurred, according to Machiavelli's analysis, when Rome was corrupt. He notes that if the events of Capua had occurred when "Rome had been corrupt in some part, without doubt that acquisition would have been the ruin of the Roman republic" (D 2.19.2).

Machiavelli draws attention to these later conquests that occurred during Rome's corruption when he offers another quotation, this one from Juvenal, a Roman writer whose lifetime extended well into the second century A.D. and whose work chronicles events later than those in Livy's history. Juvenal's life corresponds to the time when Christianity was first coming to the attention of the Romans. The passage Machiavelli quotes from Juvenal's work does not refer to Christianity: "gluttony and luxury fastened upon her and revenged the conquered world."[24] Nevertheless, Juvenal, unlike Livy, does make reference in his corpus to the early Christians.[25]

Machiavelli's discussion in this chapter of the bad effect of Capua on the Romans indicates his interest in the way the weak can triumph over the strong. Although Machiavelli states an interest in Rome's subsequent conquests and refers to a Roman writer who had knowledge of Christianity's existence, these considerations are not proof that Machiavelli discourses on the events in Capua in 2.19 with a view toward the later devastating effect of Jerusalem on its conquerors. Nevertheless, he indicates in the closing lines of the *Discourses* that the religious practices of the vanquished can pose a danger to the conqueror. In 3.49 he presents "the conspiracy of the Bacchanals that was exposed at the time of the Macedonian war, in which many thousands of men and of women were actually involved" as an example of a dangerous accident to which states are susceptible (3.49.1). The Bacchanalia was a religious

practice imported to Rome from Greece after the war with Hannibal.[26] The Romans deemed these foreign rites subversive to their
state, and, on discovering that they were being performed in Rome
itself, they punished the initiates with prison and death.[27] Machiavelli praises Rome for taking such decisive action against this
threat. Given Christianity's later success there, however, his praise
must be limited. Indeed, in commending Rome for its ability to
contain a threat emanating from a foreign religion, he cannot help
but point to a time when a foreign religion succeeded in transforming the city.

Just as in relating Rome's successful response to the threat of the
Bacchic rites he points to its later failure in meeting the threat of
Christianity, so he points to the same failure in his discussion of
Rome's ability to deal effectively with Capua's corrupting influence. Continuing this discussion of Capua in *Discourses* 2.20, he
explains that in holding the captured city of Capua the Roman "le-
gions rotting in idleness [*ozio*], began to take delight in it" (*D*
2.20.1; O 176). As a result of their *ozio*, these troops,

> having forgotten their fatherland and their reverence for the Senate,
> . . . pondered taking up arms and making themselves lords of that
> country which they had defended with their virtue. For it appeared
> to them that the inhabitants were not worthy of possessing those
> goods that they did not know how to defend. (*D* 2.20.1)

These soldiers, who conspired to make the good things of the Ca-
puans their own, were actually conspiring against their own homeland, Capua being a possession of Rome.

Although the Roman authorities were able to avert any danger
posed by the conspiracy of the soldiers (see also *D* 3.6), they later
encountered a more damaging *ozio* in Jerusalem. The Christians
preached a new idleness—*ambizioso ozio,* which, like the idleness
encountered in Capua, afflicted Rome's soldiers. Whether stationed
in Jerusalem, in another outlying territory, or even in Rome itself,
the idleness of the Christians prompted the Roman soldiers to forget their earthly homeland, for it taught them to covet good things
that this homeland could not possibly provide them, and thereby
encouraged a defection against their earthly homeland. Of course,
unlike the events in Capua, this conspiracy did not have a resolu-
tion favorable to pagan Rome, as the conspiracy of Jerusalem was
successful. Rome's soldiers brought this decadence back to their
city, and it permeated and destroyed Rome. Machiavelli discerns in

this process the revenge of the vanquished: "Truly similar cities or provinces avenge themselves against their conqueror without battle and without blood, . . . by filling it with their bad customs" (*D* 2.19.2).[28] Not only did Rome convert to Christianity, but the city became the religion's very capital.

Unlike the story of the invasion of aliens Machiavelli tells in *Discourses* 1.13, slaves and exiles occupied Rome's Capitol and successfully transformed it and its empire. Not just Rome, but the vast territory it had conquered, suffered from the deleterious effects of this successful conspiracy engendered in one of Rome's possessions. Machiavelli introduces the devastating effects of Rome's conquests on the conquered in *Discourses* 2.2, where he compares Christianity unfavorably to paganism and likens the most *virtuoso* tyranny to the reign of Christianity. Thus, surprisingly, in the very same chapter in which he uses ancient Rome as a foil for modern states composed of humble and contemplative Christians, he criticizes the conquering republic that appears to stand opposite to the focus of his criticism. After noting the defective character of modern education, he draws its political consequence: "These educations and false interpretations thus bring it about that not as many republics are seen in the world as were seen in antiquity; nor as a consequence is as much love for liberty seen in peoples as was then" (*D* 2.2.2). For all of the venom he directs at Christianity for promoting the weakness of his own times, he places the blame for the current political situation at the doorstep of the ancients:

> Still I believe the cause of this to be rather that the Roman Empire with its arms and its greatness eliminated all republics and all civil ways of life. And although that empire was dissolved, the cities still have not been able to put themselves back together or reorder themselves for civil life except in very few places of that empire. (*D* 2.2.2)

In enabling the Romans to destroy the liberty of the self-governing communities they conquered, Roman military prowess created the situation so torturous to the Florentine who vehemently exhorts political leaders to arm their people. The ancient Romans are actually responsible for the political weakness Machiavelli sees displayed before him. This is a surprising and significant charge he lodges here. He begins the *Discourses* by appealing from the weakness of his contemporaries to the strength of the ancients, but such an appeal is itself apparently pointless, for the strength of the ancients promoted modern weakness.

Strength somehow engenders weakness, and the subjugation the Romans imposed would bode ill for the political communities that were to arise in these territories after the collapse of the Roman Empire. Through the force of arms, the Romans amassed a vast empire, but ultimately their arms were ineffectual when the Christians confronted them with unfamiliar weapons—with the arts of peace rather than the art of war. Having subjugated all the other free states, the Romans assured that their state and all their conquered territory were vulnerable to the threat they could not contain. Because immediately before this discussion Machiavelli rails against Christianity and the weakness of modern education, he makes certain that the reader recognizes that the inheritors of Rome's empire are Christian states. Therefore, he blames the conquests of the Romans for the predicament of these Christian states. Having already examined the way Christianity devastated the practice of politics—if indeed the ancient Romans are ultimately responsible for this devastating political situation—he imputes to Rome a considerable burden of responsibility.

Machiavelli's examination of Rome's inability to sustain its empire and—indeed, itself—demonstrates that it was vulnerable to corruption emanating from within, in the form of appealing youths, who artfully masked their overweening desire for preeminence, and from without, in the form of foreign influences that engendered idleness in Rome's soldiers and brought subversive religious practices to its citizens. It appears from Rome's later history that such threatening youth was not an internal threat only.[29] The appearance of Christ in a conquered territory combines Machiavelli's concerns with appealing youth, idleness, and foreign religious practices. Indeed, it was this combined threat that transformed Rome and subverted its free life.

If Christ is a suitable example of a young man to whom all eyes turn, then it would appear that the Romans made a mistake in allowing him to be crucified. Just like the case of Caesar, the action taken against Christ resulted in martyrdom and the continuance of his rule. Still, Machiavelli's injunction against hasty action furnishes little solace to any state facing this threat, for the only sure benefit dilatory action guarantees is the deferment of ultimate ruin. Therefore, it appears at this point he reaches an impasse; the appearance in the state of such a youth signifies the ruin of the state by either a short route or a long one. The appearance of such a youth was not only Rome's problem but also Machiavelli's as he legislates for his new Rome. Just as it can be said that Christ built on the innovations of the Gracchi and Caesar, in the era that Machiavelli intends to usher in a most formidable threat can arise: a youth capable of building on the innovation of Christ. As we shall see, this is far from Machiavelli's last word on this issue, for the problem of youth whose seeming benevolent appeal masks a dire threat to a state is of primary interest in the *Discourses*. So effective will his new Rome be at addressing this problem that it will thwart the attempts of potential tyrants, whose appeal will be particularly insidious as they have at their disposal the historical lessons of both Caesar's ascendancy and Christianity's.

One must continue to explore the causes of the vulnerabilities of ancient Rome and in the process observe Machiavelli learning from the mistakes of this ancient city. The critical ingredient in making the promise of private benefits irresistible to the Roman plebeians, and hence in overcoming the resistance of the patricians, appears to be a claim to transcendence. A doctrine of transcendence was imported to Rome from the East and was welcomed there. As we shall see, this link appears natural enough given that the people of Rome were encouraged to look to the divine for relief. Having been so encouraged, they could easily accept succor from an alternative divine being, one offering a salvation that transcends the earth. In other words, those who vie with the patricians for the allegiance of the plebeians can utilize the instrument of the patricians to triumph over them. The claim of transcendence that Christ promoted far surpassed the promises of any of Rome's young men, and as we shall see, it was Rome's pagan religion that facilitated the Roman people's eager reception of the promises of Christianity.

❖ CHAPTER 5 ❖

MACHIAVELLI'S AMBIGUOUS PRAISE
OF PAGANISM

A careful consideration of Machiavelli's portrait of Rome suggests that in the final analysis he does not view ancient, republican Rome as the positive solution for the enfeebled people of his times. His portrait suggests that fundamental flaws in that city helped give rise to the very predicament of the Christian era that he endeavors to overcome. Ancient Rome furnished Christianity with the nutrients essential to fuel the latter's conquest of the Roman Empire. Because those aspects of Rome that proved so helpful to Christianity's conquest must be eschewed, Rome simply cannot be Machiavelli's model.

Despite his criticism Machiavelli appears to treat Rome's pagan religion in a favorable manner. Those ancient Roman commanders, who fraudulently appealed to the wrath of the gods in order to reenforce the people's dedication to the homeland, appear to be a desirable alternative to their modern counterparts, who glorify "humble and contemplative" men (*D* 2.2.2). So favorable is Machiavelli's presentation of the pagan religion that he appears to offer it as a salutary alternative to the toll he believes Christianity exacts on political life. Among Machiavellian scholars who do not consider their subject to be a Christian, there is almost universal agreement that he greatly admires the manner in which pagan religion served the purposes of the Roman state.[1] Further, virtually no student of Machiavelli doubts that he believes religion should be an instrument of politics. Exemplary of this view is Cassirer, who states: "in Machiavelli's system, therefore, religion is indispensable. But it is no longer an end in itself; it has become a mere tool in the hands of the political rulers. It is not the foundation of man's social life but a powerful weapon in all political struggles."[2]

In contrast to this view, I argue that Machiavelli's embrace of the pagan religion represents an important step to a very different destination—one that regards all appeals to divine entities as dangerous to a state. Because on the way to this final destination Machiavelli so extols the political virtues of paganism, some of his readers may be shaken in their devotion to Christianity. It is difficult to imagine Machiavelli objecting to such a result. Nevertheless, he has an additional lesson to teach. Just as a well-advised reader of Machiavelli should not close the book before confronting his less than sincere appeals to a purer Christianity, so the same should be done with his praise of paganism. Just beneath the surface of his overt appeals to paganism lies a deep ambivalence toward the use the Romans made of their religion, and when this ambivalence is brought to light, a case emerges for doubting what most commentators on Machiavelli simply do not doubt.

In this chapter I argue that Machiavelli considers the Roman leaders' use of pagan religion to maintain popular support as pernicious. It enabled the leaders of the people to put this religion to a very different purpose. The successive innovations of aspiring tyrants strengthened such appeals and eventuated in the destruction of the republic: the Gracchi looked to unseen lands and Caesar was able to entrench himself so thoroughly that even his death could not rid the state of the evil he created. Christianity, while incorporating the innovations of the Gracchi and Caesar, transcends their methods in a critical way. Christ's followers pique the passions of the people not merely with lands that many Romans have not seen, but with domains beyond human experience. This appeal to transcendence trumped all the benefits the city of Rome could offer. When the Roman people accepted the imported doctrine, they no longer needed to devote themselves to the earthly city to receive their rewards, and thus "civil life" was utterly transcended in Rome. Therefore, only when the critical element of a promise of divine provision was added to the familiar litany of private benefits did the line of ingenious aspiring tyrants, who wished to transcend civil life, achieve its goal (cf. *D* 1.7.3; *O* 88). The people of this city—a city seemingly possessed of the most resolute earthly might—was rendered susceptible to just such an appeal because almost from Rome's beginnings the leaders encouraged the people to look for divine succor. Thus these leaders were laying the foundations for an alternative appeal to the divine that would thwart their own purposes. This tool—religious manipulation—eventually escaped from the hands of the patricians. The pagan religion laid the foundation for Rome's subjugation to Christianity. The paganism of Rome, then, is less an alternative to, than a forerunner of, Christianity.

Paganism as a Political Alternative

Machiavelli's treatment of the experience of the ancient Romans shows that human beings were once guided by a religion that sustained them in their worldly enterprises. From this recognition arises the following question: Could such politically salutary beliefs reign again? We already know that with the advent of Christianity the world looks radically different, "as if heaven, sun, elements, men had varied in motion, order and power from what they were in antiquity" (*D* 1.pr.2). In Machiavelli's view these changes are not an obstacle to the recovery of the virtue of antiquity, for they affect merely the appearance of things. In the first chapter of the section of the first book of the *Discourses* devoted to the Roman religion (11–15), Machiavelli admonishes: "[n]o one, therefore, should be terrified that he cannot carry out what has been carried out by others, for as was said in our preface, men are born, live, and die always in one and the same order." In placing this encouragement to imitation in the section devoted to an examination of Roman paganism, Machiavelli appears to offer his analysis of the former, salutary religion with a view toward the possibility of achieving that which was "carried out by others" (*D* 1.11.5).

Machiavelli devotes chapter 1.11 to praise of Numa and

compares Numa's deeds to those of Romulus, founder of Rome and Numa's immediate predecessor. Machiavelli judges that Numa's deeds are more praiseworthy: whereas Romulus created the Senate as well as other institutions, Numa introduced religion to the city, thus civilizing its inhabitants and making them tractable for all the rulers who were to follow him. Indeed Numa's "arts of peace" and the "fear of God" that they promoted "made easier whatever enterprise the Senate or the great men of Rome might plan to make." As a result of this innovation the Romans "feared to break an oath much more than the laws, like those who esteemed the power of God more than that of men" (D 1.11.1).

For all of Machiavelli's insistence here on the way the ancient Roman religion promoted the health of the state, the religion Numa introduced to Rome presents a potential problem. Machiavelli presents religion as superior to politics in this discussion. One must wonder whether in Machiavelli's view politics really benefits when the citizens of a state fear the consequences of an abrogation of an oath more than those that flow from legal disobedience. Of course, as long as the religion decrees behavior that is beneficial to the state, no such problem arises; however, it is the disjunction between the demands of the state and those of religion that Machiavelli finds so harmful in modern times. In praising the accomplishment of Numa Machiavelli reminds us of the political problem of modern times. When Numa introduced into Rome so powerful a belief—one capable of exerting such influence over hearts and minds—he simultaneously introduced into Rome the possibility of divided allegiance on the political plane. We have already seen how Machiavelli describes in evocative terms the tendency of the people of ancient Rome, who had been nurtured under Numa's orders, to desire to abandon their homeland to claim the purported riches of another city, as if the defining characteristic of Christianity's influence already existed in ancient Rome.

Despite such considerations, Machiavelli's overt point is that Numa's introduction of religion was politically useful. By way of illustration Machiavelli offers two incidents in which the fear of religion worked to Rome's political advantage. The first occurs after Rome's defeat at Cannae, when Scipio went to some dejected Roman citizens, whom he had heard were planning to abandon Italy for Sicily, "and with naked iron in hand compelled them to swear they would not abandon the fatherland." Machiavelli concludes that "those citizens whom the love of fatherland and its laws did not keep in Italy were kept there by an oath that they were forced to take." The second example relates that, when Titus Manlius's father was indicted by a tribune, the son "compelled" the tribune with a threat of death to take an oath promising to withdraw the charge. The tribune took the oath out of "fear." These outcomes "arose from nothing other than that religion Numa had introduced in that city," claims Machiavelli (D 1.11.1).

In presenting Machiavelli's view of the political benefits of the pagan religion Quentin Skinner points to this discussion of Scipio's action: "The effect of this was to coerce them into *virtù:* although their 'love of their country and its laws' had not persuaded them to remain in Italy, they were successfully kept there by the fear of blasphemously violating their word."[3] This is the overt lesson Machiavelli draws from these examples; however, although he furnishes these incidents to illustrate the fear of God's power in Rome, it is the power of human beings and the fear such power inspires that he actually highlights in both stories. He emphasizes Scipio's brandishing of his sword and the fear Manlius arouses in his father's accuser. In Machiavelli's retelling, the fear of a Roman citizen, and not of a god, provided the immediate impetus for the administration of each oath. Moreover, while the fear of God's power may very well have constrained these oath takers to keep their vows, Machiavelli's recounting of these incidents does not emphasize such fear, as he describes the administration of the oaths rather than their enforcement. Hence one might wonder whether it was actually the fear of *"la potenza di Dio"* or the fear of the angry return of a Scipio or a Manlius that contributed more to the keeping of these oaths (O 93). By so emphasizing the fear of human power in these stories, Machiavelli fails, perhaps deliberately, to prove his point that the Romans were particularly tractable because of their fear of divine power. One wonders whether Machiavelli is suggesting ultimately that human force is a better instrument of coercion than the fear of an omnipotent divinity.

Machiavelli's argument thus far in this chapter is that Numa's introduction of religion was a great boon to Roman politics. Reflection on the general implications of Numa's accomplishment and its practical effect in the cases of Scipio and Manlius has, however, led to different—and perhaps contradictory—indications of Machiavelli's ultimate view. On the one hand, in asserting that oaths generated greater respect than laws, Machiavelli opens up the possibility of a conflict between religion and politics that points to the tremendous influence religion can wield over human action. On the other hand, in offering the spectacle of powerful and fearful Roman heroes forcing the administration of those oaths, Machiavelli suggests the possibility of the dread engendered by human rather than divine beings as a means to desired political ends. In the one case, Machiavelli points to the power of religion; in the other, to the power of human beings. These divergent indications could be reconciled if Machiavelli means that, given the power of divine belief (and hence the danger to politics if it were to escape from the clutches of the leaders of a state so as to be interpreted in a manner that enervates the state), the safer course in bringing about desirable political outcomes is to rely solely on fear engendered by human beings.

The above considerations have taken us far from Machiavelli's manifest argument in this chapter that religion can facilitate political virtue by manipulating citizens. Despite these reflections on the problems Numa's religion may have introduced into Rome, Machiavelli dwells in the succeeding chapters of this section on the utility of Numa's institution of a religion that "was founded on the responses of oracles and on the sect of the diviners and augurs," which easily lent itself to the belief that the god who could predict one's future could also ensure its occurrence. Indeed, Machiavelli begins 1.12 by declaring that religion is essential in maintaining political health:

> Those princes or those republics that wish to maintain themselves uncorrupt have above everything else to maintain the ceremonies of their religion uncorrupt and hold them always in veneration; for one can have no greater indication of the ruin of a province than to see the divine cult disdained. (D 1.12.1)

Later he asserts that "[a]ll things that arise in favor of that religion [leaders] should favor and magnify, even though they judge them false; and they should do it so much the more as they are more prudent and more knowing of natural things" (D 1.12.1).

Machiavelli illustrates the political utility of such appeals to the divine by offering examples of their use in later times during the republic. For instance, an appeal to the anger of the gods assured that elections produced only patricians to fill the offices of the republic, and a favorable prognostication produced new hope in an army disheartened by a long siege (D 1.13). Thus, in presenting the

successes of the Roman patricians in manipulating a credulous people, the central contention of his section devoted to a consideration
of the pagan religion is the political utility of contrived appeals to
the divine.[4] This quintessential Machiavellian combination of devi-
ousness and wry playfulness tends to lull commentators into believing that, in understanding it, they have plumbed the depth of
Machiavelli's teaching on religion. Friedrich Meinecke's conclusion
with regard to this subject is typical:

> Machiavelli spoke out very forcibly on the subject of the indispens-
> ability of religion . . . ; at any rate, he was strongly in favour of a re-
> ligion which would make men courageous and proud. He once
> named "religion, laws, military affairs" together in one breath, as
> the three fundamental pillars of the State. But, in the process, reli-
> gion and morality fell from the status of intrinsic values, and became
> nothing more than means towards the goal of a State animated by
> *virtù*. It was this that led him on to make the double-edged recom-
> mendation, which resounded so fearsomely down the centuries to
> come, inciting statesmen to an irreligious and at the same time dis-
> honest scepticism: the advice that even a religion tinged with error
> and deception ought to be supported, and the wiser one was, the
> more one would do it.[5]

Meinecke accurately recapitulates Machiavelli's overt point in this
section but, like Skinner, neglects to consider whether the examples
Machiavelli provides actually bear it out.

Paganism's Political Uses

Deeper consideration of Machiavelli's examples of the utility of
the Roman religion indicates that in his view the Romans employed
these contrived appeals for two purposes. The first was to inspire
troops in the field with confidence before a battle. Machiavelli
claims that the Romans would never "go on an expedition unless
they had persuaded the soldiers that the gods promised them victory" (D 1.14.1). The other was to maintain the dutiful obedience
of the plebeians to the patricians and hence to maintain patrician
predominance in the city. Machiavelli indicates here and elsewhere
in the *Discourses* that religion's role was not vital in serving either
of these purposes. Other methods could have served these ends just
as well and perhaps even more effectively and with less danger.

The inculcation of the belief among one's soldiers that properly
propitiated divinities will come to their aid would appear to be a

commonsensical expedient in steeling the hearts of the city's warriors against fear before a battle. Machiavelli explains that for this very purpose the Romans maintained a class of diviners called *pullari,* who before a battle would take the auspices. If the chickens ate, the Romans would fight; complications arose, however, if the chickens were recalcitrant when the commanders had determined that the time was right for battle. Machiavelli remarks on such an eventuality:

> when reason showed them a thing they ought to do, notwithstanding that the auspices had been adverse they did it in any mode. But they turned it around with means and modes so aptly that it did not appear that they had done it with disdain for religion. (D 1.14.1)

Despite his insistence that this religious custom did not inconvenience the Roman commanders, Machiavelli proceeds to recount the unfortunate result of just such a circumstance. Appius Pulcher determined that the time was at hand for battle when opposing the Carthaginian army in Sicily, but the chickens withheld their approval of his timing by refusing to eat. Machiavelli reports that Appius, frustrated with this complication, dismissed the religious ritual with the announcement that he would see if the chickens would drink "and had them thrown in the ocean" (D 1.14.3). Appius's army lost the battle. Apparently, by so publicly dismissing divine augury, Appius lost the opportunity of fighting with confident troops and was instead burdened with a dispirited army.

Although Machiavelli also relates how the inconvenience of incompliant chickens can be treated successfully (an uncooperative poultryman can be easily placed in front of the army's lines to receive an errant Roman spear, an event that will produce at once both his death and a sign of the gods' favor), one wonders whether there exist alternative methods of rendering an army confident that do not so constrain its commander. Indeed, much later in the *Discourses* in a chapter entitled "If one wishes to win a battle, it is necessary to make the army confident both among themselves and in the captain," he returns to the subject of inspiring troops, and suggests that the straits in which the Roman commanders found themselves owing to the demands of their city's religious rituals were wholly unnecessary (D 3.33).

He begins this chapter by asserting that an army must believe it will win the impending battle. Such confidence is produced in soldiers when they are well armed, well ordered, and well acquainted

with each other. The best way to assure that they are well acquainted is to see that they were born and reared in the same place.
He then enumerates the qualities of a captain that inspire confidence. The last quality he names is the captain's ability to make the
road to victory appear easy, which requires that he conceal or make
"light of things that at a distance could show as dangers." "Such
things, well observed, are the great cause that the army trusts, and
by trusting wins" (D 3.33.1). At this point Machiavelli states that
the Romans engendered such confidence in their armies through
the *"via di religione"* (O 240), thus returning to the theme of
1.11–15. But by speaking generally of confidence in an army and
citing contributing factors that in no way partake of religion, and
then only later mentioning the Roman method of utilizing religion,
he induces the reader to conclude that other "ways" exist which do
not entail religion—that the Roman *"via"* is just one of many.[6] The
Romans did not need the recourse to religion that required their
commanders to choose either to cloak cleverly their deviations
from the auspices' dictates or to be less subtle and to be punished,
as was Appius Pulcher who drowned the chickens.[7]

Even in the earlier section devoted to religion, Machiavelli reveals the darker side of appeals to the divine. This revelation occurs
in 1.15, when he endeavors ostensibly to illustrate "how much confidence can be had through religion well used." His only example
in this chapter, that of the Samnites, surely does not prove this
point. He explains that, owing to the long wars with Rome, this
people had come to such straits they could no longer sustain themselves. But they were so attached to their liberty that they could not
abstain from war. Believing that "there was no better means" of inducing "obstinacy in the spirits of the soldiers" than that of religion, the Samnites as a last resort reinstituted an ancient religious
ritual abounding in the blood of its sacrificial victims (D 1.15.1).
According to Machiavelli the Roman commander who faced the
Samnites consoled his own soldiers by telling them that the Samnites' ornate garb could not harm Romans, and that the Samnites'
ritual served only to make them afraid of their fellow citizens, the
gods, and the enemy. The Samnites lost this battle to the Romans,
and the Roman commander inspired his own troops by actually
making light of the importance of religion.

Although this example does not show, as Machiavelli claims,
how much confidence can be acquired by religion,[8] it does serve as
a comment on some of Machiavelli's other claims in the *Discourses*

regarding religion. First, in 1.12 Machiavelli had criticized the Church for having allowed its original principles to lapse. Here the Samnites sought to go back to the origins of their religion, and this recourse did not bring them the success for which they had hoped. Thus 1.15 can be taken to be a comment on Machiavelli's prescription in 1.12. Second, in 1.11 Machiavelli had praised the Romans for the fear they had of God. Here he shows that such fear of the divine may not, in all cases, be beneficial to an army. Third, the example of the Samnites provides a contrast to the modern states that Machiavelli castigates in 2.2 for not tenaciously defending their liberty. In that chapter Machiavelli points to religion as being responsible for the weakness of modern states and cites a religion that calls for sacrifice "full of blood and ferocity . . . , with a multitude of animals being killed there" as being more conducive to the protection of liberty (D 2.2.2). In 1.15 he shows that even a most ferocious religion cannot recover "lost virtue" (D 1.15.1). Machiavelli indicates in these ways that religious appeals are both inconvenient and unnecessary. Indeed, he indicates further that such appeals are sometimes counterproductive in attempting to inspire an army with confidence.

The other use of religion Machiavelli treats in detail, that of constraining the plebeians to acquiesce in the political purposes of the patricians, also appears superfluous. Whereas in the earlier section 1.11–15 he illustrates the utility of such appeals, he suggests later that these means were ultimately ineffective. This reappraisal becomes evident in Machiavelli's further consideration of the way the patricians overcame the plebeians' demands for the passage of the Terentillian law. This law proposed that five citizens be appointed to codify the law pertaining to the power of the consuls, thus placing limits on the administration of the office.[9] When Machiavelli first treats the controversy over this law in 1.13, he states that one of the first remedies the nobility used in averting its passage was religion, and one such use of religion was the nobility's reference to the Sibylline books, which predicted that the city was in danger of losing its liberty due to sedition. Livy says that the tribunes charged the patricians with fraud, whereas Machiavelli gives more credit to the tribunes by asserting that the fraud was actually "exposed by the tribunes [*fusse scoperta*]" (D 1.13.2; O 97). Machiavelli's change in terms carries the additional implication that in his view the patricians had indeed falsified the prognostication for political reasons. Machiavelli says that despite this exposure, the plebeians, frightened by the books' warning, did not wish to pursue the promulgation of the law, whereas in Livy's account war intervenes.[10]

Although Machiavelli's explicit purpose in 1.13 is to praise the use the Romans made of their religion, he undermines his own thesis even here when he states that the recourse to religion was the first remedy that the nobles pursued. The implication is that they subsequently had to try at least one other method to avert passage of the law, and hence that their recourse to religion was not entirely successful. Later, in chapter 1.39, Machiavelli treats subsequent methods of the patricians that did not partake of religious maneuvering, and hence makes evident the insufficiency of religious posturing. Machiavelli relates later—without any mention of religion—how the patricians eventually overcame the inconvenience of this proposal; while their first recourse was to religion, the patricians resolved the problem through purely political means:[11] they replaced the two consuls with tribunes possessing consular powers, offices for which the plebeians were eligible. Machiavelli says in 1.39 that the patricians changed the name of the office but managed to keep the same authority in the republic. Eventually the plebeians realized their mistake and went back to the original office of the consuls.

While the tribunes with consular power existed, the patricians had ways of keeping plebeians from holding these offices. In 1.13 Machiavelli says that the patricians frightened the people into electing only patricians to be tribunes with consular power by attributing a plague to the gods' anger because of the plebeians' earlier control of these high offices. In describing the same episode Livy differs by saying that the patricians had only their best men stand for the offices and as an added precaution also attributed the city's misfortune to the gods' anger over the plebeians' predominance.[12] Whereas in the section on religion Machiavelli only mentions the method relating to religion, later in the *Discourses* he completely discards this particular method. Machiavelli devotes an entire chapter, 1.48, to describing the way the patricians managed to keep the plebeians from holding these offices. He mentions two methods, neither of which relates to religion: the patricians either had their best men stand or used devious means to guarantee that the worst of the plebeians stand along with the better men of their number. Machiavelli says that this first method made the plebeians ashamed not to give the offices to the patricians, and the second made them ashamed to accept them. So Machiavelli's argument progresses as follows: in 1.13 he gives only one method of keeping the plebs from office, that of the clever manipulation of religion— Livy gives two. Later in 1.48 Machiavelli gives two methods, neither of which relates to the manipulation of religious beliefs—one is the method Livy mentions, but which Machiavelli ignored in 1.13, and the other is not to be found at all in Livy's account of this incident.[13] Thus Machiavelli has replaced the method in Livy's text relating to religion with his own which pertains not to religion, but to devious political maneuvering.

In this manner the religious contrivances of the Romans, the central focus of Machiavelli's section on religion and apparently indispensable to the health of the state, now seem to be ineffective. Nevertheless, although seemingly not necessary in the mundane contrivances of the patricians, religion is certainly necessary on extraordinary occasions:

> And truly there was never any orderer of extraordinary laws for a people who did not have recourse to God, because otherwise they would not have been accepted. For a prudent individual knows many goods that do not have in themselves evident reasons with which one can persuade others. (D 1.11.3)

Even in this account of Rome's beginnings Machiavelli allows an exception to his maxim, for he asserts that in the case of Rome's very founder, Romulus, "the authority of God was not necessary" (D 1.11.2).[14]

This distinction between Romulus and Numa might be explained by Numa's achievement being "extraordinary," whereas Romulus's was not; this explanation does not seem satisfactory given that Machiavelli ranks Romulus, not Numa, among the four great founders.[15] Moreover, Machiavelli changes Livy's account of Rome's founding in a manner that accentuates Romulus's authority, as well as his lack of religion, in contrast to Numa's religion and corresponding lack of authority. In drawing these distinctions between Romulus and Numa, for example, Machiavelli contradicts Livy, who indicates that religion existed in Rome prior to Numa's kingship. In Livy's account, augury is used to determine the gods' will as to which brother should name and govern the new city; because of a disagreement over the interpretation of the auspices, Romulus slew Remus to become sole authority. As king, Romulus attended to the worship of the gods.[16] The lack of religion in Rome under Romulus, on which Machiavelli insists, is, in fact, his own invention. The unwary reader of Machiavelli's account of Rome's founding would readily assume that a belief in the gods was introduced only with Numa's ascension. In offering this new account of Rome's founding, Machiavelli appears to believe that not all innovators require recourse to a higher power to gain the adherence of their people. Whereas Machiavelli comments here that Numa doubted his own authority, there is no comparable statement regarding Romulus's authority in the chapter; Romulus apparently had no cause to doubt it. Moreover, this change in Livy's history reveals Machiavelli's insistence that sole responsibility belong to Numa for the introduction of religion in Rome.

The Pitfalls of Paganism

The above considerations suggest that in Machiavelli's view recourse to the gods is not necessary in extraordinary or ordinary politics and that Rome was expending energy pointlessly on its religious rituals. Moreover, he shows further that Rome's recourse to religious duplicity was not only ineffective but politically pernicious. In Machiavelli's depiction of turbulent Rome the patricians' use of religious appeals is consistently related to class conflict: the people of Rome seem always to be teetering on the brink of defection. From the perspective of the plebeians, defection does not appear unreasonable given that they are exposed to more danger in the city's wars and that their brawn maintains Rome's freedom (*D* 1.47). Machiavelli comments that at times the plebeians attributed Rome's constant stream of wars not to "the ambition of neighbors who wished to crush them" but to the wish of the nobles who wanted to divert the plebeians from demanding more power in the city (*D* 1.39.2).[17] When such thoughts threatened to dislodge plebeian allegiance from their leaders, a well-executed appeal to the gods on the part of the patricians brought the plebeians back from the edge of sedition. Later, when the city had conquered territory in the East, a new understanding was imported into Rome, one that appealed not to the old pagan gods, who were said to demand martial dedication to Rome, but to a new god, who required a new kind of virtue that insisted on the way of peace. Rome came into contact with this new understanding when the city had already been convulsed by the appealing claims of would-be tyrants. Because the city had assiduously fostered the religious credulity of its people, its citizens and soldiers were susceptible to this religious appeal and its promise of transcendent goods.

Moreover, as we shall see, Machiavelli suggests that some leaders of the people grasped the tremendous possibilities inherent in the politically devastating combination of a promise of private benefits with a religious appeal, permitting them the opportunity to propel themselves to preeminence. Their victory consists in the utter destruction of the people's dedication to an earthly homeland. Therefore, although Numa's innovation of religious manipulation was intended to maintain the people's dedication to Rome, it ultimately served as an important instrument for the subversion of such dedication.

Machiavelli reveals his understanding of how this subversion took place when he suggests that the leaders of the people initiated themselves into the mysteries of the patricians' fraudulent religious appeals. Recall that in discussing the first way the patricians attempted to avert passage of the Terentillian law in *Discourses* 1.13, Machiavelli states that they appealed fraudulently to a dire prediction in the Sibylline books. Whereas Livy says the tribunes merely accused the patricians of falsifying the prognostication, Machiavelli claims these tribunes actually discovered the fraud. In the context of the earlier discussion in this chapter, his change in Livy's story appears significant in revealing that for Machiavelli the patricians in fact were not pious but only affected religious awe to manipulate the people. At this point Machiavelli's change in terms takes on even more significance because it reveals also that, in Machiavelli's understanding, some tribunes understood the purposes to which religious appeals could be put.

Having discovered the patricians' fraud, clever plebeians—perhaps plebeians like these clever tribunes of 1.13—possess the knowledge necessary to employ the same tool in the pursuit of their own interests. After the constitution of Rome had permitted the Gracchi and Caesar to make so much headway in appealing to the people with promises of private benefits, a religious doctrine was imported to Rome from the East. This doctrine contained the type of promises of transcendent goods that the tribunes needed to gain the people's allegiance to their cause, for they promised in another life the victory of the plebeians over the nobles. To gain that victory, the plebeians no longer dedicated themselves to the martial causes of their city.

Machiavelli suggests, of course, that the promised benefits are illusory. Having taken the bait, the people find themselves oppressed by those offering them salvation. We have already considered

Machiavelli's analysis of the way the Church's hierarchy oppresses the people. A "wise" tyrant will always take such a course: "[H]e will wait to eliminate the nobility with the favor of the people; and he will never turn to the oppression of the people until he has eliminated them, at which time, when the people recognizes it is a slave, it has nowhere to take refuge" (*D* 1.40.5).

It was in this manner that clever tribunes thwarted the patricians who had used the plebeians in the aggrandizement of themselves and their country. In other words, a dangerous possibility lurks when a state encourages the religious gullibility of its people: clever plebeians will realize that they can trump the patricians at their own game. The result would be a religion very much like Christianity; Machiavelli blames pagan Rome for Christianity's success in that city.

In the Florentine's rendition of Rome's history, it is Numa who is ultimately responsible for Christianity's victory; Machiavelli makes Numa solely responsible for introducing religion into Rome and hence for the ultimate perversion of that religion and the subversion of Rome that results. Although Machiavelli is initially liberal in his praise of Numa, even going so far as to rank him above Romulus, eventually Machiavelli becomes scornful of this religious founder. His criticism first comes to light in *Discourses* 1.19, when Machiavelli compares Numa's peaceful nature to Romulus's warlike nature and concludes:

> From this all princes who hold a state may find an example. For he who is like Numa will hold it or not hold it according as the times or fortune turn under him, but he who is like Romulus, and like him comes armed with prudence and with arms, will hold it in every mode unless it is taken from him by an obstinate and excessive force. (*D* 1.19.4)

Numa's recourse to religion, then, made him dependent on fortune, a dangerous position for a leader and his state. Machiavelli reiterates this point in 1.21 when comparing Numa (again to his detriment) to his successor, Tullus. Upon taking the throne, Tullus found that the Romans were no longer trained for war and resolved to retrain them for military service rather than rely on foreign arms. Numa depended on fortune in two ways: he did not arm his own subjects and he appealed to a belief in divine entities.[18] This is a serious charge that Machiavelli registers against the one whom he claims introduced religion into Rome.

Machiavelli's criticism of Numa for being unarmed leaves the reader with the uneasy feeling that in appealing to divine entities this king somehow weakened Rome—that he somehow left Rome itself unarmed. The tool of religious manipulation that Numa bequeathed to the patricians apparently left Rome unarmed because it left that city vulnerable to another type of religious appeal, which subverted the very purpose of the patricians' appeals—that of retaining the people's dedication to Rome's wars. In this manner one sees how Christianity's way of peace was prefigured in Numa's "*arti della pace*" (1.11; O 93).

Machiavelli's presentation of the Roman "*via di religione*" suggests his ultimate dissatisfaction with this method, which allowed the Roman commanders to obtain their desired ends. Many of his examples show that the Roman recourse to religion was at best superfluous and at worst pernicious. One wonders if Machiavelli means to suggest that a state would be better served by forgoing appeals to extrahuman forces altogether.

PART III

MACHIAVELLI'S NEW ROME

Race du Caïn, au ciel monte et sur la terre jette Dieu.
—Baudelaire

In examining Rome's decline into corruption, Machiavelli observes that Rome should have introduced new orders. It becomes clear that these new orders are his own, which he claims to have discovered and which historical Rome could not possibly have introduced because Machiavelli constructs them as a response to events that occurred after the city had begun its decline. His orders incorporate his understanding of the strength residing in the religion that so enfeebled the humanity of his age. To be saved, ancient Rome must be infused with modern vigor.

His response, then, is premised on the historical lesson of Christianity's ascendancy. Machiavelli condemns Christianity, but he learns much from its victory and its rule. Indeed he selects the harshest elements of Christian teaching and transforms them to function as the solution to the problems confronting his new republic. Nowhere in his application to his new politics of these selected elements of Christianity is there an appeal to a transcendent being. As his analysis of Rome's downfall suggests, such appeals combined with the machinations of would-be tyrants to bring Rome under the domination of that virulent tyranny of his age—Christianity.

Upon further consideration, however, Machiavelli's criticism of Rome seems too severe and too selective. Other provinces were converted to Christianity without benefit of Rome's history. To find Christianity's promises compelling, a province did not need a Numa or ambitious men such as the Gracchi, who induced the people to accept promises of unseen riches. Indeed, peoples lacking Rome's history readily acquiesced to the religion's rule. Machiavelli appears to acknowledge this extreme attractiveness of the religion when he sternly insists on the importance of vigilance against the encroachments of aspiring tyrants. Given the lessons that derive from Christianity's attainment and maintenance of rule among various types of peoples, anyone founding a new city after Christianity's victory must be especially attentive to both the promises of potential tyrants and appeals to transcendent powers. Just as aspirants to tyranny in Rome built on the innovations of their predecessors, so aspirants in the new era will attempt to build on the innovations of Christianity in an endeavor to construct an even more resilient tyranny. Machiavelli appears to offer his too-severe and too-selective criticism of Rome with a view to founding a new Rome for which the avoidance of ancient Rome's mistakes is even more critical.

To understand the grounds of Machiavelli's new Rome, one needs to confront his mastery of artful equivocation. In his most forthright criticisms of Christianity, for instance, he infused that criticism with a measure of ambiguity by appealing to an alternative interpretation of that religion, as well as to the form of that religion as given by its *datore*. Upon consideration, these appeals did not seem genuine, as they could not serve his political purpose while remaining a faithful interpretation of Christianity. He now appears in the guise of a *datore* of that alternative interpretation, who will interpret "our religion" according to *virtù* rather than to *ozio* and who will, therefore, promote the exaltation of the homeland (cf. *D* 1.12 and 2.2). But his equivocation continues, because his dispensation cannot really be termed a religion; he has excised any reference to divinity.

Similarly, he equivocates as to whether he presents an entirely new understanding in the *Discourses* or merely appeals to something old—the Rome of Livy's history. Because he confesses to having altered Livy's history, it would appear that his use of Livy provides the vehicle for his new teaching. The character of his thought is more complicated still; his use of the Roman historian is deceptive, in part because it masks his deceptive use of Christianity. His new understanding contains alterations of two understandings: the pagan and the Christian. It is new in transforming elements of the old.

Finally, in coming to view Machiavelli as a *datore* of this understanding, one sees how his dedication to republics is itself compatible with the teaching of *The Prince*. For a republic to thwart tyranny, it must become more tyrannical. To overcome the tyranny of his time by propagating this understanding, Machiavelli himself needs to assume some of the characteristics of a tyrant.

❖ CHAPTER 6 ❖

OLD LANDS AND MACHIAVELLI'S NEW ONE

Machiavelli furnishes two contradictory characterizations of himself and his enterprise: on one hand, he declares with seemingly dispositive authority that he is merely a humble antiquarian who hopes the results of his dusty researches will impel the people of his time to undertake the task of imitating their forebears; on the other, he announces equally authoritatively that he is a bold pathfinder in the realm of politics, who hopes that others will have the fortitude to follow him into a territory he alone has explored. To understand Machiavelli's enterprise, it is necessary to determine which characterization represents Machiavelli's true understanding of himself.

If Machiavelli's criticisms of ancient Rome indicate that he regards pagan Rome as furnishing the necessary foundation for the Christian Rome he so excoriates, then he cannot demand an imitation of ancient Rome, however sincere his appeals to antiquity appear at times. In other words, to provide a solution to the problem of the divided city that was inherent in ancient Rome and that became prominent in Christian times, Machiavelli must go beyond Livy's depiction of Rome.

He offers indications that his embrace of Livy's Rome is a calculated and provisional step to win the sympathy of his Renaissance readers, who are imbued with an abiding admiration of antiquity. His final destination is a new Rome that corrects the problems of ancient as well as of Christian Rome, and he arrives there by making changes in Livy's account. The problems inherent in both ancient and Christian Rome are corrected by his sketching the outlines of a new, more resilient Rome. The solution he suggests is distinctively modern because it emerges from his own understanding of the manner in which the Christians defeated the pagans. In short, Machiavelli's new Rome utilizes elements of both paganism and Christianity in order to subvert both.

The Reformation of the Corruption of the World

When treating the issue of corruption in the set of chapters, *Discourses* 1.16–18, Machiavelli broaches several issues that apply to his own time and declared intention. By asserting, for example, that Rome should have managed its corruption by introducing not only new laws but also new orders because "one should order different orders and modes of life in a bad subject and in a good one" (*D* 1.18.4), he recalls the terminology he applies to his own undertaking as the work opens. In the preface to the first book of the *Discourses* he so emphasizes the innovative character of his thought that he appears to suggest a comparison of his discovery with that of the most famous explorer of his time. Even though the search for "new modes and orders" is no less dangerous than the search for "unknown waters and lands," he announces that he has "decided to take a path as yet untrodden by anyone" (*D* pr.1). This new path apparently leads to his new modes and orders. According to him, the quests for both a new continent and a new political understanding require resolve and courage. Despite this similarity, what appears initially to be a presumptuous comparison to Columbus actually takes on the character of a contrast even more presumptuous: because Columbus sought a new route for trade and discovered an already inhabited continent instead, it cannot be said that he actually trod on new ground. Machiavelli, by stressing that he treads on hitherto unexplored political ground, suggests that in sheer novelty his achievement actually surpasses that of Columbus. He corroborates his own claim to novelty—as well as his own presumptuousness—in that famous passage in *The Prince* where he asserts the necessity of eschewing the example of imaginary republics and principalities: "And because I know that many have written of [the manner in which a prince should deal with subjects and friends], I fear that in writing of it again, I may be held presumptuous, especially since in disputing this matter I depart from the orders of others" (*P* 15.61). Machiavelli again declares the distinctiveness of his own political solution. If Rome fell because it failed to innovate thoroughly, as the discoverer of new modes and orders he cannot be said to be responsible for committing a similar mistake in his own era.

Machiavelli's discovery of these new modes and orders is particularly timely because corruption has permeated his own age. Indeed his new modes and orders are a response to that corruption. He specifies that although Germany is exempt from this scourge, France, Italy, and Spain are thoroughly corrupt; these three countries taken together constitute "the corruption of the world." In accordance with his discussion of corruption in 1.17 and 34, he indicates here that inequality is the source of this corruption. Incorrupt republics, he explains, "do not permit any citizen of theirs either to be or to live in the usage of gentleman; indeed, they maintain among themselves an even equality" (*D* 1.55.3).

As already noted, certain members of the clergy meet the definition of the gentlemen he here excoriates; both the gentleman and the prosperous churchman live idly [*oziosi*] on the returns from their abundant possessions without doing any work necessary to live (*O*, 137–38). An even more pernicious type of gentleman, in addition to possessing such fortunes, commands castles and has obedient subjects. Although states can become corrupt without the admixture of Christianity into their political life, it would appear that this religion has introduced a particularly virulent form of corruption into politics.[1]

Because the modern age is so thoroughly corrupt, it is in particular need of renovation, of new modes and orders. These essential sweeping changes must originate from a single man. In *Discourses* 1.17 he posits the necessity of such an individual: "if a city that has fallen into decline through corruption of material ever happens to rise, it happens through the virtue of one man who is alive then, not through the virtue of the collectivity that sustains good orders." The mere existence of such a man is hardly a solution, however, for Machiavelli adds that the material is likely to return to its earlier form after the reformer's death. What is needed, therefore, is a reformer of "very long life or two virtuous ones continued in succession" (see also *D* 1.20). When the succession of two such virtuous leaders is "lacking, as was said above, it is ruined—unless indeed he makes it be reborn with many perils and much blood" (*D* 1.17.3). With this condition added, the idea emerging from Machiavelli's continued insistence that the task of reformation is difficult—if not altogether impossible—is that the end must be reached through repugnant means. Because these means are likely to be shunned, so too will be the end.

In the next chapter he confirms this conclusion, as he continues to emphasize the difficulties of the lone individual who undertakes the task of reformation in the midst of corruption: "For if one wishes to renew [the orders] little by little, the cause of it must be someone prudent who sees this inconvenience from very far away and when it arises." Quite possibly such a prudent one will not appear when prudence is most needed, and even if he did appear, quite possibly such an individual would not "be able to persuade anyone else of what he himself understands." In addition to renovating in stages, the orders can also be renewed "at a stroke," but this method entails severe difficulties of its own:

> For to do this, it is not enough to use ordinary terms, since the ordinary modes are bad; but it is necessary to go to the extraordinary, such as violence and arms, and before everything else become prince of that city and be able to dispose it in one's own mode. Because the reordering of a city for a political way of life presupposes a good man, and becoming prince of a republic by violence presupposes a bad man, because of this one will find that it very rarely happens that someone good wishes to become prince by bad ways, even though his end be good, and that someone wicked, having become prince, wishes to work well, and that it will ever occur to his mind to use well the authority which he has acquired badly. (*D* 1.18.4)

When so phrased, the dilemma that Machiavelli posits is a formidable one. As suggested in 1.17, the dilemma arises from the unsavory character of the necessary means.

Despite this problem's apparent intractable character, in *Discourses* 1.9 entitled "That it is necessary to be alone if one wishes to order a republic anew or to reform it altogether outside its ancient orders," Machiavelli has already furnished a motive for the good man to take not only the reins of sole authority but also the most extreme measures to achieve his end:

> nor will a wise understanding ever reprove anyone for any extraordinary action that he uses to order a kingdom or constitute a republic. It is very suitable that when the deed accuses him, the effect excuses him; and when the effect is good, as was that of Romulus, it will always excuse the deed; for he who is violent to destroy, not he who is violent to mend, should be reproved.

So generous is Machiavelli's forgiveness in this case that he pardons a crime of Romulus not even mentioned in Livy's history.[2] Whereas Machiavelli declares that Romulus "deserves excuse in the deaths of his brother and his partner" (D 1.9.2), Livy is far from charging Romulus with responsibility for the death of Titus Tatius, Romulus's colleague in rule. In Livy's account, Tatius is killed not by Romulus but by a mob of vengeful Laurentians. The only suggestion of wrongdoing that Livy imputes to Romulus occurs when he reports that Romulus, in choosing not to go to war with Lavinium, showed less resentment of Tatius's death than was thought to be proper.[3] It appears that Machiavelli makes Romulus's deeds bloodier to exonerate him for even greater crimes.

Romulus is not the only example in this chapter of a murderer intent on sole authority of whose deeds Machiavelli approves. He also tells of Agis, a king of Sparta, who desired to return to the orders of Lycurgus but who was himself murdered as one who "wished to seize tyranny." When the successor of Agis, Cleomenes, came across

> the records and writings . . . of Agis in which his mind and intention were seen, he knew that he could not do this good for his fatherland unless he alone were in authority, since it appeared to him that because of the ambition of men he could not do something useful to many against the will of the few.

To this end Cleomenes had all "the ephors killed and anyone else who might be able to stand against him" (D 1.9.4). Because Machiavelli appeals to potential founders and reformers in this chapter and because he insists that bloody deeds need not mar one's eternal glory, he suggests that the attainment of glory is a primary concern of those whom this chapter addresses.

In addition to quelling any fears that the severity of the remedy may work to a reformer's eternal infamy rather than to his perpetual fame, Machiavelli draws a clearer picture of the end that can outweigh such harsh methods. A founder should contrive "to help not himself but the common good, not for his own succession but for the common fatherland." Initially such a purpose appears impossibly altruistic in a Machiavellian universe, but he shows the way in which this seemingly selfless end can actually work to the founder's own benefit. He cautions that "the thing is ordered to last long not if it remains on the shoulders of one individual, but rather if it remains in the care of many and when its maintenance stays with many" (D 1.9.2). Thus a state will not be long-lived when only a founder's heirs might benefit from its institution. In the interest of perpetuating the glory of his deeds, the founder must order a state that depends on the many rather than on the few; the good of many magnifies the glory of one. Machiavelli thus reassures the good man that deplorable methods can be reconciled with both the good end he envisions and the pursuit of perpetual fame. In the process, Machiavelli also suggests to the bad man—for whom bad means are not so repugnant—the way to use his authority so as to perpetuate his glory in a manner that never would have occurred to such a "mind" otherwise (cf. D 1.18).[4] Indeed, in concluding his discussion of the conundrum of the good man who shuns bad means and the bad man unable to descry the good end, Machiavelli points to the hopeful examples of Romulus and Cleomenes. Nevertheless, he draws a distinction between their actions and those required of a reformer in the midst of thoroughgoing corruption: "one should take note that neither one of them had a subject stained with the corruption that we have been reasoning about in this chapter, and so they were able to wish, and in wishing, to color their plan" (D 1.18.5).

In *Discourses* 1.55 Machiavelli returns to the difficulty of reform in the midst of corruption, this time with a view to the stubborn character of corruption that stains the Italy of his own day. Because a great number of gentlemen reside in such places as Naples, Rome, and the Romagna, these localities are suited for kingship. Conversely, due to the happy scarcity of such gentlemen in Tuscany, "there is so much equality that a civil way of life would easily be introduced there by a prudent man having knowledge of the ancient civilizations." Indeed, that this material is suitable for the imposition of such a form is shown by the long existence of three republics there.[5] Despite the ease with which such an innovation could be introduced into Tuscany, "its misfortune has been so great that up to these times it has not been made subject to any man who has been able or known how to do it" (D 1.55.4).

Although Tuscany could be easily redeemed by the existence of so prudent a man, Italy itself could not be happy unless it were united under the obedience of one prince or republic (D 1.12).[6] If Italy is to become united under a prince or a republic, the establishment will be easy for one part of Italy and difficult for the other, for whichever alternative is chosen, part of Italy is ill suited to that alternative's form of governance. If a republic is to have sway in Italy, Rome, in particular, due to its large contingent of gentlemen, is not suited to the republic's rule.

Could the material of Rome be rendered suitable to a dominant republic in Italy—a republic that would itself accord with a civil way of life? He responds that the introduction of a republic into the regions dominated by gentlemen "would not be possible; but if any one were arbiter and wished to reorder them, there would be no other way than to make a kingdom there" (D 1.55.4). Although he so resoundingly rejects the possibility of the establishment of a republic in this region, he continues that such an undertaking is not strictly speaking impossible: "he who wishes to make a republic where there are very many gentlemen cannot do it unless he first eliminates all of them" (D 1.55.5). From this terse statement one understands the sheer difficulty of the undertaking. Not only would the execution of so many be difficult to arrange,[7] but it would be morally repugnant, conforming precisely to the difficulty as Machiavelli defines it in *Discourses* 1.18.

Again, this problem need not be decisive. Machiavelli's study of the Bible allows him to augment his examples of Romulus and Cleomenes as individuals capable of killing for good purposes with the exalted example of Moses: "whoever reads the Bible judiciously will see that if he wished his laws and his orders to go forward, Moses was forced to kill infinite men who, moved by nothing other than envy, were opposed to his plans" (D 3.30.1).[8] Nevertheless, if the gentlemen whose deaths constitute the prerequisite for the establishment of a republic in modern times are understood to be the wealthy members of the clergy, the additional problem of pious compunctions must enter the picture. One need only recall Machiavelli's account of Baglioni's disastrous encounter with Pope Julius and his cardinals to confirm the power of such compunctions.

Although Baglioni flouted morality by committing incest with his sister and killing his cousins, he was reduced to utter cowardice when the defense of his rule required resolute action against the leaders of the Church. Thus the action Machiavelli appears to demand is extremely difficult.

Nevertheless, the reader confronting this declaration of the enormous difficulty of such reform has already been schooled by Machiavelli to regard just such a situation as a political windfall. As Machiavelli exclaims in *Discourses* 1.10: "And truly, if a prince seeks the glory of the world, he ought to desire to possess a corrupt city. . . . And truly the heavens cannot give to men a greater opportunity for glory, nor can men desire a greater" (*D* 1.10.6).[9] Furthermore, he offers the general view that as the difficulty of a task increases, so too will the glory bestowed upon the one who completes it successfully. His four great founders, for instance, introduced "new orders and modes" as a response to difficult circumstances. Machiavelli actually terms their difficulties "opportunities" and claims that "[s]uch opportunities . . . made these men successful, and their excellent virtue enabled the opportunity to be recognized" (*P* 6.23).[10] The current devastating political situation, then, holds out the promise of great glory for one who possesses the willingness and acumen necessary to undertake its reformation. Thus, his recital of insurmountable obstacles in *Discourses* 1.17, 18, and 55 would excite rather than quash ambition in one eager to attain glory.

Moreover, in Machiavelli's universe there is a character who confirms that pious compunctions need not be decisive. Stefano Porcari, "who relished glory," tried to restore Rome to its ancient way of life by wresting it from the hands of the prelates in order to do something "worthy of memory" (*FH* 6.29.263). Although Porcari failed in the attempt, his enthusiasm for the task showed that there can exist an individual who will be moved to the deed by its sheer enormity, and hence by the prospect of the glory that will go with its successful completion.

In considering Machiavelli's discussions on possibly eradicating the corruption of his times, it appears that in some manner he regards himself as the farsighted man—capable of seeing the problem and knowing its solution—whom he discusses in 1.17, 18, and 55. Nevertheless, a distinction exists in his discussions between such a man and himself: unlike the man he describes, Machiavelli cannot be alone, for the completion of his enterprise depends on the aid of others. As he proclaims in the preface to this book, he has discovered a new way; he has not instituted it, nor can he, for he also acknowledges that the realization of his intention depends on the actions of others who read his writings (1. and 2.pr.). Still he appears to be alone by virtue of the quality of his mind. Are his writings, which reveal his mind and intention, the medium through which Machiavelli as a latter-day Agis seeks to inspire a latter-day Cleomenes to undertake the needed reform? Will those who read his writings conclude, as did Cleomenes when he came upon the writings of Agis, that the members of the aristocracy must be eliminated for a successful reformation?[11] Does he really mean for individuals to become so hardened by his many references to the necessity of criminality that they go out and slaughter the idle and rich rulers of the Church?[12] Or does he mean for his caustic comments only to cause others to change their behavior with regard to the churchmen so that at least some would not so readily overlook their many transgressions (cf. *D* 3.1)? If political men were as a result to become less complacent and thus to resist more actively the evil designs emanating from the Church's hierarchy, then perhaps the power of the Church would be eclipsed, and a more vigorous politics and a more united Italy would result. On this particular question it is difficult to say what practical effects Machiavelli intended; nevertheless, it is clear that if either alternative were to be implemented as a result of his writings, Machiavelli would in some sense rule over the actions of the individuals who took that course.

True to his praise for the use of both force and fraud, Machiavelli also appeals to a less violent and more duplicitous course. His less-than-faithful presentation of Livy's Rome can insinuate itself quite peacefully into the understanding of succeeding generations, furnishing Machiavelli's own understanding of the necessary principles of political life under the cover of an appeal to antiquity. Thus again he would rule over those individuals who embrace his depiction of ancient Rome as a standard for modern states.

Innovation or Imitation?

From the start of the *Discourses* Machiavelli calls his reader's attention to the tension between his claim to novelty and his obvious recourse to ancient history; in the preface to the first book he claims to be both the discoverer of something new and merely the recoverer of the ancient understanding of politics. Despite his unabashed claims to novelty in both *The Prince* and the *Discourses,*

he immediately dilutes this declaration in the *Discourses* by lamenting that, although the ancient understanding serves as a guide in
art, law, and medicine, "neither prince nor republic . . . has recourse to the examples of the ancients . . . in ordering republics,
maintaining states, governing kingdoms, ordering the military and
administering war, judging subjects, increasing empire" (*D* 1.pr.2).
Because he wishes to overcome this state of affairs, he has

> judged it necessary to write on all those books of Titus Livy that
> have not been intercepted by the malignity of the times whatever I
> shall judge necessary for their greater understanding, according to
> knowledge of ancient and modern things, so that these statements of
> mine will more easily be found to possess the utility for which one
> should seek knowledge of histories.[13] (*D* 1.pr.2)

Moreover, when considering this great problem of modern weakness elsewhere, he confirms that the solution is not innovation but
merely imitation:

> One sees . . . every day miraculous losses and miraculous acquisi-
> tions. For where men have little virtue, fortune shows its power very
> much; and because it is variable, republics and states often vary and
> will always vary until someone emerges who is so much a lover of
> antiquity that he regulates it in such a mode that it does not have
> cause to show at every turning of the sun how much it can do. (*D*
> 2.30.5)

As in his other discussions of the disheartening political situation
of the times, he still insists that a gifted man is needed. But here, as
in his treatment of the less demanding task of introducing "a civil
way of life" into Tuscany, he indicates that the required individual
need not be capable of innovation but only of a thorough grasp of
the past (cf. *D* 1.55.4; see also *D* 2.pr.). Does Machiavelli seek a
new understanding of politics or an unadulterated return to the ancients?

A later chapter of the *Discourses,* 2.5, clarifies Machiavelli's understanding of his relation to antiquity. In treating the variation of
religions and languages, he expresses an interest in the process by
which one epoch succeeds another. His discussion reveals that in all
instances in which one epoch subverts another the new power will
actively undertake to extinguish all memory of its predecessor.
Here he raises the topic of Christianity's relationship to its antago-
nist, paganism, at a time when Christianity had already acquired a

great deal of influence. He observes that to solidify its power, the "Christian sect . . . canceled all [the gentile sect's] orders and all its ceremonies, and eliminated every memory of that ancient theology"; however, Christianity was ultimately unsuccessful in its endeavor to expunge all memory of its predecessor because the Christians "maintained the Latin language, which they were forced to do since they had to write this new law with it."[14] Noting the "obstinacy" with which "Saint Gregory and . . . the other heads of the Christian religion . . . persecuted all the ancient memories, burning the works of the poets and the historians, ruining images, and laying waste every other thing that might convey some sign of antiquity," he observes that if the Christians had only had a new language at their disposal, they would have eradicated any memory of antiquity (D 2.5.1). But they did not, and as a result their work of obliteration remains incomplete. Therefore, the first revelation that emerges here is that "the malignity of the times" to which he so vaguely refers in the preface to the first book is really the malice of St. Gregory (cf. D 1.pr.2).[15]

What the Christians attempted against paganism the pagans in all likelihood perpetrated against their predecessors. In considering the long parade of alternating human dominions, he asserts that "sects vary two or three times in five or in six thousand years" (D 2.5.1). The second revelation of this chapter thus takes the form of a prophecy: by not endeavoring to exempt Christianity from this cycle of birth and decay, he predicts that Christianity's reign will end not in the second coming of Christ, but rather in the ascendancy of yet another sect that will attempt to expunge all vestiges of the Christian age.

In addition to those changes that result from human action, other changes owe their origin to heaven, as when floods, plagues, and famines "eliminate the human race and reduce the inhabitants of part of the world to a few." In a truly odd passage he posits the particular importance of a flood in this process of devastation "both because it is more universal and because those who are saved are all mountain men and rude [rozzi], who since they do not have knowledge of antiquity cannot leave it to posterity" (D 2.5.2; O 154). To these humble alpine people who might survive such a flood he applies the same adjective, rozzi, that he had applied to the simple Romans who had trusted in Numa's tales of the nymph; also he had implied that the Florentines of his own day merited the same term when they believed Savonarola spoke with God,

although these city dwellers do not think themselves "either ignorant [*ignorante*] or rude [*rozzo*]" (*D* 1.11.5; *O* 94). By pointing to
the gullibility of his contemporaries in such matters, Machiavelli
appears to question the assertion he made earlier in the same chapter when reflecting upon Numa's success with his credulous people:

> Indeed it is true that since those times were full of religion and the
> men with whom he had to work were coarse [*grossi*], they made
> much easier the carrying out of his plans, since he could easily im-
> press any new form whatever on them. Without doubt, whoever
> wished to make a republic in the present times would find it easier
> among mountainmen [*uomini montanari*], where there is no civi-
> lization, than among those who are used to living in cities, where
> civilization is corrupt; and a sculptor will get a beautiful statue more
> easily from rough marble than from one badly blocked out by an-
> other. (*D* 1.11.3; *O* 94)

Clearly, by speaking of rude mountaineers in 2.5, Machiavelli is re-
suming a consideration that he had begun in 1.11, the first chapter
of the section devoted to the Roman religion.

When he later considers the introduction of a new order, he
takes a broader view of history. Whereas his earlier reflection treats
the beginnings of the Roman religion, in the later discussion he explicitly considers the epochs that must have preceded the Roman
and also anticipates the end of the Christian era. Given this context, then, he continues his discussion of a great flood by considering the opportunity such a disaster would afford:

> And if among them someone is saved who has knowledge of it, to
> make a reputation and a name for himself he hides it and perverts it
> in his mode so that what he has wished to write alone, and nothing
> else, remains for his successors.[16] (*D* 2.5.2)

It is unsettling, to say the least, that Machiavelli views such devastation so sanguinely. Of course, one could defend his view by offering that such a flood is ultimately a boon for humanity: by destroy-
ing corrupt civilization it allows a more worthy manner of living to
be established.[17] But just such a defense of Machiavelli points to the
most troubling aspect of this discussion: he does not make the defense himself. The only good to derive from this catastrophe is that
which will benefit this perverter of antiquity: if this one is clever, he
will gain for himself a *"riputazione e nome"* (*O* 154).

After considering *Discourses* 1.11, however, one must wonder why the occurrence of such a flood is necessary at all for the founder to impose his own stamp on a given population. Of course, the prospective founder of a new order is left with rude mountaineers on which he can impose "any new form whatever" (*D* 1.11.3). Granted, such a reordering is made easier by the existence of so malleable a populace, but the point of his subsequent discussion of the miracle wrought by Savonarola—that of convincing the apparently sophisticated Florentines that he conversed with God—suggests that one can inculcate belief in those who have been corrupted by civilization. Therefore, although more difficult, the task of founding a new order for people who think themselves worldly does not appear to be utterly impossible.

Such reflections on this passage in 2.5 must presuppose that, in looking to the next epoch beyond the Christian, Machiavelli speaks of a flood in a metaphorical sense. He views the corruption with which Christianity has permeated his contemporary civilization as equivalent to an inundation of water. To cope with this inundation humanity has no alternative but to make a new beginning.

To test this supposition, let us for a moment suppose the contrary. Let us suppose that Machiavelli is serious in his consideration of the prospect of a flood. Recall that in claiming this particular type of disaster to be the most important among the three he names in this chapter, he points out that floods are "more universal" and that those who remain are rude mountaineers. Clearly the results indicate that the few survivors of this particular flood are lacking in learning, and Machiavelli does specify that "they do *not* have knowledge of antiquity [emphasis added]." Indeed, such rustics would in all likelihood be illiterate.[18] But if this were the case, why does Machiavelli claim that these unique circumstances allow the knower of antiquity to hide his knowledge and "pervert . . . it in his mode" (*D* 2.5.2)? In other words, if the records of the previous civilization were lost in this disaster and the remaining population were wholly ignorant of antiquity, the knower could create entirely out of whole cloth a new understanding of the past to suit his own needs. For added security he could hide, as Machiavelli suggests, any records that happened to remain. His material would present him with a tabula rasa. In these circumstances there would be no need for perversion as such. Thus, using the technique of perversion of ancient sources of knowledge would appear to be a necessity not among the survivors of a flood, who exist on isolated mountaintops, because there is simply no need for such subtle circumspection, but rather in contemporary civilization, where people do possess some knowledge of the past or at the very least some access to its remaining records.[19] In this manner one can draw a distinction between Machiavelli's contemporaries and the mountaineers of *Discourses* 1.11 and 2.5: although in acumen he may consider his contemporaries to be similar to the *rozzi* people of the mountains, they are not wholly devoid of knowledge of the previous epoch or, at least, of the resources by which to acquire such knowledge. This difference makes the perversion of ancient sources necessary, if one is to undertake to introduce surreptitiously a new understanding in the current era without the aid of a devastating flood. (Of course, if nature were to be so cooperative as to furnish an actual flood to aid the imposition of a new form, nature, by this paradoxical act of kindness, would actually detract from the founder's glory.)

Consideration of 1.11 and 2.5 therefore indicates the following about Machiavelli's understanding of his own time with regard to the past and future: a new epoch is needed and can be expected as early as the seventeenth century; and, although various epochs differ, the susceptibility of the people to clever manipulation does not. Machiavelli seems here to be hinting at the means by which the Christian epoch is to be superseded. Indications also abound that he means to serve as the impetus behind its supersession himself. We know, for example, that he claims to have discovered "new modes and orders" and that the dire conditions of his generation promise great glory for a successful redeemer, in the same way that the obstacles confronting Moses, Romulus, Theseus, and Cyrus rendered their deeds most glorious. Moreover, we know that the survivor of the flood, who is uniquely situated to provide the basis for the new dispensation, is both a knower and a perverter of antiquity; the information that Machiavelli provides about himself allows us to see that he fits both descriptions.

He certainly is a knower of antiquity. In the dedicatory letter of *The Prince,* for example, he maintains that he has come to his "knowledge of the actions of great men" not only by virtue of his practical experience with practical politics, but also by "a continuous reading of ancient ones" (*P* d.l. 3). Similarly, in the dedicatory letter of the *Discourses,* he claims that the work presents "as much as I know and have learned through a long practice and a continual reading in worldly things" (*D* d.l.). As this work purports to be a commentary on Livy's history, one can safely assume his reading on the subject of the affairs of the world certainly includes ancient history.[20] But no better testament exists to his pursuit of the knowledge of antiquity than his letter to Vettori in which he describes the loving care he gives to the ritual that renders him worthy of approaching their discourse:

> On the coming of evening, I return to my house and enter my study; and at the door I take off the day's clothing, covered with mud and dust, and put on garments regal and courtly; and reclothed appropriately, I enter the ancient courts of ancient men, where, received by them with affection, I feed on that food which only is mine and which I was born for, where I am not ashamed to speak with them and to ask them the reason for their actions; and they in their kindness answer me; and for four hours of time I do not feel boredom, I forget every trouble, I do not dread poverty, I am not frightened by death; entirely I give myself over to them. (CW 3:929)

Despite a declared reverence for ancient writings, he makes changes in Livy's account, changes that suggest a measure of disrespect toward his ancient master and, hence, a conflict with his declared reverence for the ancients. In attempting to reconcile this apparent conflict, one might conclude that he possessed greater respect for antiquity than actual knowledge of it. According to this view, Machiavelli would not be so disrespectful as to alter his sources intentionally, but he was not so great a knower of antiquity as he thought. The changes to be found in his writings were the product of his carelessness, and hence were inadvertent; confident that he knew what his esteemed predecessor had said, he neglected to check his facts. This solution is plausible. Nevertheless, given his own explicit and presumptuous claims to originality, his analysis of the political devastation caused by Christianity, his understanding of Christianity's approaching decline, and his statement that a perversion of the past can be useful in introducing a new epoch, it seems prudent to leave open the possibility that Machiavelli makes these changes self-consciously, and thus give more weight to his knowledge of antiquity than to his reverence for it.

The perverter of antiquity after a flood begins to sound remarkably like the Florentine who writes about the ancient Roman republic during the inundation of the Christian epoch. Machiavelli presents himself as a type of Noah who perverts the records left to him after the flood of Christianity and the efforts of Saint Gregory. By furnishing a filter through which Livy's history of Rome will henceforth be read, Machiavelli appears to hide an unadulterated

Livian account of Roman events for the generations to follow, just
as the knower of antiquity of *Discourses* 2.5 hides any records that
remain in his possession. Machiavelli's perversion of Livy's history
seems intended to furnish the understanding that will guide a new
epoch—the epoch that is to succeed Christianity's rule.

Why, though, does Machiavelli go to the trouble—and trouble
not only for himself but also for his readers—of couching something new in the guise of something old? The answer lies in his
unique historical circumstances. An understanding of these circumstances emerges from a reconsideration of the relation between what Machiavelli himself does to Livy's history in the *Discourses* and his description of the deed of the knower and
perverter of antiquity in *Discourses* 2.5. There is a difference between their actions. Whereas the character in 2.5 alters the understanding of the *previous* epoch for his own purposes, Machiavelli,
if he intends to introduce a new epoch, concentrates more on perverting not the reign of Christianity, but rather the epoch that pre-
cedes the Christian one.[21] His ability and his need to alter these
records both arise from Christianity's incapacity to obliterate the
records of its predecessor. Because of this failure, the people of his
time were able to look back with admiration at the times that preceded the Christian era.

If his intent is to offer something new, his historical circumstances certainly would warrant a perversion of the ancient history
that survived the scourges of Christianity. He was, after all, writing
during the Renaissance. However one defines the Renaissance, it
was a time when many educated individuals revealed their admiration of the past by endeavoring to recover the ancient understanding.[22] In addition, Machiavelli identifies a general tendency for people of all times to be "partisans of past things" (*D* 2.pr.1). As a
result of this general and specific disaffection abroad during his
times, Machiavelli had a sympathetic audience in the humanists as
long as he could overtly appeal to the ancients; as I indicated in
part 2, however, Machiavelli is keenly aware of the defects of ancient Rome. Because his understanding is deeper than that of the
humanists in this regard, he sees that a simple appeal to the ancients is not enough. As much as he admired Rome, he must reject
it as an untransformed model because his nemesis, Christianity (the
source of what he understands to be the political problem of his
time), flourished on Roman soil. Although a different understanding of Rome separates Machiavelli from his humanist friends, there

is no reason for Machiavelli to alienate them unnecessarily.[23] A subtle perversion of Roman history may allow him at once to present a new understanding and to maintain their sympathy. Therefore, on one hand, because he announces the enormity of the project, he endeavors to attract seekers after glory to his side; on the other, to maintain the dedication of these lovers of glory and admirers of the past, he must conceal his understanding in the apparel of the Rome his followers so admire.

Further, he himself indicates there is good reason for him to attempt to maintain their goodwill, taking care not to challenge their convictions and sensibilities too overtly, for the success of his enterprise depends upon the sympathy of some of his readers. In the preface to the first book of the *Discourses* he indicates that his project is of such a magnitude that he can only begin and others must finish. Indeed, he claims only to have discovered new modes and orders; he makes no claim to being capable of introducing them. To complete his task he needs the help of others: "Although this enterprise may be difficult, nonetheless, aided by those who have encouraged me to accept this burden, I believe I can carry it far enough so that a short road will remain for another to bring it to the destined place" (*D* 1.pr.2). What better group to appeal to than those who long for the past because they are disaffected with the present? (*D* 2.pr.).

The Travails of Finding a New Land in Christian Times

Given Machiavelli's own statements then, we can seriously consider that, when he refers to Livy's Rome, he intentionally presents not a historically accurate depiction of that old Rome but rather what might be called a blueprint for his own new Rome. This new Rome is his new land—the land on which he claims to be the first to tread. Only by presenting his envisioned future in the guise of a recovered past will he be able to maintain the adherence of those who long for the seemingly glorious Rome contained in Livy's history. Machiavelli's originality is demanded because Christianity has devastated politics and because that ruin is ultimately a product of antiquity's mistakes. Machiavelli's new Rome is new precisely because it is designed to prevent the people from abandoning their earthly city; his new Rome will avoid the mistakes of the old Rome because he will attempt to assure that human beings no longer appeal to any transcendent power.

This is indeed a grandiose plan, and one that must confront

great difficulties. The character of these difficulties, as well as Machiavelli's grounds for believing they can be overcome, come to light in two chapters in the second book of the *Discourses,* which address topics relevant to his own enterprise. In *Discourses* 2.8, "The cause why peoples leave their ancestral places and inundate the country of others," he distinguishes between two types of war: one fought for the sake of ambition, which occurs when a prince or a republic attempts to establish an empire; and the other fought from necessity. He claims that this latter cause for war produces the most devastating form of conflict. In the former case, he asserts, the conqueror is often satisfied with "the obedience of the peoples" and therefore "most often lets them live with their laws, and always with their homes and their goods." In contrast, when a people seeks a new land through the necessity of either hunger or war, they fight a "very cruel and very dreadful" war (*D* 2.8.1).

He finds that Rome fought three such dangerous wars: two against the "French" and one against the Germans and Cimbri, in all of which Rome was victorious. It becomes clear later, however, that Rome actually fought additional wars of this kind, but with quite different results: "the Goths, the Vandals, and the like . . . seized the whole Western empire" (*D* 2.8.1). In other words, in the most dangerous type of wars the Romans eventually lost their empire. The aggressors in such wars are dangerous because "they enter with violence into the countries of others, kill the inhabitants, take possession of their goods, make a new kingdom, and change the province's name, as did Moses and the peoples who seized the Roman Empire" (*D* 2.8.2). Therefore, the Hebrews, as well as the barbarian conquerors of Rome were peoples, driven by necessity, who successfully attained the territory of others.

In describing the effects of such a territorial war, he discusses the consequences of the Hebrew invasion for "the Maurusians, a people in Syria in antiquity." These people, when they ascertained the approach of the Hebrews, judged that they themselves should seek a new land rather than attempt to defend the land they now occupied for fear that, by staying, they risked losing not only their land but "themselves also in trying to save it." As a result of this decision, the Maurusians went to Africa to make a new home for themselves. Machiavelli adds that the historian Procopius reports the existence of certain columns in Africa bearing the inscription: "'We are the Maurusians, who fled before the face of Joshua the robber son of Nun'" (*D* 2.8.2).

Machiavelli renders this quotation in Latin, and as a result the name Joshua appears in his text as "*Jesu*" (*O*, 157).[24]

Does Machiavelli, too, flee before the face of Jesu? Given his assertions that the work constitutes an endeavor to find a new land and that he believes political life in his time to be ravaged, it seems legitimate to consider whether a certain correspondence exists between Machiavelli's predicament and that of the Maurusians. If Machiavelli does flee, he must be prepared to find a new land. If that land is inhabited, his search could initiate a war whose cause originates in necessity. Consideration of this question points to the gulf between Machiavelli's own endeavor and the wars of the barbarian invasions of Rome and the Hebrew conquest of Canaan: he is unarmed and thus cannot hope to launch an invasion to rival those emanating from war of either type. Indeed, so far is he from engaging in such a war, he does not have a people that recognizes the necessity of the discovery of a new land. If he has any sympathizers at all, they do not recognize the insufficiency of a return to the old land represented by the paganism of Livy.

After alluding to the two successful invasions of the Hebrews and the barbarians, he elaborates on the way such invaders change the names of the places they occupy, and reflects that "the new names that are in Italy and in the other provinces do not arise from anything other than from having been thus named by the new occupants" (*D* 2.8.2). Clearly the names existing in modern Italy and the remainder of Europe owe their origin not only to the invasion of foreign peoples but also to the existence of Christianity. In his *Florentine Histories* he acknowledges this:

> Moreover, not only have the names of provinces changed, but the names of lakes, rivers, seas, and men: for France, Italy, and Spain are filled with new names altogether foreign to the ancient. Thus one sees, leaving aside many others, that the Po, Garda, the Archipelago do not conform to the old names; men too, once Caesars and Pompeys, have become Peters, Johns, and Matthews.[25] (*FH* 1.5.14–15)

Hence Christianity itself can in some way be understood as a conqueror.

The existence of Christianity provides the unspoken link between Moses and the barbarian invaders of Rome, whom Machiavelli sets up in *Discourses* 2.8 as exemplars of dangerous conquerors. Moses' successors conquered Canaan, and later a new religion emanated from the land they occupied. At the time of the

barbarian invasions of Rome this religion had insinuated itself into
the city, and the invaders themselves were to become Christians.
Although the Christians are, therefore, a type of conqueror, their
methods must be distinguished from those of the barbarians and of
the Hebrews; their means were peaceful. Just as he does not broach
the peaceful conversion of the Roman Empire to Christianity in this
chapter, he does not here treat the manner in which he intends to
claim this new land. This chapter is devoted instead to war, and to
war of the most devastating type; thus such discussions would be
out of place, for these cases do not entail violence. Nevertheless, to
recognize the way Christianity conquered must be heartening for
Machiavelli's own prospects. In utilizing a metaphor for his own
undertaking of the claiming of a land on which no one has yet trod,
Machiavelli disavows the use of violence. Quite simply, because the
place he seeks is uninhabited, he promises that there will be no
need to drive away the current inhabitants of the place, and hence
no need of arms.[26]

He furnishes important reflections on the strength of the unarmed in *Discourses* 2.13. Machiavelli—the thinker who so admires the arms of ancient Rome and exhorts rulers of his time to
arm their people—finds the use of force ultimately unsatisfactory.[27]
The peaceful method he finds more effective is that of fraud. In
comparing force and fraud he declares: "Nor do I believe that anyone placed in low fortune is ever found to attain great empire
through open force alone and ingenuously, but it is done quite well
through fraud alone" (*D* 2.13.1). This bears repeating: force alone
will not be enough. He even finds that his Roman republic, exemplary in the force of its arms, relied to a large extent on fraud: "The
Romans therefore are seen in their first increases not to be lacking
even in fraud, which it was always necessary to use for those who
wish to climb from small beginnings to sublime ranks" (*D* 2.13.2;
see also *P* 18).

In so recognizing the effectiveness of fraud, Machiavelli explains
how he can have any hope for success for his own enterprise, and
also furnishes a needed explanation for the evident success of
Christianity in a world in which, he often claims, the mightiest prevail. Christianity's success is problematic for Machiavelli precisely
because he so emphasizes the need for arms. In considering the successes of his four great founders in *The Prince*, he asserts that when
such innovators "depend on their own and are able to use force,
then it is that they are rarely in peril." He concludes that "all the

armed prophets conquered and the unarmed ones were ruined." To corroborate this maxim, Machiavelli offers the example of Savonarola, who he claims "was ruined in his new orders as soon as the multitude began not to believe in them, and he had no mode for holding firm those who had believed nor for making unbelievers believe" (P 6.24). With reference to the fate Savonarola met on the pyre, Isaiah Berlin observes, "an unarmed prophet will always go to the gallows."[28] Whereas this lack of arms may be a satisfactory explanation for Savonarola's failure, it leaves unexplained the success of that extraordinary unarmed prophet—Jesus Christ—whose impact is much on Machiavelli's mind. Surely, Jesus too went to the "gallows," but his enterprise succeeded after his death. *Discourses* 2.13 reveals that in Machiavelli's view it is possible for the unarmed to achieve victory; fraud must be considered an implement in the arsenal of the ambitious (see also P 7 and 18). With regard to his own hopes, Machiavelli is quite unabashed about their magnitude on the one hand (i.e., D 1. and 2.pr.), and about his humble and needy state on the other (i.e., P d.l.; D d.l. and 2.pr.). Given his own "little beginnings" then, fraud seems to be an evident choice for him in his desire to climb to a high place.

If, in Machiavelli's view, fraud is the one alternative or a desirable supplement to force, we find with relief that speculation regarding what Machiavelli considered the character of Christ's fraud or of his followers is beyond our immediate purpose. Nevertheless, because Machiavelli desires to emulate Christ in introducing a new teaching without the benefit of arms, he should certainly be suspected of having recourse himself to the same tactic of fraud.[29] From this recognition arises the question of the character of Machiavelli's fraud. The most obvious answer is that he misleadingly uses a pagan source when he desires to transcend the pagan understanding: he presents himself as a follower but understands himself to be a perverter of antiquity.

In this understanding of himself as perverter of antiquity, a distinction exists between the role undertaken by Machiavelli himself and that of the perverter of *Discourses* 2.5. Machiavelli claims there that the perverter of antiquity would act for the sake of "a reputation and a name" (D 2.5.2). Machiavelli must have been aware that the notorious maxims contained in *The Prince* and in the *Discourses* would certainly earn him a name from posterity. He published neither book during his lifetime. After their publication his name became synonymous with evil.[30] Differences between the

144 MACHIAVELLI'S THREE ROMES

perverter of 2.5 and Machiavelli appear at this point: whereas the knower of antiquity appears to undertake his endeavor of perversion for the sake of a good name, Machiavelli's enterprise converted his name into an uncomplimentary adjective. Moreover, whereas the knower of 2.5 is motivated only by a selfish concern for reputation, Machiavelli claims that he has undertaken his dangerous project for the "common benefit to everyone" (D 1.pr.1). He hopes that his understanding will remedy the defective politics to which his lifetime bore witness. Reflection on his self-proclaimed intent and its very real effects on his name and reputation indicates that he willingly sacrificed himself for the benefit of humanity. He appears to understand himself as a martyred savior—as Christ-like.

Such beneficence on Machiavelli's part seems incompatible with his own analysis of human motives, however, for in his view even those great benefactors who utilize kingly power for a good end act for their own reputations. It is not entirely clear that Machiavelli's devotion to humanity is entirely selfless, however; his motivation, the *"comune benefizio a ciascuno,"* would appear to include his own benefit as well (O 76). At the very least he must have gotten amusement from his own sly equation of himself and Christ. Moreover, although the one who destroys a ruling understanding will be vilified by those who take their guidance and sustenance from it (D 1.9), Machiavelli also must have received satisfaction from knowing that those who would attempt to replicate his portrayal of ancient Rome or to found a politics on a Machiavellian foundation would have to acknowledge—to themselves, at least, if not publicly—that he was their ruler in these endeavors.

Machiavelli reveals his own method with regard to scripture more candidly in *The Prince.* In a passage discussing the need for arms, the source he perverts to his own ends is the Old Testament. He adduces the example of David as particularly "apt for this purpose." According to Machiavelli, when David went to Saul to volunteer to fight Goliath, Saul offered David his arms, which David refused, "saying that with them he could not give a good account of himself, and so he would rather meet the enemy with his sling and his knife" (P 13.56). As Harvey Mansfield notes in his translation, Machiavelli's version differs significantly from the account given in the Old Testament. In the biblical account David was not armed with a knife when he fought with the Philistine. The biblical account runs:

> So David prevailed over the Philistine with a sling and with a stone, and struck the Philistine, and killed him; there was no sword in the hand of David. Then David ran and stood over the Philistine, and took his sword and drew it out of its sheath, and killed him, and cut off his head with it.[31]

Machiavelli arms David with a knife, which he lacks in the original. He appeals to the authority of the Bible in order to teach a lesson regarding the necessity of fighting with one's own arms; however, because he changes the story, he teaches a lesson regarding self-reliance that the Bible cannot be said to teach. His specific use of Scripture in this instance serves as a guide to the use to which he puts scriptural religion generally. As the following chapter will detail, his lessons in self-reliance continue as he transforms elements of scriptural religion to demonstrate how human beings need not depend on divine forces to sustain their political lives.

One comes to understand that Machiavelli has recourse to certain elements of biblical understanding as he considers the way his own enterprise might meet with success. To counter effectively the strategy of the Christians, it is necessary to understand just how effective their alternative methods can be. Of course, before he employs these methods, he will transform them.

Machiavelli's fraud therefore consists not only in his recasting Livy's history to suit his own purposes but also in his use of biblical religion as a stalking-horse for his teaching. This method of appealing to something new in the guise of something old seems all the more prudent given that Machiavelli ascertains that "the collectivity of men feed on what appears as much as on what is; indeed, many times they are moved more by things that appear than by things that are." As a result, "[t]his should be observed by all those who wish to cancel an ancient way of life in a city and to turn it to a new and free way of life, for since the new things alter the minds of men, you should contrive that those alterations retain as much of the ancient as possible" (D 1.25.1; see also, P 18). As the ruling understanding is Christian, he would appeal not only to Roman antiquity but also to Christianity if he were to follow his own advice to introduce a free way of life. Thus, beyond the genuine utility of certain transformed elements of Christianity, an appeal to them also furnishes a measure of protection, as many will not discern that the understanding he propagates is actually a repudiation of the old. In appealing to elements of both pagan and Christian Rome, Machiavelli is doubly safe. Having thus observed Machiavelli's insistence on the utility of fraudulent appeals, we can return to a consideration of Rome, confident that it leads us to his new land—new because he infuses ancient Rome with his own unique modern understanding that at once will overcome the problem of the divided city and prevent for all time its reoccurrence.

❖ CHAPTER 7 ❖

A TEMPORAL CHRISTIANITY AND THE PRINCES OF THE REPUBLIC

In staging the spectacle of republican Rome in the *Discourses*, Machiavelli edifies his contemporaries by demonstrating a domestic policy that at once promotes an acquisitive foreign policy and prevents the elevation of a single individual to preeminence. As we know, although the history of ancient Rome furnishes Machiavelli with a large measure of satisfaction on this score, ultimately it cannot fulfill his demands: history reveals that as the city expanded, the *principi* of republican Rome were displaced by the rule of a single man. Machiavelli differs significantly from Livy, his source, by infusing his depiction of the events in Rome's downfall with terms and images evocative of the later ascendancy of Christianity; he discerns a nascent Christian Rome in pagan Rome. This pagan Rome—which bears such a resemblance to Christian Rome, and which he roundly censures as a result—cannot be the Rome found in the pages of Livy, because Machiavelli utilizes knowledge of historical events unavailable to the Roman historian.

Despite these decisive criticisms of ancient Rome, however, there is another Rome to be found in the pages of the *Discourses*. Like the one Machiavelli criticizes, it is not to be found in Livy's history, for it too is informed by Machiavelli's modern historical understanding. This Rome is equivalent to the new land Machiavelli claims to have discovered. With recourse to the strength that Machiavelli discerns in Christianity's devastating rule over human beings, his new Rome solves the problem that defied ancient Rome. He thus will not become dejected by the lamentable events that overwhelmed Italy: the moderns have a distinct advantage over the ancients, for the moderns, in ordering their political lives, have at their disposal the example of Christianity's rule. Machiavelli utilizes this example to avert the danger that the new age must confront: the possibility of a supertyrant, who would be able to draw on the lessons of both Caesar's and Christianity's ascents.

Specifically, Machiavelli improves on ancient Rome by altering its method of punishment. The Rome of Livy's depiction vacillated in punishing its captains, and in Machiavelli's view its irresolution resulted in its subjugation to tyranny. In his own inimitable, wickedly wry manner, he finds a principle of punishment in Christian doctrine—the religion that espouses love and the news of human salvation—and wrests that principle from its theological context to apply it to his new and improved Rome.[1]

But how can we locate his new land, without mistaking it either for the Rome of Livy's history or for the Rome that he criticizes with the benefit of hindsight? I have already noted how Machiavelli both praises and criticizes Rome. Without reducing interpretation to a mere formula, I will make it my general practice to assume that those changes Machiavelli makes, and of which he ultimately approves, will be a part of his new Rome, whereas those he makes and ultimately criticizes indicate where in his view critical pitfalls lie. By pointing to these pitfalls he warns those who will complete his project to avoid them assiduously.

Machiavelli's Roman Captains

In *Discourses* 3.19–23 Machiavelli poses the question of how a commander should conduct himself: kindly so as to inspire love in his subordinates, or cruelly so as to inspire fear? At the beginning of this section he appears to favor kindness, but it soon becomes evident that he believes cruelty must predominate. Moreover, as his argument unfolds, it becomes clear that kindness must be shunned because it furnishes a leader with a path to tyranny. Machiavelli begins by considering the results produced when two consuls of opposite dispositions shared command. The harsh commander Appius Claudius, who despised the plebeians, was so poorly obeyed that he had to depart from his province as if defeated, whereas his colleague, Quintius, whom Machiavelli describes as having a "kind and . . . humane disposition," defeated the enemy. On the basis of this empirical evidence, Machiavelli states, "it appears that in governing a multitude, it is better to be humane rather than proud, merciful [*pietoso*] rather than cruel" (*D* 3.19.1; *O* 225; cf. *P* 17). Incredibly, he appears here to embrace a form of the Christian teaching regarding mercy.[2]

Apparently Machiavelli's embrace of mercy here is incredible even to himself, for he looks immediately to the authority of Tacitus, who, he says, holds the opposing view. Machiavelli cites in Latin a sentence that he attributes to this Roman historian: "'in ruling a multitude punishment is worth more than compliance'" (*D* 3.19.1).[3] Unsettled by this contradiction between Tacitus's declaration and the results of his own investigation, Machiavelli attempts to reconcile them by concluding that Tacitus must have intended for such severity to be applied in cases where the leader is dealing with inferiors. Having thus resolved the apparent contradiction, Machiavelli concludes that when one commands colleagues, as in the example of the two consuls of the Roman republic, one must favor considerateness: "[o]ne may often see that the Roman captains who made themselves loved [*amare*] by their armies and who managed them with compliance had better fruit than those who made themselves extraordinarily feared" (*D* 3.19.1; *O* 225).

One has to wonder whether such "better fruit" to which he vaguely refers here would actually redound to the benefit of an individual captain at the expense of his republic, given that a captain who has won the loving fealty of his army could actually present a formidable problem to his republic. This potential problem is in the background of Machiavelli's discussion, for immediately following this section of chapters devoted to examining the issues concerning a captain's character, he finds that extended military commands constituted a critical factor in the ruin of the Roman republic. With his period of command lengthened, a captain was given the opportunity to make his army his "partisan." The existence of partisans, as we know, foreshadows the downfall of a republic: "Because of this, Sulla and Marius could find soldiers who would follow them against the public good: because of this, Caesar could seize the fatherland" (D 3.24.1; cf. FH 7.1). These considerations of the way a captain makes partisans of his soldiers are not explicitly part of his analysis at this point, however. Indeed, at the end of 3.19, having restricted the application of Tacitus's maxim to monarchies, Machiavelli puts forward the humane Quintius as the exemplar of correct conduct in a republic.

At this point Machiavelli is struggling to maintain that in a republic, as opposed to a monarchy, love must be supreme. Nevertheless, by the end of this section of chapters, he maintains that fear must be primary in a republic as well. By the end of this same section he indicates that punishment and the fear it engenders should at least be as prominent a pair of weapons in the arsenal of a republic as in that of a monarchy.

Machiavelli's explicit retraction of his first position occurs in 3.22, when he compares Manlius Torquatus, who utilized cruelty, to Valerius Corvinus, who utilized kindness. Again, as in 3.19, these two Roman commanders were contemporaries; here, however, the relevant scope for evaluation is the entire career of each rather than a single battle. Machiavelli begins the chapter by claiming that they are equal in virtù, in the number of their triumphs, and in the extent of their glory; the only distinguishing feature between them is disposition.[4] Whereas Manlius proceeded "with every kind of severity," Valerius treated his soldiers "with every humane mode and means." Machiavelli draws an even starker contrast between the two commanders when he tersely reports, "to have the obedience of the soldiers, one killed his son and the other never offended anyone" (D 3.22.1). Willingness to kill one's son in order to elicit obedience from one's army reveals a frightening, inhuman singularity of purpose. In Machiavelli's universe, however, the use of such fearful tactics is more of a recommendation than a disqualification for rule, as Manlius's manner of proceeding is similar to that of Brutus, whose resoluteness in executing his sons at the republic's inception elicits Machiavelli's praise (D 1.16 and 3.3).

Despite Manlius's likeness to Brutus, Machiavelli will not at this point tip the balance in favor of this harsh captain: "Nonetheless, with so much diversity of proceeding, each produced the same fruit. . . . For no soldier ever drew back from fighting or rebelled from them or was in any part discrepant from their wish" (*D* 3.22.1). This declaration of their equality notwithstanding, Machiavelli finds it necessary to choose between the way of fear as exemplified by Manlius and the way of love as exemplified by Valerius. Machiavelli rules in Manlius's favor, thus reversing the conclusion he had reached in 3.19. In the remainder of chapter 3.22, Machiavelli makes it evident that Valerius's kindness is detrimental to a republic and that Manlius's cruelty is most beneficial.

Machiavelli declares unequivocally that Manlius's way is more appropriate for "a citizen who lives under the laws of a republic" because it is impossible to detect in this captain's conduct any "private ambition." The way of Manlius benefits the state solely; his methods will not win him "partisans" as he is "always harsh to everyone and loving only the common good" (*D* 3.22.4). People will not endeavor to become his adherents in the hope of receiving private benefits. If a republic were led by a cohort of commanders with this disposition, then a parity among the leaders would be maintained, and corruption would be kept at bay (cf. *D* 1.34).

In contrast to Manlius's way of fear, Valerius's way of love generates partisans. Whereas Manlius's method causes a republic to endure, Valerius's method could bring about its collapse; a commander who collects such partisans prepares "the way for tyranny" if his rise to preeminence were not checked (*D* 3.22.6). Machiavelli has thus successfully inverted his conclusion of 3.19.

If Valerius's conduct is harmful to a republic, and Manlius's beneficial, what happens to the individual who chooses one or the other? Which path is more likely to benefit the individual who takes it? Machiavelli broaches this issue in the last chapter of the section, 2.23, entitled "For what cause Camillus was expelled from Rome." If the way of love prepares the way for tyranny, as he asserts at the conclusion of the previous chapter, the greatest reward for one who desires supreme command would lie at the end of this path. Machiavelli will not even acknowledge the presence of such a prize, however, and focuses instead on those who have taken this path only with deplorable results: "We have concluded above that proceeding like Valerius hurts the fatherland and oneself" (*D* 3.23.1). The alternative method appears to be the better choice because the captain who utilizes it will benefit his country and only occasionally injure himself. In this manner Machiavelli

promulgates the politically salutary lesson that Manlian behavior is more beneficial to the individual.

As the chapter continues, however, the case of Camillus appears
to offer a challenge to this lesson, for it represents one of those
rarer instances in which an individual suffered harm when proceeding in a manner akin to Manlius's. Machiavelli notes that, even
though Camillus's temperament inclined toward that of Manlius,
he suffered exile.[5] Both facts must be recognized; yet the chapter indicates only that Camillus's exile was not a necessary result of his
severe nature. Camillus crossed a line he need not have: his soldiers
not only feared him, they hated him. According to Machiavelli's
analysis Camillus broke the cardinal rule against depriving people
of property (cf. *P* 17). After the sack of Veii he not only refused to
turn the proceeds from the sale of Veientian property over to his
soldiers along with the other plunder, but threatened to use the
goods that had already come into the hands of his soldiers to fulfill his vow to Apollo (*D* 1.55).

In placing this emphasis on Camillus's hateful actions that
threatened his soldiers' profit, Machiavelli differs from Livy, who
points to Camillus's likening himself to Jupiter in his triumphal
procession, which was, according to Livy, "an act which struck
men as being not only undemocratic, but irreverent."[6] Machiavelli
does mention the incident in which Camillus had his chariot drawn
by four white horses, and remarks that the Romans "said that because of his pride he wanted to be equal to the sun." Machiavelli
refuses to link Camillus's expulsion to this impious act, for after
mentioning it, he admonishes, in predictable Machiavellian fashion, that the surest way to incur the people's hatred is to deprive it
of "something useful" (*D* 3.23.1). One can be feared without being hated, because the proper measure of severity does not necessitate that a leader deprive the people of property.

Due to his ill-advised threat to seize the possessions of his soldiers, Camillus was unlikely to gain their acquiescence in his desire
to be regarded as divine. But what if a commander who proceeded
in the opposite manner—one who was neither hated nor feared,
but loved—were to possess the same desire? Surely one who desired *"transcendere il vivere civile"* (*O* 88) by establishing a
tyranny might also desire to transcend human life by being regarded as divine. We have already encountered the problem that a
republic faces in having its leaders adored by the people. When
condemning the Roman practice of prolonging the period of com-

mand in *Discourses* 3.24, Machiavelli offers the examples of Marius, Sulla, and Caesar and the tyranny that finally resulted. Of the three, Caesar's rule was extended for the longest period, for after his death, others ruled in his name. It would appear that when one who strains for tyranny has acquired partisans who love him, his rule can be prolonged indefinitely. Again, during Machiavelli's time, Rome was the seat of power for those who claimed to rule in Christ's name. The problem of the people's benefactor being so adored by the people that he becomes a god to them is best exemplified by Christ.

Commanders who employ Manlian methods do not pose such a problem for a republic. These leaders simply do not possess benevolent masks under which they can conceal their aspirations to tyranny. As a result they are neither liberal nor lovable, and cannot generate followers who adore them. Thus a republic whose commanders resembled Manlius would avoid such a problem as led to the collapse of Rome when Marius, Caesar, and Christ attracted such devoted followers, who demanded that the commands of their beloved leaders be prolonged.

Machiavelli declares the primacy of fear and rejects the way of love for a republic. Eschewing the way of love has implications for his view of Christian doctrine, which teaches the way of love. We have already seen how Machiavelli considers Christian mercy to be devastating to the politics of his own times. Important for the matter at hand, however, is that his modern understanding informs his presentation of Roman history. He finds facets of the ancient republic that must be shunned, as well as others that should be embraced. Manlius becomes his exemplar because such a harsh type of character, if properly cultivated, would forestall the ascendancy of what Machiavelli endeavors to eschew: the reign of the Caesars and of Christianity. Moreover, he displays even more interest in Manlius's character because harshness is a prominent feature of Machiavelli's transformation of Christianity.

A Remedy for Political Decay

The role of Manlian captains in a republic as delineated above is merely negative: because of their stern characters, Manlian captains do not have the wherewithal to garner partisans, and therefore they cannot threaten their state with the establishment of a tyranny. Such commanders do provide an important benefit, however: their commands reinvigorate the state.

Indeed, on the basis of the salutary effect of a Manlius, Machiavelli makes a grandiose promise:

> [Extraordinary commands] are useful in a republic because they return its orders towards their beginning and into its ancient virtue. As we said above, if a republic was so happy that it often had one who with his example might renew the laws, and not only restrain it from running to ruin but pull it back, *it would be perpetual.* So Manlius was one of those who retained military discipline in Rome with the harshness of his commands; constrained first by his nature, then by the desire he had that what his natural appetite had made him order be observed.[7] (*D* 3.22.3)

Machiavelli claims to have found the way to guarantee eternal life to a republic. He refers here to *Discourses* 3.1: "If one wishes a sect or a republic to live long, it is necessary to draw it back often toward its beginning." He begins that particular chapter as follows: "It is a very true thing that all worldly things have a limit to their life; but generally they go the whole course that is ordered for them by heaven so that they do not disorder their body but keep it ordered so that . . . it does not alter . . . to its harm" (*D* 3.1.1). Thus his statement in 3.22 that the consistent application of Manlian commands could make a republic perpetual is not an exact recapitulation of this earlier statement to which he points. In the earlier chapter he acknowledges that a state has a limit to its existence. In the later chapter he makes a much greater claim: that no such limit need circumscribe the life of a republic.

Even though *Discourses* 3.1 acknowledges the existence of this external limit, which must moderate human aspirations for politics, this chapter emphasizes that human beings need to take an active role in guiding their political life. For a sect or a republic to attain even this heavenly ordained limit, those who live under its orders must take action: they must assure that the orders be renewed. Renewal results from a return to the condition of fear that was present at the state's beginnings, and can be accomplished through either external or internal events. He illustrates this distinction by referring to events in the history of the Roman republic and offers the French capture of Rome as an example of an "extrinsic accident" that had such a salutary effect. Because the Romans were neglecting their institutions as "ordered by Romulus and by the other prudent princes," they lost their ability to withstand such an incursion; after suffering this shocking humiliation at the hands of the French, however, they renewed their laws and their religious rites (*D* 3.1.2). Thus, according to Machiavelli's argument, this seemingly unfortunate accident was a boon to Rome.

Similar benefits can result from actions taken within a state, such as the continual establishment of laws that go "against the ambition and the insolence of men" (*D* 3.1.3). In addition, a citizen can vigorously enforce the law. As examples of such enforcement that occurred before the French invasion Machiavelli enumerates "the death of the sons of Brutus," of "the ten citizens," and of "Maelius the grain-dealer," and after that invasion, the deaths of Manlius Capitolinus and Manlius Torquatus's son; Papirius's prosecution of Fabius, his Master of Horse; and the accusations against the Scipios. These actions had a restorative effect "[b]ecause they were excessive and notable, such things made men draw back toward the mark" (*D* 3.1.3).

Among the internal methods of renewal, Machiavelli points to the extreme importance of these extraordinary commands in recovering the fear inherent in the beginnings. On the basis of the terrifying commands that Manlius issued, Machiavelli can offer the promise of a republic's perpetual existence. Of course, because such commands originate entirely within the state, they offer a far safer course than reliance on external accidents. External accidents may not come at all or, if they do, may be too extreme. In either case, reliance upon them could threaten rather than renew a state's existence. In contrast, prudence can guide internal renewal to assure that it occurs at the proper time and with the required severity.

In this chapter Machiavelli also treats the way that sects can be reinvigorated. He reports that Dominick and Francis saved Christianity by pulling it back toward its beginnings. Here Machiavelli mentions the name of Christ—its only appearance in the *Discourses*. Again, he says of these saints that "with the example of the life of Christ . . . brought back into the minds of men what had already been eliminated there" (*D* 3.1.4). The example of the *"vita di Cristo"* to which these saints appealed enabled them to regain the complacent acquiescence of the people (*O* 196). Although many Christians still discern the evil ways of many of the religion's ministers, they accept the saints' plea to leave these transgressors to God to punish.

In reconsidering Machiavelli's discussions of the Roman deeds that revitalized the republic—after he has drawn attention to the utility the Christian sect derived from the example of the life of

Christ—a commentator must conclude that Machiavelli finds political utility in the example of Christ's death. His promise here—
for example, that "excessive and notable" deeds (deeds that are
best exemplified by the executions of the sons of the republic or-
chestrated by these sons' fathers) lengthen the life of the state—
draws on an understanding of modern events. A distinct parallel
exists between the awe elicited by God's sacrifice of his son for
the sake of the redemption of humanity in eternal life on the one
hand, and Machiavelli's claim regarding the life-giving properties
of such awe-inducing executions on the other.[8] Moreover, when
Machiavelli elevates Manlius in *Discourses* 3.22 to be his exemplar of proper conduct in a republic, his peculiar emulation of
the claims of Christianity grows even more emphatic, for he
speaks not merely of the life of a republic being stretched to the
limit that heaven affords, but of a republic's existence in perpe-
tuity. Machiavelli apparently attempts to replicate on a purely
temporal plane the Christian promise of eternal life. His promise
is purely political as he extends it not to individuals who have
faith in a divine redeemer, but rather to a state whose principles
are founded in fear. The earthly generation of fear for this political purpose replaces fear of God.[9]

Because his understanding of these Roman events is informed
by his own knowledge of the power of Christian doctrine, it must
be concluded that the Rome of which he speaks in 3.1 is not the
Rome of Livy's history. This Rome is a creation of Machiavelli.
That his depiction of the Rome he so praises here is a creature of
his own peculiar modern understanding and dark imagination becomes clear when it is recognized that his recitation of events in
Rome is not entirely accurate. Among those spectacular executions, for example, he lists "the death of the sons of Brutus, [as
well as] the death of the ten citizens" (*D* 3.1.3). These ten citizens
were appointed to codify Rome's laws, but under the leadership of
Appius Claudius, they aspired to tyranny. When Rome freed itself
from their oppression, the ten were not killed. Livy indicates that
although Appius Claudius and Spurius Oppius were charged, they
killed themselves in prison before either one could be tried. The remaining members were sent into exile.[10] Machiavelli, for his part,
acknowledges elsewhere in the *Discourses* (1.45) that Appius
killed himself in prison before his trial. Therefore, by praising
Rome for killing the ten, thereby suggesting that it had executed
them as it had the sons of Brutus, he actually praises Rome for

staging an event that did not occur. Because he believes that the Roman people should have witnessed the execution of these ten aspiring tyrants, he slights historical Rome by suggesting that its practices fell short of his own standard. He damns historical Rome with false praise.

His tacit criticism becomes explicit when he remarks that a failure to act promotes the type of corruption from which Rome suffered: "as the memory of that beating is eliminated, men make bold to try new things and to say evil." After offering examples of excellent men who had the same beneficial effect as these executions, he declares: "If the executions written down above, together with these particular examples, had continued at least every ten years in that city, it follows of necessity that it would never have been corrupt" (D 3.1.3). Here we have Machiavelli's elusive remedy for corruption.

The fact of Rome's decay indicates that the ancient Romans did not understand the principle informing their salutary actions, because if they had, they would not have allowed the practice to lapse. In this way Rome could have prevented the accumulation of partisans and the elevation of a single man in the republic. But how could these ancient Romans, who lived before Christ's life and death, understand the life-giving properties of such spectacular executions? Under Machiavelli's tutelage, of course, "whoever wished to make a republic in the present times" (D 1.11.3) would apply this principle consistently so that, when faced with a similar exigency, the republic would be reinvigorated by the death of those who sought to subvert it.

Machiavelli's Divine Exemplar

With the promise of a perpetual political life, then, Machiavelli plays on the meaning of some prominent facets of Christian doctrine. As imitation is the sincerest form of flattery, his recourse to these elements of Christian doctrine suggests his admiration for the way that religion exercises rule over human beings. Nevertheless, he does pervert these doctrines; he wrenches them from their otherworldly context, giving them an entirely this-worldly meaning for the very purpose of overcoming the people's tendency to look to the otherworld by compelling them to focus on their temporal existences.[11] In forcing such myopia, Machiavelli seeks to endow political leaders with the means to achieve effectual politics.

His use of biblical teaching to empower human rulers is nowhere more evident than in the *Discourses* when he takes up the subject of *The Prince:* that of a new prince in a new principality. He begins with the stipulation that his advice here is extended to a prince whose "foundations are weak" and who "may not turn to civil life either by way of kingdom or of republic." In such a case Machiavelli advises that the best means for keeping the princedom is "to make everything in that state anew." He states how this is to be done as follows:

> that is, in cities to make new governments with new names, new authorities, new men; to make the rich poor, the poor rich, as did David when he became king: "who filled the poor with good things and sent away the rich empty."[12]

Machiavelli's demand that the ruler of a state be acknowledged as the cause of all things recalls a theological claim that God is the ultimate cause of all things.[13] Machiavelli makes these theological undertones explicit when he uses the only quotation from the Bible that appears in the *Discourses* to support the necessity of this prince's actions. Machiavelli's quotation, however, comes not from the Old Testament, as his reference to David would suggest, but from the New, and the Scripture refers not to David, but to God.[14] These are the words that Mary speaks after the Annunciation and before the birth of Christ. The harsh and "very cruel" methods that Machiavelli advocates for the new prince are those of the Christian god (*D* 3.1.1; *O* 121).[15]

So cruel are these methods that Machiavelli claims they are "enemies to every way of life [*d'ogni vivere*] not only Christian but human" (*D* 1.26.1; *O* 109). This terse comment suggests that, because such practices are so far removed from the dictates of the Christian religion, any Christian ruler should shun them as a matter of course, and they are so terrible that a ruler need not even be a Christian to find them repulsive. Machiavelli then continues, "any man whatever should flee them and wish to live in private rather than as king with so much ruin to men" (*D* 1.26.1). Although he offers this respectable alternative to wide-scale rapine, later in the *Discourses* Machiavelli indicates that such a private life is not a viable choice for a person of notable qualities. In 3.2 he claims that it will be to no avail to plea: "'I do not care for anything, I do not desire either honors or useful things, I wish to live quietly and without quarrel!'" (*D* 3.2.1).[16] Moreover, it would be difficult to maintain that he actually rejects such methods, for they remain the political solution for a new prince.

This particular political solution, then, is modeled after the methods of the Christian god. In describing these methods as enemies of Christian communities, Machiavelli appears to suggest that they are themselves "unchristian" and thus points to a disjunction between the precepts of Christianity on one hand and the actions of that religion's god on the other. Whereas adherence to the precepts of that religion has enfeebled the political life of human beings, the actions of its god, in Machiavelli's view, are worthy of emulation. As an alternative to the enfeebling rule of Christianity, he puts forward the deeds of the Christian god as a model for human rule.[17] It would thus appear that he prefers a human tyranny to one buttressed by a claim to divinity and administered by the parasitic nobles of the Church.

Machiavelli's ultimate view of lone rule bears directly on the relation between *The Prince* and the *Discourses*. As an advisor to potential tyrants in *The Prince*, he more than sanctions harsh and autocratic methods. Although the *Discourses* appears to embrace republican methods, it also sheds important light on the subject matter of *The Prince*, because in his work on republics Machiavelli reveals that the way of the most despicable type of tyrant is the way of God (*D* 1.26 and 2.2). Machiavelli can recommend—even praise—the methods of tyrants in his work on republics because his Rome will be a republic of a peculiar sort, one that incorporates the harshness of the tyrant without ever succumbing to the rule of one.

Although Machiavelli can recommend the methods of a tyrant, particularly at the founding of a republic, he ultimately favors the rule of many (*D* 1.9). In his view it overcomes the difficulties of succession to which autocratic states are susceptible, and thereby produces a more resilient state better equipped to acquire. In *Discourses* 1.26, for example, he touches on the issue of succession in monarchies when he refers to the father of Alexander the Great: "Philip of Macedon, father of Alexander, who with these [harsh] modes from a small king became prince of Greece" (*D* 1.26.1). Of course, Philip's son on inheriting his father's rule did not remain merely prince of Greece; rather, the son conquered the world. Machiavelli had presented this pair earlier as evidence that "two virtuous princes in succession are sufficient to acquire the world" (*D* 1.20.1). Although Machiavelli expresses admiration for the combined acquisitive capacities of Philip and Alexander, he rejects their example: "A republic should do so much the more, as through the mode of electing it has not only two in succession but infinite most virtuous princes who are successors to one another. This virtuous succession will always exist in every well ordered republic" (*D* 1.20.1).[18] Here he clearly articulates his preference for republics on the basis of their ability to acquire. They can acquire successfully because they have solved a facet of the problem of succession—the problem that Machiavelli introduced in *Discourses* 1.2 when he observed how dissolute sons caused the various forms of an unmixed regime to collapse.

Although Rome's mixed regime overcame the problem that such dissolute sons presented to the city's longevity, the Roman republic, as we know, succumbed to appealing sons who became steadily more adept at making guileful promises to the people. Machiavelli offers a solution to this problem based on his modern understanding of the way the lone ruler dominates the Christian dispensation. But before we examine the specifics of Machiavelli's solution, we must acknowledge the degree to which his depiction of a praiseworthy republic relies on his understanding of the necessity of princes. The state that has solved both aspects of the problem of succession is no ordinary republic; it is a republic full of princes, a fact Machiavelli emphasizes when he insists on calling the leading men of the Roman republic *"principi"* (e.g., *D* 1.12; *O* 95). In having so many princes at hand, the state need not eschew the passions of a monarchy, while at the same time it does not confront the disabling monarchical problem of an inferior son inheriting rule from a virtuous prince (*D* 1.19). This preference for republics is actually wholly consistent with his teaching in *The Prince,* for there he offers the Romans—the Romans of the republic—as a model for "wise princes" on the basis of their ability to expand (*P* 3.11–12; *D* 2.1).[19]

Again, the lone ruler plays a prominent role in the story that unfolds in the *Discourses.* A single man must found a republic and reorder a corrupt one (e.g., *D* 1.9, 18, 55), and a thriving republic therefore owes its very existence to him. And as my previous chapter argues, Machiavelli suggests himself as just such a lone man, in his undertaking to order the understanding that is to succeed the Christian epoch; Machiavelli is alone in having discovered this solution. Moreover, in being alone in ordering the type of republic that solves the problem of succession, he simultaneously orders a republic that solves the problem of religion. Because Numa's arts of peace slipped from the hands of the patricians to be utilized by enterprising young men willing to promise the people transcendent benefits to fuel their own rise to preeminence, appeals to the divine can be a danger and something to be averted, given the disastrous consequences of such an accident for a state.

Machiavelli has already explored how a state can avert this danger: fear induced by human beings can replace the fear induced by divine beings. In this discussion he had not pursued the possibility in detail because the solution appeared to be necessarily short-lived. This consideration emerges from the thought that "where the fear of God fails, it must be either that the kingdom comes to ruin or that it is sustained by the fear of a prince which supplies the defects of religion." He continues, "[b]ecause princes are of short life, it must be that the kingdom will fail soon, as his virtue fails" (D 1.11.4). Although this statement prominently displays the difficulties such a state would confront, Machiavelli does present the alternative: a state can exist without religion. In his view the people's religious impulse need not be fulfilled in every instance, as the prince possesses the ability to inspire fear.

Despite his consideration of this possibility, Machiavelli points to the constraints to which an irreligious state would be subject. He indicates here that an irreligious state would have to be a monarchy to supply the proper measure of terror. And because this state is a monarchy, it would face impending collapse when a prince's successors failed to replicate his *virtù*. Further, Machiavelli makes his readers witness to this process of decline when he considers how religion did not exist in Rome before Numa's reign; according to Machiavelli's own account, Romulus possessed sufficient *virtù* to maintain an irreligious state, while his weak successor did not.

In response to the devastating possibility of such a weak succession, Machiavelli fashions an unconventional republic that is replete with *"infiniti principi virtuosissimi"* (D 1.20; O 105).[20] Thus at any given time any number of princes are capable of assuming rule. Moreover, many of the virtuous princes populating this republic will be of the Manlian persuasion. They maintain the life of the republic by infusing it with a large measure of fear—fear, in Machiavelli's view, being the critical factor in maintaining a republic's life. If fear of a prince can sustain an irreligious monarchy, it would appear that Machiavelli's fearsome princes can sustain an irreligious republic; there need be no appeals to the divine.

Machiavelli's "Christian" Republic

Machiavelli's republic incorporates princes, and hence the passions of princes, into its framework. For this state to remain a republic, it must prevent any one of its infinite princes from attaining the preeminence that their princely natures covet. In thwarting the aspirations of these princes, Machiavelli has recourse to the elements that he finds so cruel in Christianity's rule. These elements are used to prevent any single prince from acquiring the reverence of the people. His republic will not make the mistake of being pious toward any of its leading men. This strategy originates in Machiavelli's perversion of the Christian doctrine of human corruption. If Christianity is the tyranny of his times, Machiavelli, by replicating some of its methods of rule, infuses tyrannical elements into his republic.

Christian doctrine in Machiavelli's hands enhances the power and fearsomeness of a republic's leaders. Nowhere is this more apparent than in his terrifying discussion of the proper manner of punishing a multitude; in *Discourses* 3.49 he praises the Roman republic for such an action. Machiavelli observes that "when a multitude errs when the author is not certain," punishing one in ten creates the most fear (*D* 3.49.2).[21] This method, while inflicting the penalty only on a fraction of the offenders, serves to chasten all because, not knowing who will receive the penalty, all must fear it. Although the ancient Romans utilized this practice, Machiavelli's praise of it in the Christian era gives it an additional meaning. His teaching on the subject is reminiscent of the Christian belief that everyone is tainted with the original sin, but not all will be punished.[22] Not knowing who will be damned, all Christians must fear the possibility of damnation and all are chastened. Machiavelli appears to learn from the methods of the Christians. The "sins [*peccati*]" of which he speaks in this chapter, however, are punished not in the hereafter by God, but on earth by a military or political leader (*D* 3.49.3). Here Machiavelli infuses Rome with his own modern understanding of the effectiveness of Christian doctrine rendered political. By praising a Rome infused with elements of his transformed Christian doctrine, he thus offers for imitation his own creation arrayed in antique garb.

Further, in the section on ingratitude in the *Discourses* (1.28–32) one sees in greater detail the way Machiavelli transforms the harsh methods of the lone ruler of the modern age so as to make them applicable to his republic.[23] He raises the question of why the Romans were less ungrateful to their citizens than the Athenians. The presumption appears to favor gratitude, and Rome, which he claims was "more merciful [*più pia*] toward its citizens" than was

Athens (*D* 1.28.1; *O* 110). A state should acknowledge and reward those citizens who benefit it. Nevertheless, we have already encountered Machiavelli's admonition against allowing an apparent benefactor to be revered. And as this section continues, he makes it quite clear that gratitude is dangerous. In his view, a republic must suspect all its citizens of corruption no matter what services they have performed for their state.

The danger of not doing so becomes manifest in the next chapter when Machiavelli discusses a problem likely to confront any prince or republic. Having dispatched a captain, what is a "lord [*signore*]" to do when the captain performs his task too well? By winning "an empire for his lord" he also wins the glory and the allegiance of a battle-tested army for himself (*D* 1.29.1; *O* 111). The ruler or rulers seemingly owe gratitude to this hero, but he is as much a threat as a benefactor to the state. In the case of a prince, Machiavelli advocates the harshest measures possible. The prince in looking to his own security should put this conquering captain to death or should deprive him of his reputation.

Machiavelli adds that if such measures are necessary to the security of a prince, "[i]t is not a miracle . . . , if a people" must do the same. Thus, a republic must, in looking to its security, be as harsh as is a prince. This lesson is very much in accord with his teaching on the character of a captain: a properly constituted republic must be a frightening place. He confirms the necessity of fear when he continues in 1.29 that a "city that lives free has two ends, one to acquire, the other to maintain itself free, it must be that in one thing or the other it errs through too much love" (*D* 1.29.3).

As he continues he appears to blunt the harshness of this warning against an excess of love. He explains that these errors can occur when a republic injures citizens whom it should reward and fears citizens whom it should trust. Rome did exhibit ingratitude in the case of Caesar, and this case led to tyranny. His example suggests that a republic errs through an excess of fear, not of love. He immediately corrects this impression that harsh ingratitude is always an error on the part of a republic as he draws a distinction between a corrupt and an incorrupt state:

> Although these modes are the cause of great evils in a republic that has come into corruption, and often it comes all the sooner to tyranny, as happened to the Rome of Caesar, who took for himself

by force what ingratitude denied him, *nonetheless in a republic that is not corrupt they are the cause of great goods and make it live free, since men are kept better and less ambitious longer through fear of punishment* [emphasis added]. (*D* 1.29.3)

Therefore, in accord with his dramatic assertion of *Discourses* 3.1, he affirms that harsh punishment—indeed, capital punishment—maintains a republic.

Nevertheless, in adducing the example of Caesar he warns against the use of such potent medicine in a republic weakened by corruption. When Brutus undertook to rid Rome of its menace, Caesar had already amassed a great number of followers. As we know, the type of inequality that such a following suggests is for Machiavelli the clearest sign of corruption in a republic. Because Caesar had acquired these followers, Brutus, by murdering his enemy, served only to make Caesar a martyr to them. An execution, when a republic suffers from such corruption, results in tyranny—the death of the republic rather than its continued life. He again reminds us that the problem he confronts is one of Caesar's ascendency—of the ascendency in a republic of a single man who garners the reverence of the people.

As if the point needed reinforcement, he adds the example of Scipio. Rome was ungrateful to this hero. This ingratitude sprang from fear, because Scipio showed himself to surpass in ability all of Rome's other commanders when he conquered so formidable an enemy at so young an age. Indeed, so extraordinary were Scipio's talents that Cato Priscus, "reputed holy," justified his action against Scipio by declaring that a city could not be called free when a citizen existed whom the magistrates feared. Machiavelli approves of Cato's reasoning: "if the people of Rome followed the opinion of Cato in this case, it merits the excuse that I said above those peoples and those princes merit who are ungrateful through suspicion" (*D* 1.29.3). In fearing, a republic does fearful things to its benefactors. If such fear furnishes the impetus for immediate action, then the republic prevents any given individual from gaining ascendency.

Although he maintains it is not miraculous that a republic must be just as ungrateful as a prince, because of their differing organizations a republic must be harsh in a manner that is different from that of a prince. For a prince, Machiavelli offers an easy solution to the problem of those captains who might attempt to usurp power. He advises that a prince should go to the site of the battle, thus depriving the captain of the power that would accrue from his victory and assuring that "the glory and the acquisition" gained belong solely to the prince (D 1.30.1). This method of ensuring credit for oneself is similar to the advice Machiavelli extends to the new prince in *Discourses* 1.26 to see to it that there be "no rank, no order, no state, no wealth there that he who holds it does not know it as from you" (D 1.26.1). The ruler of a particular state must make himself the ultimate cause of the good his captain brings to the state.[24] Whereas Machiavelli places the prince in the position of God, he places the captain in the position of any Christian whom God sees fit to test; in order to avoid punishment, the captain or the Christian must humbly renounce any attachment to his gains (D 1.30). Machiavelli seems to have found a totally secular application for the biblical pronouncement that a man will not profit if he gains the whole world and forfeits eternal life.[25] In Machiavelli's formulation, of course, the captain fears only for his temporal existence.

Here, as in *Discourses* 1.26, Machiavelli endows a human being with some salient attributes of God, and again these same attributes, when ascribed to God, constitute the tyranny that Machiavelli endeavors to overturn. For this reason, perhaps, he states in 1.30 that there is an alternative to the captain's renunciation—the captain can determine to use his newfound power to rebel against his "lord" (D 1.30). Machiavelli's articulation of such an alternative may steel the hearts of his contemporaries in a rebellion against their Lord. Although he expresses admiration for a mortal capable of making himself the sole fount from which all good and ill flow to his people, we know that he favors the political organization of a republic (D 1.20).

An established republic, however, requires a solution to the problem of a conquering captain that is different from the one Machiavelli delineates for a prince. Machiavelli notes in 1.30 that a republic, unlike a principality, cannot have the prince accompany the expedition in order to steal credit for the victory. Instead, he recommends the example of the Roman republic. It made use of everyone in war, noble and commoner alike, so that every age had so many virtuous men with so many victories to their credit "that the people did not have cause to fear any one of them." This lack of fear arose from a belief not in the innate goodness of these leaders but rather in their innate badness: "since they were very many and watched one another," reports Machiavelli (*D* 1.30.2). He thus applies the doctrine of original sin to a republic, because everyone there is suspect: "an orderer of a republic should order that every citizen in it can accuse without any fear or without any respect" (*D* 1.8.2). Because no one was above suspicion, each was understood to be corrupt—to be a potential tyrant whose ambition needed to be checked—the only way to glory was to renounce one's gains. A dictator, for example, gained more glory the sooner he renounced the office (*D* 1.30). A threat of force, of course, must quicken such renunciations. The harsh measures of the prince do seem applicable to a republic even in this case, particularly if those inclined to such severity are vigilant.

According to Machiavelli's analysis such vigilance is critical. In the chapter "That one should be mindful of the works of citizens, because many times under a merciful [*pia*] work a beginning of tyranny is hidden," he observes that men who benefit others through private favors make these others their partisans, which, in turn, "give spirit to whoever is so favored to be able to corrupt the public and to breach the laws" (*D* 3.28.1; *O* 234). In this manner a republic's reluctance to regard all its citizens as corrupt will result in corruption.[26] This is the course of ordinary republics. He says of republics that citizens normally can strive to overturn them with impunity "both because republics are slower than a prince, suspect less, and through this are less cautious, and because they have more respect for their great citizens, and through this the latter are bolder and more spirited in acting against them" (*D* 3.6.19). Machiavelli has thus solved this problem to which ordinary republics are vulnerable by infusing his new republic with some tyrannical impulses.

One sees the Christian belief in the corruption of all—the belief that no one can claim reward by right—informing also Machiavelli's praise for the Roman method of punishing in *Discourses* 1.24. He entitles this chapter "Well ordered republics institute rewards and punishments [*pena*] for their citizens, and never counterbalance one with the other," and he asserts here that such a republic never "cancels the demerits of its citizens with the merits" (*D* 1.24.1; *O* 107–8). This is necessarily the case because a citizen who has performed excellent work for the city acquires not only the reputation that his deed has brought him but also the audacity and confidence to commit evil deeds without fear of penalty. To this Machiavelli replies ominously:

For if a citizen has done some outstanding deed for the city, and on top of the reputation that this thing brings him, he has an audacity and confidence that he can do some deed that is not good without fearing punishment, in a short time he will become so insolent [*insolente*] that any civil life will be dissolved. (*D* 1.24.1; *O* 108)

In acting on this principle to avert such an outcome, Rome executed its savior.[27] Because Manlius Capitolinus endeavored to instigate a sedition in Rome, he was thrown from the Capitol which "with so much glory for himself, he had saved" (*D* 1.24.2).[28]

Machiavelli overtly praises Rome in these discussions and modifies these stories merely by infusing Christian terms into his description of Roman practices. Elsewhere, however, he criticizes Rome for lacking the necessary punishments—for not correctly utilizing Christian doctrine in an entirely temporal context. He relates the story of Horatius, for example, who, as the only surviving Roman brother of a set who had slain a set of Alban brothers, won a great victory for Rome. Returning from battle as Rome's victor, he slew his sister when she grieved openly for one of the Alban brothers to whom she had been betrothed. Although Horatius was a Roman hero, the Romans put him on trial for this crime. Machiavelli comments on the Romans' actions: "To whoever considers it superficially, such a thing would appear an example of popular ingratitude" (*D* 1.24.1). In contrast to such a superficial observer, he will not blame the Romans for placing their champion on trial. In his opinion, as we know, republics err through too much love and cannot afford to express too much gratitude to their great men.

Although he approves of the trial, he still finds cause to blame Rome: "nonetheless whoever examines it better and inquires with better consideration what the orders of republics should be will blame that people rather for having absolved him than for having wished to condemn him" (*D* 1.24.1). Because he understands what the methods of republics should be, he claims that the Romans erred in not convicting Horatius; Rome, in his view, should have been even more ungrateful in this instance.

In an earlier consideration of this trial Machiavelli explains the cause for the Romans' ill-advised leniency toward Horatius when he declares that Horatius "after many disputes was freed more because of his father's prayers [*prieghi*] than for his own merits" (*D* 1.22.1; *O* 106). In Livy's account the father cuts a sympathetic figure when he points out that if this son is taken from him, he will be left childless. In Livy's version, however, the father's pleas are not referred to as prayers.[29] By utilizing this term in his version of the story, Machiavelli calls attention to the Christian practice of praying to God for forgiveness. Here again we witness Machiavelli's presentation of a Rome not derived from the pages of Livy's history.[30] In this case Machiavelli seems to alter Livy's account in order to criticize his own creation. By characterizing the father's appeal for forgiveness in a manner that likens it to an appeal to the divine, Machiavelli hints at a potential pitfall in applying Christian doctrine to a political context—that of a simultaneous adoption of Christian forgiveness. Machiavelli's criticism of Rome for yielding to the prayers of the father illustrates his own rejection of forgiveness.[31] While embracing the Christian notion of corruption and applying it to his republic, he shuns Christian forgiveness.[32]

Machiavelli reinforces his insistence on a severe version of temporal Christianity when he again makes another change in Livy's presentation of Rome's methods of punishment. In this instance, however, he appears to criticize Rome for failing to apply an element of Christian teaching to a temporal context. He observes that Rome never punished its captains "extraordinarily" for an error even when it resulted in harm to the republic. In the body of this chapter he relates how Rome's captains, Sergius and Virginius, were not punished severely for an error that was "committed not through ignorance." Clearly their error was committed through malice: each captain was in charge of a part of the army that was encamped before Veii; when Sergius's troops were set upon by the Faliscians, this captain preferred to allow his army to be defeated than to ask for the help of his colleague; Virginius, for his part, anticipated Sergius's humiliation and chose not to come to his aid, preferring instead "the dishonor of his fatherland and the ruin of the army" (*D* 1.31.2).

Thus, in contrast to *Discourses* 1.30, Machiavelli illustrates a negative consequence of competitors watching each other in a republic. Because he finds the correct application of this principle so vital to a republic and because he has offered Rome as the model that both practiced it and punished most severely, one would expect that such a misapplication of this principle in acts of "truly wicked" malfeasance would elicit the harshest penalty from the republic he praises. Machiavelli too appears to expect such a result: "It is true that whereas another republic would have punished them with the capital penalty, this one punished them with fines"

(*D* 1.31.2). He has already noted in this chapter that the Romans were not known to have "crucified or otherwise put to death" their captains for losing a battle (*D* 1.31.1). As a result, Sergius and Virginius were not punished in a similarly harsh manner, "not because their sins [*i peccati loro*] did not merit greater punishment but because . . . the Romans in this case wished to maintain their ancient customs" (*D* 1.31.2; *O* 114). This strongest and most resolute ancient republic did not give these captains the punishment they merited; it appears to have been too "pious" toward its leaders (cf. *O* 113). To describe what such malefactors merited, Machiavelli resorts to Christian terminology. He finds the strength he is searching for in Christian belief and criticizes Rome for not utilizing it. A new republic can learn from Rome's failures as well as from its successes.

The importance of punishing for Machiavelli, along with his disapproval of historical Rome for failing to do it correctly, become more evident in his discussions of Papirius at the end of this same chapter. Machiavelli mentions Papirius's charges against the young Fabius, his Master of Horse, as an instance of Rome's not punishing its captains severely. In Papirius's absence and against his orders, Fabius fought a battle against the Samnites and won. Papirius demanded Fabius's death, but Papirius's father interceded, arguing that because the Roman people had not exacted such a penalty from their captains in defeat, they should not exact it from them in victory.

Clearly Machiavelli takes the part of Papirius in this matter, for he cites "the execution of Papirius against Fabius" as one of the "excessive and notable" executions that brought Rome "back toward the mark" (*D* 3.1.3). Moreover, he does not hesitate to condone punishment that is meted out in victory, for, as we know, among other executions that served the republic well in this capacity is Manlius's deed of killing his own son when, without orders, the son fought and killed a soldier in the Latin army. These changes in Livy's Rome are lessons to anyone endeavoring to construct a new Rome that the republic must be most harsh in punishing—both in victory and in defeat—and must not be swayed by prayers for forgiveness.

Machiavelli thus offers his solution to the problem of the way a republic, having unleashed the passions of its citizens, is to deal with the most potent of political ambitions. The liberal use of harsh punishments solves the problem of obligation, which so confounds a republic that confers honors only for "certain honest and determinate causes." A recipient of honors distributed on an equitable basis knows that he is deserving of them, and hence "does not confess that he has an obligation to those who reward him" (D 1.16.3). The significance of Machiavelli's recommendation to "kill the sons of Brutus" as a solution to this problem is now evident. Such a stern action vitiates the arrogance that would otherwise be instilled in its leading men (D 1.16.4). There must be a certain measure of tyranny inherent in the republic to keep its ambitious princes under control.[33] These actions against the aristocrats serve the additional purpose of purging the hostility that the people develop against the few (D 1.4 and 7).[34] Machiavelli does not seem to fear that the greatest ingratitude toward some of its captains will dampen the willingness of others to sacrifice for their republic. Apparently their desire for glory will continue to motivate their courageous exploits, and because they know that an infinite number of virtuous princes are eager to replace them, they keep to honest paths in acquiring the renown they covet.

Moreover, in the process Machiavelli simultaneously furnishes the solution to the apparent conundrum in *Discourses* 1.33, that of a young man who rises to preeminence in a republic. As he presents the problem there, it seems to have no solution, as it is impossible to recognize this inconvenience before it has made significant headway, and once "the citizens, when they become aware of their error, have few remedies to avoid it. If they try to work as many as they have, they do nothing but accelerate his power" (D 1.33.2). Machiavelli recommends the un-Machiavellian course of temporizing, which only puts off the young man's rise to tyranny. Because this recommendation is unsatisfactory, a beguiling alternative is assassination. To understand that this seeming expedient is injurious, one need look no further than the case of Caesar, who aroused fear in the citizens too late: "That fear made them think about remedies; and the remedies they made accelerated the ruin of their republic" (D 1.33.4). This solution was applied too late because Caesar had already amassed partisans—a sure sign of a republic's corruption. As Machiavelli warns, otherwise salutary punishment, when utilized in the midst of corruption, is destructive and, as the case of Caesar illustrates, makes a republic come "all the sooner to tyranny" (D 1.29.3). The solution therefore is to apply this severe solution earlier, when the young man has yet to accumulate the followers who are sure to gather at his side.

An obvious objection to such a policy is that it is impossible to administer the remedy early enough because the difficulty of seeing early enough that an appealing youth will pose a problem. This difficulty, however, will not present itself in Machiavelli's republic, which he apparently has designed with a way of avoiding it. His Rome will function so that the actual apprehension of a given leader's black intent will be unnecessary; the republic will function automatically to defuse the impulse to supreme rule which would otherwise grip its enterprising youth. First, because Machiavelli teaches both the goodness of severe captains who are incapable of collecting partisans and the wickedness of benevolent captains who are more than capable in this regard, the appealing veneer of any given youth will be suspect from its first appearance. Second, because the republic will furnish a climate favorable to the proliferation of Manlian captains—men who are princes willing to take the extreme courses that political life demands—punishment will be prevalent. Manlian punishment most likely will cut down a potential tyrant before he has reached his prime.[35] Nevertheless, the consistent occurrence of such fortuities is unnecessary: "If the executions written above, together with these particular examples, had continued at least every ten years in that city, it follows of necessity that it would never have been corrupt" (D 3.1.3). His Rome will improve on ancient Rome because he has determined that such examples will appear at consistent and healthful intervals, "since men are kept better and less ambitious longer through fear of punishment" (D 1.29.3). He intends to avoid the ascendancy of an alluring youth, such as a Caesar, a Cosimo, a Christ, or, indeed, in the epoch that is to follow, a super-Christ.

❖ CHAPTER 8 ❖

MACHIAVELLI'S RULE AND HUMAN LIBERTY

Machiavelli emerges from behind his masks often enough for us to determine that, by perverting the previous understandings to which he explicitly appeals, he furnishes the impetus for a new understanding. He thus can be taken to be a type of ruler. A consideration of his rule—its envisioned extent, its intended effects, and its manner of attainment—allows us to liken his dispensation to, and to distinguish it from, the rule he wants to overturn. Although fear will reign in the republic he envisions, in gathering adherents he avails himself of an appeal to love. He claims to love the people. Unlike the current prince, however, he offers his love for the people on the condition that they hear his call to arms. In assuming the mantle of the prince of war, he attempts to overturn the rule of the Prince of Peace, which has had such a devastating effect on politics. In his capacity as ruler he intends to allow human beings what they

have been denied for so long: honor and glory for their earthly exploits. Indeed, he endeavors to replace the divine and natural
realms with the human one. By his assumption of his exalted position and his imposition of human necessity, human beings will cultivate the faculties—those of the soldier—that will allow them to
establish a human republic.

Whither Machiavelli's Rome?

If Machiavelli seeks to be the ruler who will correct the corruption that characterizes his age, what does he envision as the locus
of his rule, and what type of political community or communities
would result from it? Although he does not address these questions
explicitly, he does offer numerous reflections that permit grounded
speculation on possible answers.

In one place Machiavelli's concern seems provincial: he tries
merely to encourage the people of his native region with the example of their ancient forebears, the Etruscans, whom he tends to call
by the modern name of Tuscans. After elaborating on the greatness
of the Etruscans before the conquests of the Romans, he expresses
the temperate hope that the example of these ancient people can be
replicated by their descendants:

> And if the imitation of the Romans seems difficult, that of the an-
> cient Tuscans should not seem so, especially to the present Tuscans.
> For if they could not, for the causes said, get an empire like that of
> Rome, they could acquire the power in Italy that their mode of pro-
> ceeding conceded them. (D 2.4.2)

The hope he expresses here for his own people is compatible with
his statement in *Discourses* 1.55 that, because there is no corruption in Tuscany, "a civil way of life would easily be introduced
there by a prudent man having knowledge of the ancient civilizations" (D 1.55.4). At this point the force of Machiavelli's reforming spirit seems to extend only to his native Tuscany.

Although Machiavelli seems to pin his hopes on his native Florence and Tuscany, other considerations suggest that the Etruscans
are a bad example for reform and that Machiavelli has more
grandiose designs. In the same chapter in which he presents the
Etruscans as a model for imitation, he points to some fundamental
defects in the Etruscan political organization. He explains that
within Etruscan territory were several independent republics organized in the form of a league. The league held no one republic

preeminent and expanded by making the territories it conquered "partners." This method of expansion limited the extent of territory that could be gained: "The like mode of proceeding is also seen by experience to have a fixed limit, of which we have no example that shows it may be passed." Fourteen communities marked the outside limit, and as a result, the Etruscans "could not go with their acquisitions beyond Italy" (*D* 2.4.2 and 4.1).

Machiavelli's sincere wish that the modern Tuscans emulate their ancient ancestors must thus be tempered by the limited ability of the Etruscan league to expand. As he makes emphatically clear from the beginning of the *Discourses,* a republic unable to digest ever new acquisitions cannot endure. If a state is unwilling or unable to wage a constant succession of wars, it will face collapse from the domestic turmoil that is sure to flourish in times of peace (*D* 1.6). A league such as that of the Etruscans, which is incapable of expanding beyond fourteen communities, will be hobbled by such dire difficulties. Machiavelli suggests the weakness of the league when he mentions in ominous tones that even before the Tuscans were extinguished by the might of the Roman republic they were vulnerable to lesser forces: "two hundred years before the Romans grew into much strength, the said Tuscans lost the empire of the country called Lombardy today." The French under "their duke Bellovesus" was able to wrest that territory from them (*D* 2.4.1).

Moreover, states modeled on the Etruscan league—even before they could become susceptible to the problems inherent in the method by which they expanded—would be vulnerable in the short term due to the corruption emanating from Rome. The Church clearly is responsible for the ills of Italy. Just as clearly, a fledgling state or states in Tuscany would only serve as a tasty morsel for a foreign power as a result of the international intrigue that the Church orchestrates on Italian soil. Recognizing the Church's continuing role of furnishing an entrée to Italy forces Machiavelli to conclude that "no province has ever been united or happy unless it has all come under obedience to one republic or to one prince" (*D* 1.12.2). Therefore, reform in a province distant from Rome would necessitate reform in Italy's heart, and a united Italy would be the result. Again, we recognize that the very difficult task in *Discourses* 1.55—that of rendering Rome fit for *il vivere politico*—is the one Machiavelli sets for himself.

If Machiavelli envisions an Italy "happy" because it has come under the sway of a single prince or republic, he would also permit himself the vision of the dominance there of the republic outlined in the previous chapter—the one that he creates by offering criticism and correction of the historical Rome. This republic holds such promise for Machiavelli that he claims it could be perpetual. Now, surely, he makes this claim as a challenge to the eternity that Christianity promises. His promise serves as a motivating tool for temporal enterprises in that it will encourage people to operate with the prospect of an earthly future before them rather than a heavenly one.

Much in Machiavelli's thought suggests that he cannot be serious about his promise of political eternity. One need look no further than five chapters prior to the one in which he discusses a perpetual republic to hear him gainsay its possibility: "Because one cannot give a certain remedy for . . . disorders that arise in republics, it follows that it is impossible to order a perpetual republic, because its ruin is caused through a thousand unexpected ways" (D 3.17.1). Moreover, he maintains emphatically that all worldly things are transitory. In the *Florentine Histories,* for instance, he states:

> Usually provinces go most of the time, in the changes they make, from order to disorder and then pass again from disorder to order, for worldly things are not allowed by nature to stand still. As soon as they reach their ultimate perfection, having no further to rise, they must descend. (*FH* 5.1.185)

Similarly, in the *Discourses* he maintains that the world has always been in the same condition, but that the "wicked and the good [have varied] from province to province" (D 2.pr.2).

In Machiavelli's view, apparently, any given state must be transitory. Even his own envisioned republic, long-lived because of its harsh resoluteness, must ultimately succumb to the decay to which all human things are susceptible. In the face of this evidence to the contrary, Machiavelli might nevertheless posit his republic as a challenge to this cycle of growth and decay that has held sway only because of insufficient human understanding and activity. After all, as the previous chapter showed, he offers his reflections on the rejuvenating effects of spectacular executions in *Discourses* 3.1 as a means to extend the life of worldly things; and then in 3.22 he goes so far as to assert that the existence of those who take Manlius, the exemplary executioner of 3.1, as their model is key to the continuance of a perpetual republic. Despite Machiavelli's possible faith in his promise, those to whom he extends it, just as in the case of the Christian promise, cannot know whether it can or will be fulfilled. Machiavelli takes full advantage of this fact.

Nevertheless, a way of understanding Machiavelli's promise exists, consistent with his sincerity and his understanding of the perpetual cycle of growth and decay in politics. It necessitates that Machiavelli covet an influence greater than what can be encompassed even by Italian territory. As "it is a very natural and ordinary thing to desire to acquire" (P 3.14), the motive for Machiavelli's seeking this extension of his influence could be said to be clear, but he points to another compelling reason to justify it. He seeks this innovation not only for his own good but also for the good of others. He consistently points to the need of reform not only in Rome, or in Italy, but also in the world. The "world" appears to have been rendered "weak" (D 2.2.2), and "the corruption of the world" resides not only in Italy, but in France and Spain (D 1.55.3). The reformation of such extensive corruption would be a great boon to humanity.

If Machiavelli's motives in this grandiose project can be so clarified, so too can his means. Admiration of ancient Rome need not be—and surely was not—limited to the descendents of the ancient Romans, or, in fact, to the descendents of those who were romanized by the city's early conquests in the peninsula. The type of politics he insidiously elaborates through his changes in Livy's history can have effect anywhere Rome is admired and Machiavelli's commentary read. In this way, perhaps he envisioned himself as the progenitor of numerous militaristic and resolute republics, each striving for preeminence over the others. In the same way as in his claim that the world has always been in the same condition despite the rise and fall of individual states (D 2.pr.2), Machiavelli suggests that, within the whole, individual states would rise and fall, but the whole would remain constant. Thus, as a result of Machiavelli's innovation, the whole of these states would constitute a perpetual human republic, which would owe its origin to him and would rival Christianity's promise of eternity as well as the extent of its territorial conquest. The potential locus of the rule of Machiavelli's Rome is the world. Again he confronts us with the magnitude of his hopes: the establishment of a new epoch.

Machiavelli's Way of Love

To found this expansive new Rome, Machiavelli seeks a type of rule for himself. Should his readers be as suspicious of his motives as he has taught them to be of those who sought lone rule in the Roman republic? He has fostered this suspiciousness by making his readers aware of the manner in which those who attempt to chart their way to preeminence cultivate the people's love for them as they express their own love for the people in their provision of private benefits. A student of Machiavelli will know, of course, that such declarations are mere subterfuges—that if these appeals have their intended effect they portend subjugation rather than liberation. Having been schooled in this Machiavellian understanding, we must confront Machiavelli's own profession of love for the people as he seeks preeminence.

His profession of love is bold, for he announces in a chapter heading of the *Discourses* that "the multitude is wiser and more constant than a prince," and declares in the beginning of the chapter that in rendering this judgment he differs from "all the writers" (*D* 1.58.1).[1] At this point, however, that Machiavelli makes such an announcement should come as no surprise. Machiavelli's populism has been noted throughout this study: he denounces the clergy for oppressing the people; he doggedly refuses to blame the people for Rome's downfall, even though it becomes apparent that the plebeians' hopes to satisfy their passions easily played a significant role in that city's descent to tyranny. To exonerate the people, he blames instead the constitution of Rome for allowing the corruption that issued from its ambitious men.

This description of Machiavelli's open defense of the people should give pause, as it furnishes a basis for likening his own endeavor of setting forth a new understanding of politics to any ordinary effort to establish a tyranny. His endeavor takes on an even more ominous dimension when it is recognized that he offers himself as a competitor of Christ. As we have noted, by his writings he wishes to rule over the understanding that is to inform the next epoch; he is the *datore* of a new dispensation. He also portrays himself as the self-sacrificing redeemer of humanity who promises salvation for political entities. Because Machiavelli likens Christ's accumulation of influence to that of any other aspiring tyrant, must not Christ's competitor also be viewed as a potential tyrant?

Machiavelli had seemed to construct a new Rome for the express purpose of preventing the rule of a tyrant, and now, if his new Rome is to exist, it appears that this will occur through the elevation of Machiavelli himself as a type of ruler. Is it possible that those to whom he appeals for help in completing his enterprise are really being asked to exchange one tyrant for another? An examination of the claims of *Discourses* 1. 58 clarifies the character of his populism, and thereby the character of his rule. We come to see that Machiavelli must be likened to any ordinary tyrant who seeks influence through an appeal to the people: this appeal is not wholly genuine as he will not allow the people the liberation they seek. And in understanding this element of deception in Machiavelli's appeal to the people, we see how he differs from Christianity, the tyranny he aims to overthrow.

In his defense of the people he chooses Livy as his opponent. He cites in Latin Livy's judgment of the nature of the multitude: "either it serves humbly [*humiliter*] or it domineers proudly [*superbe*]" (*D* 1.58.1; *O* 140). Although the source is pagan, the terms themselves are reminiscent of Christian doctrine, which mediated between the humble and the proud by exalting the humble. Part of Christianity's appeal to the people was its claim to exalt the poor, the meek, and the humble over the rich, the mighty, and the proud. Despite this appeal, the practical result of Christianity's temporal victory was the elevation of a new form of nobility that both oppressed the people and did nothing useful for life (*D* 1.55). Moreover, we have examined the Machiavellian repudiation of Christianity's embrace of humility on the grounds that it paradoxically rendered human beings complacently weak but also proud. This seemingly incongruous combination results from Christianity's denial of the resources necessary for human self-defense, on the one hand, and from teaching them to look for the workings of divine providence in their earthly undertakings, on the other. According to Machiavelli, Christianity is mistaken in believing that humility can drive out pride (cf. *D* 2.14). The effects of this mistaken belief are devastating because, in both their humility and their arrogance, Christians are left unarmed.

As Livy cannot, of course, subscribe to the Christian reinterpretation of humility as a virtue, Machiavelli reports that the historian indicts the multitude for its prideful dominance and its humble servility. Machiavelli's response to this accusation is to put forth the example of the "Roman people, which never served humbly [*umilmente*] nor domineered proudly [*superbamente*] while the Republic lasted uncorrupt; indeed with its orders and magistrates, it held its rank honorably" (*D* 1.58.2; *O* 140). He is willing to confer even more praise: "Whoever considers the Roman people will see it to have been hostile for four hundred years to the kingly name and a lover of the glory and common good of its fatherland" (D 1.58.3). Machiavelli offers himself as the Roman people's champion against the historian's indictment. In this manner, what had appeared to be a defense of the people in general is a defense of a specific people— the people of the Roman republic.

This bold champion, then, is not so precipitate as to attempt to fulfill the promise he extends in the chapter heading—the promise that on the basis of the people's wisdom and constancy it should rule. He reneges on his promise to the people—as all prospective tyrants are wont to do. Machiavelli has furnished elsewhere ample ammunition for the bombardment of the position he promulgates in the chapter's heading. He has shown, for example, that the Roman populace had a foolish and dangerous propensity to be moved by the rashest promises (D 1.53). Because of their credulity, the plebeians were easily deceived by the patricians, about particulars as well as generalities (D 1.48). Therefore, although Machiavelli claims that the Roman patricians gave vent to the ambition of the plebeians, he demonstrates thoroughly and convincingly that the *"popoli"* of the Roman republic were precluded from rendering the most important decisions through the clever machinations of the republic's "princes." Machiavelli discloses that the exemplary populace does not exercise rule (e.g., D 1.13, 39, 44, 48, and 54).[2]

In the text of chapter 1.58 he becomes much more cautious. At one point he characterizes his position as "conclud[ing] . . . against the common opinion which says that peoples, when they are princes [*principi*], are varying, mutable, and ungrateful, as I affirm that these sins [*peccati*] are in them no otherwise than in particular princes." Thus he confers his praise quite sparingly; the people's constancy consists merely in their being no less constant than "varying, mutable, and ungrateful" princes. The charges would be true, he continues, if they were also applied to a prince, because the *"popoli"* and the *"principi"* do not have a "diverse nature" (D 1.58.3; O 141).

Machiavelli thus rescinds the promise he appeared to have extended. Because assertions of the people's constancy and wisdom seemingly back up its claims to rule, he appears to support the people's liberation from domination by the few. He does not follow through on this promise, however. Instead, he intends to subjugate the people anew to the demands of politics. Like others possessed of tyrannical ambition, he reneges on his promise to the people. Although Caesar was liberal until his murder, had he attained the principate, Machiavelli says, he would have had to curb his expenses (*P* 16). Machiavelli will not fulfill the rashest desires of the people, because he endeavors to institute a resilient politics.

With this broken promise to his credit, Machiavelli stands with all tyrants. Nevertheless, an element in his thought indicates that he truly loves the people—albeit in the name of politics. This element distinguishes him from the ruling tyranny he seeks to overturn. Machiavelli has already discussed the arguments that the people itself put forth in support of its claim to the supreme offices of the state. Because the plebs constituted the larger party in the city, which faced the greater danger in war, and because their "limbs kept Rome free and made it powerful," the plebs thought that their party should hold the office of the consulate (*D* 1.47.1). When, however, the plebeians submitted a member of their party as a candidate, they recognized his unsuitability for this office; the plebeians, recognizing their own weakness, thus elected someone worthy of the office from among the patricians (see also *D* 1.57).

Because Machiavelli acknowledges the claims that the people put forth on their own behalf, one finds in his thought a true defense of the people—or of human beings generally—against the current tyranny that robs them of their dignity. He recognizes that their numbers and muscle combine to render a state free and powerful. On this basis he loves the people in a manner that is not intended to mislead. By weaving the claims of Christianity into his depiction of Roman history, he approves of Rome's way of "love," which entails making the people it has subjugated into soldiers in Rome's army (*D* 2.3). As we know, this love is not the way of peace but the way of war.

Like the demagogue who contends for tyranny, then, Machiavelli utilizes the way of love. Unlike the tyrant, however, his love promises not private benefits but the public greatness of a city. Moreover, he allows honor to the valiant and good, in stark contrast to the current tyrant (cf. *D* 2.2). In his beneficence Machiavelli will allow honor to those who would complete his task of the reformation of political life. Unlike the priests who claim to act in the name of God, those who will act on Machiavelli's directives will not invoke his name, given its disreputableness. Thus, Machiavelli permits glory seekers the rewards they covet and simultaneously frees them from the effects of the tyranny he denounces.

Machiavelli's Praise of Necessity

Machiavelli's praise of necessity and its ramifications reveal the manner in which his political arrangements would constrain the human beings who live under them, as well as the degree to which he stands over and above these arrangements. Machiavelli's purpose as he opens the *Discourses* is to overcome the *ambizioso ozio* that characterizes the Christian era. What is to overcome *ozio*— any type of *ozio*—is the proper application of necessity. Certainly God and nature can both be understood to impose necessity on human beings; nevertheless, what Machiavelli emphasizes in his treatment of necessity is its purely human application for the purpose of producing an effective political order. He attempts, as far as possible, to make human beings its source. Indeed, even the human resourcefulness that emerges through a fallacious appeal to the divine is nowhere evident in his most extended treatments of necessity in the *Discourses*. Human power apparently does not need to be diluted through such an appeal to transcendent powers. Moreover, he disparages nature's role in the endeavor to force men to behave well. He expresses no gratitude to nature for endowing human beings with their higher faculties and emphasizes instead the need to cultivate the faculties of a soldier.

"[M]en never work any good [*bene*] unless through necessity," declares Machiavelli (*D* 1.3.2; *O* 82). This point furnishes his central contention for the creation of a self-sustaining political order, and so a legislator must understand how to impose the necessity that acts as a balm for politics. In attempting to replace both natural and divine forces with human force, Machiavelli stands above this enterprise as its director. Ultimately, he is the source of the necessity that will redeem political life.

Machiavelli begins the first chapter of the *Discourses* with praise of necessity. This discussion opposes the necessity that the human environment imposes on a city to the necessity that emerges through the imposition of laws. By recommending the latter, he appears to shun the helpful role that nature can play in maintaining a healthy city. Thus he seems ungrateful to nature but mitigates this harshness when he readily accepts nature's aid in another way: he embraces nature's fertility. He maintains a respectful stance toward nature in acknowledging the manner in which human beings depend on its provision. As the *Discourses* proceeds, however, he cannot maintain this gratitude. What becomes primary for him is the human imposition of necessity without regard to nature's gifts.[3]

In *Discourses* 1.1 Machiavelli asserts that the virtue of a city's builder becomes manifest in two ways: in the builder's choice of a site and in the character of the city's laws. These two indicators of the builder's virtue are closely related, for the choice of site determines the type of laws the city must have:

> Because men work either by necessity or by choice, and because there is greater virtue to be seen where choice has less authority, it should be considered whether it is better to choose sterile places for the building of cities so that men, constrained to be industrious, less seized by idleness [*ozio*], live more united, having less cause for discords, because of the poverty of the site. (*D* 1.1.4; *O* 78)

Here Machiavelli articulates his view of the necessity of necessity and then puts forth the additional view that nature, by disposing of its own gifts in a niggardly fashion, can actually be said to aid human beings in the critical imposition of necessity.[4]

Machiavelli, for his part, categorically rejects this use of nature in order to impose necessity of another sort. Although the view he has just presented has merit in that the sterility of the site would counteract *ozio* by guaranteeing that its occupants were occupied with providing for their own maintenance, Machiavelli abandons the austere and united city with the introduction of the additional consideration of human nature:

> This choice would without doubt be wiser and more useful if men were content to live off their own and did not wish to seek to command others. Therefore, since men cannot secure themselves except with power, it is necessary to avoid this sterility in a country and to settle in the most fertile places where, since [the city] can expand because of the abundance of the site, it can both defend itself from whoever might assault it and crush anyone who might oppose its greatness. (*D* 1.1.4)

His reasoning here is very similar to that of *Discourses* 1.6, where he rejects the true political life and true quiet of a city when he forces a city to grow in size so as to defend itself. It is on this very basis that he rejects Sparta's harmony and Venice's serenity: "when a republic that has been ordered so as to be capable of maintaining itself does not expand, and necessity leads it to expand, this would come to take away its foundations and make it come to ruin sooner" (*D* 1.6.4).

There is in the contrast between the view Machiavelli rejects and the one he embraces in *Discourses* 1.1 a distinction in the manner in which nature is to aid in the imposition of necessity. The former view asserts that the city that is to flourish must enlist nature's help in endeavoring to restrain the appetites that cause discord among citizens. Nature's beneficence actually comes to view through its provision of infertile places, for the existence of scarcity gives human beings the opportunity to subdue their own nature—to subdue their passions. In this manner the city, through its laws and with nature's help, struggles against the passions imposed by human nature. According to this view human freedom comes to sight in the attempt to assert control over the passions imposed by human nature. One sees the effect that the city's site has on its laws as Machiavelli considers this possibility of a sterile site: the laws need not be as stringent in a place that demands much effort from its residents to sustain themselves. Nature rather than law imposes the requisite necessity on the residents of such a site.

In rejecting this possibility, Machiavelli demands that the builder choose a site that will tender nature's gifts in abundance. To overcome any complacency that the fertility of the site might foster, the founder must formulate laws that impose stern necessity on the inhabitants:

> As to the idleness [*ozio*] that the site might bring, the laws should be ordered to constrain it by imposing such necessities as the site does not provide. Those should be imitated who have inhabited very agreeable and very fertile countries, apt to produce men who are idle [*oziosi*] and unfit for any virtuous exercise, and who have had the wisdom [*savi*] to prevent the harms that the agreeableness of the country would have caused through idleness [*ozio*] by imposing a necessity to exercise on those who had to be soldiers, so that they became better soldiers there than in countries which have naturally been harsh and sterile. (*D* 1.1.4; *O* 78)

Machiavelli thus accepts the consequences inherent in the choice of a rich site: internal discord and conflict with foreigners.

Machiavelli does not seek liberation from the passions engendered by human nature, for he advises his founder to build in a place where they will flourish. Accordingly, Machiavelli's founder accepts not only nature's gifts in the form of the most fertile site, but also the implications for human nature that such prosperity engenders: riches unleash the appetites, and these appetites in turn result in domestic discord. Machiavelli accepts these implications of nature's gifts for human nature with an appreciation of the power they can engender. We have already encountered his argument that the domestic discord to which these very appetites give rise is the cause of a city's greatness; Rome allowed its people a voice in its government, was gripped by the conflicts between the many and the few, and turned these passions toward the acquisition of a vast empire. Because a city needs to be powerful, Machiavelli greedily accepts nature's most lavish offerings.

Coming to the forefront in his argument is the requirement of the human imposition of necessity. In a fertile site, when nature plays its part by furnishing its fruits in abundance, laws become of the utmost importance. After recapitulating that "it is a more prudent choice to settle in a fertile place, if that fertility is restrained within proper limits by laws," he relates an anecdote concerning Alexander's plans for his new city:

> When Alexander the Great wished to build a city for his glory, Deinocrates the architect came and showed him that he could build it on top of Mount Athos,[5] which place, besides being strong, could be adapted to give that city a human form, which would be a marvelous and rare thing, worthy of his greatness. When Alexander asked him what the inhabitants would live on, he replied he had not thought of that. At this the former laughed, and setting aside that mountain, built Alexandria, where the inhabitants would have to stay willingly because of the fatness of the country and the convenience of the Nile. (D 1.1.5)

Because a mountainside would be by far the most sterile place for a city, the architect's proposal appears to be a radicalization of the view that a builder of a city should choose a sterile site. Because of this sterility, the inhabitants would not be acquainted with overabundance, and as a result their passions would not be piqued; accordingly, they would live in harmony with each other. Perhaps the city could overcome all division to live as a one. Indeed, the architect specifies that the form of the city is to resemble that of a single man.[6] Deinocrates' proposal appears to be the architectural analogue of the view of certain moral philosophers that the city should strive to replicate the best attributes of a single human being, and thus the city should cultivate the highest in human beings.

Alexander, student of Aristotle but possessed of infinite political ambition, rejects with a laugh the designs of his architect.

Machiavelli concurs wholeheartedly with Alexander's rebuff. The city that will perfect the art of acquisition cannot be founded on any such idealization of humanity.

Machiavelli's lesson, then, is to take all that nature can offer and apply human force in addition. In teaching this lesson, of course, he does exaggerate the extent to which nature can be said to provide rich sites in such abundance that they need only to be inspected and claimed. In all likelihood, war would be a prominent part of the process, and he knows this (*D* 2.8). Nature is not kind, contrary to what he indicates at the opening of the work. But a state need not be concerned with nature's provision of a favorable site: Rome was able to put so many men under arms "not from Rome's site's being more benign than [that of Sparta or Athens], but only from its different mode of proceeding" (*D* 2.3.1; *O* 151).

Machiavelli's position on nature and necessity becomes clearer in *Discourses* 3.12, entitled "That a prudent captain ought to impose every necessity to do combat on his soldiers, and take it away from those of enemies." This chapter contains illuminating instances of the generation of necessity gleaned from history, as well as a general discussion of the role of necessity in human development. He nods to the thought of moral philosophers on the subject, but his treatment indicates that he has a very different view of nature than they, for he withholds his gratitude toward nature for its provision of human reason. He begins the chapter with the reflection:

> At other points we have discoursed of how useful is necessity to human actions and to what glory they have been led by it. As it has been written by certain moral philosophers, the hands and the tongue of men, two very noble instruments for ennobling him, would not have worked perfectly nor led human deeds to the height they are seen to be led, if they had not been driven by necessity. (*D* 3.12.1)

In attempting to identify these moral philosophers to whom Machiavelli refers, Leslie Walker points to the discussions of Aquinas and Aristotle, which treat the ways human communities arose.[7] What is striking in Machiavelli's vague reference to such discussions is that he neglects the human faculty of reason. In the discussions of Aquinas and Aristotle the topic is quite prominent. Human beings, unprovided with the instruments of defense that other animals possess, have "instead the power to reason,"

Aquinas notes. "Now, every man is endowed with reason, and it is by the light of reason that his actions are directed to their end."[8] In contrast to Aquinas's Latin, in Greek one word—*logos*—designates both speech and reason. Aristotle distinguishes human beings from the brutes on the basis of their possession of *logos:*

> For nature, as we declare, does nothing without purpose; and man alone of the animals possesses speech [*logon*]. The mere voice, it is true, can indicate pain and pleasure, and therefore is possessed by the other animals as well (for their nature has been developed so far as to have sensations of what is painful and pleasant and to signify those sensations to one another), but speech [*logos*] is designated to indicate the advantageous and the harmful, and therefore also the right and the wrong [*to dikaiov kai to adikon*]; for it is the special property of man in distinction from the other animals that he alone has perception of good and bad and right and wrong and the other moral qualities.[9]

Although Aristotle recognizes that human beings and animals share the possession of voice, the human voice is to be distinguished from that of the other animals because it is informed by reason.

Machiavelli seems to play upon the bifurcation of *logos* into speech and reason and refers only to the former capacity—that is to say, speech without the admixture of reason. What Machiavelli describes as "tongue," human beings share with the beasts of the field. Although Machiavelli asserts that the tongue and the hands were the instruments by which man became noble, by neglecting to mention the human faculty of reason he leaves obscure the ends toward which Aquinas and Aristotle point.[10] He does not lead us to either the ennobling activity of politics, consisting in the deliberation of the just and unjust, or the application of reason in religious or philosophical contemplation. Machiavelli shuns such contemplation for it eventuates in *ozio*, either the *ambizioso ozio* of the Christians or the *onesto ozio* of the ancient philosophers.

Without these ends Machiavelli's view of nature is quite different. Whereas Aquinas and Aristotle can be grateful that the harshness of human surroundings provides the impetus for the development of human communities,[11] and hence for the development of human beings' higher faculties that occurs when they live together, Machiavelli sees only a necessity for people to arm themselves. Therefore he rejects the view that nature is benevolent in allowing a few to attain perfection. His emphasis instead is on the many, and

Machiavelli places it simultaneously on the arms that the many are capable of bearing and on those characteristics of human beings that he so cherishes.

This is evident in the remainder of the chapter, in which he treats the circumstance of war. Human beings are to react to their surroundings by imposing a greater necessity on themselves. He begins his treatment of these martial considerations with these observations:

> since the virtue of such necessity was known by the ancient captains of armies, and through that how much the spirits of soldiers became obstinate in doing combat, they would do every deed so that their soldiers were constrained by that. . . . Thus he who desires either that a city be defended obstinately or that an army in the field do combat obstinately ought to contrive above every other thing to put such necessity in the breasts of whoever has to do combat. (*D* 3.12.1)

Considerations of this sort explain why a city in rebellion is much more difficult to subdue than when captured in the first instance. During the second siege the defenders of the city's liberty fight with more vigor out of fear—fear of human punishment:

> in the beginning they surrendered easily, not having cause to fear punishment because they had not offended; but since it appears to them that they have offended when they have rebelled afterward, and because of this they fear punishment, they become difficult to capture. (*D* 3.12.1)

As fear of retribution produces stalwart soldiers, he notes that one can make opponents less resolute in their own defense by assuaging their fear of punishment as a result of their capitulation. To this end, one could, for example, promise them pardon or reassure them that one seeks to punish only the ambitious few in the city. Machiavelli makes it quite evident that these pledges are not to be extended in earnest: "Although coloring like this is easily recognized, and especially by prudent men, nonetheless people are often deceived in it who, greedy for present peace, close their eyes to whatever other snare might be laid under the big promises" (*D* 3.12.2). Again he reveals his understanding of the susceptibility of the many to fraud; nevertheless, he does not here suggest that captains capitalize on this credulity with religious appeals. Although the familiar Machiavellian endorsement of fraud is present in this chapter, fraudulent appeals to divine entities are conspicuously absent.[12]

Machiavelli emphasizes the credulity of the people in many contexts and how they will quite likely continue to harbor superstitions. Despite the appealing opportunity offered the leaders by the people's superstitious nature, Machiavelli issues tacit warnings of both minor and major import against the recourse to the technique of religious fraud. From the loss of a battle to the establishment of a most virulent tyranny, he suggests that appeals to transcendent powers can produce disastrous political outcomes. Even though the promises of distant and intangible goods from both the Gracchi and the Christians provided the people's impetus for action, Machiavelli indicates that the acquisition of immediate and tangible goods can furnish equally compelling motivation. To illustrate this point he offers the example of the people of the Roman republic. The plebeians were so desirous of keeping the immediate and tangible goods yielded by their capture of Veii that they refused to fulfill Camillus's vow to Apollo. Although this incident does not reveal the deeply religious character of the Roman people, as Machiavelli claims there (D 1.55.1), it does show some grounds on which Machiavelli's earthly religion might exalt the homeland. Earthly goods—not divine ones—can provide the sole impetus for action.

His chapter on necessity in *Discourses* 3.12 further reveals the kind of methods that will strengthen human rule. He entirely ignores the divine realm here. He reports part of the speech of an enemy of Rome, who, when he found himself trapped between Roman installations with his army, exhorted: "'Go with me, neither wall nor ditch but the armed stand against the armed; equal in virtue, you are superior in necessity, which is the last and greatest weapon.'" Machiavelli neglects to report that earlier in this same speech this enemy had asked his colleagues, "Do you think that some god will protect you and deliver you from this plight?"[13] Having so truncated the speech, Machiavelli adds that the necessity to which this captain appeals "is called by Titus Livy 'the last and greatest weapon'" (D 3.12.3). Machiavelli need not even mention the possibility of divine intervention to embrace what he takes to be Livy's conclusion. What makes people operate well, according to Machiavelli, is the immediate fear of the direst consequences—a threat to their mortal existences. Such circumstances compel human beings to act better than would either the hope of a divine balm or the threat of a divine scourge. Because they act better, Machiavelli has a renewed faith in human abilities. Having relied on Christianity himself as he taught his own lessons regarding the necessity of relying on one's own arms, he has produced a new interpretation of that religion: one that recognizes only earthly sins and offers only earthly salvation (cf. *P* 13 and *D* 2.2).

If his earthly city is to emphasize arms, laws must be imposed. He says in *The Prince* that "because there cannot be good laws where there are not good arms, and where there are good arms there must be good laws, I shall leave out the reasoning on laws and shall speak of arms" (*P* 12.48). Although he is attentive to arms in the *Discourses,* he certainly does not shirk the discussion of laws. Even in *The Prince* he concedes the importance of laws for a republic: "The republic has to send its citizens [to command its armies], and when it sends one who does not turn out to be a worthy man, it must change him; and if he is, it must check him with laws so that he does not step out of bounds" (12.49–50). We have seen the type of laws with which he would check the ambition and insolence of his republic's captains, as well as the fearful manner in which he would enforce these laws with dreaded necessity. In correctly assessing nature's gifts, he has armed a republic that will contend with the reality of all human things being in motion (*D* 1.6).

With his republic so armed, he makes religion superfluous: "where there are arms and not religion, the latter can be introduced only with difficulty" (*D* 1.11.2). He confirms that an abundance of arms and a lack of religion is no obstacle to good government: "where there is good military, there must be good order" (*D* 1.4.1). In the chapter that considers the beginning of the city Machiavelli does not see fit even to mention the divine. When classical political philosophy treated the beginning of cities, the gods' role in the provision of laws was a prominent consideration.[14] Not only does Machiavelli not mention the divine in this chapter, he does not indicate that any appeal to the divine is required to enforce the laws human beings must impose.

Machiavelli is the one who alone furnishes the understanding of necessity that will drive out *ozio* and reform the politics of his time. But again, he intends for his imposition of necessity to create a sphere for human action, where the many will be free to pursue their gains and the few their renown. In the process, human beings will create political and military monuments to their power.

Although Machiavelli is ultimately the source of necessity that will redeem political life, he is also subject to necessity. The necessity that arises from the inundation of the Christian era impels him to strike out in search of a new land. The master of equivocation will have it both ways: he is the source of necessity and subject to it; as subject to it he has at his disposal the palliative that necessity forces the wars of the worst kind (D 2.8, see also D 1.pr). In this necessity, he suggests, there is excuse for the harshness of his teaching.

NOTES

Introduction

1. Quentin Skinner, *The Renaissance*, vol. 1 of *The Foundations of Modern Political Thought* (Cambridge: Cambridge University Press, 1978), 157. Skinner revises this assessment in *Machiavelli*, Past Masters Series, ed. Keith Thomas (New York: Hill and Wang, 1981), 50. Similarly, Alfredo Bonadeo concludes with regard to Machiavelli's thought generally that "it is necessary to remember that the main purpose of the exercise of Machiavellian power is the establishment and preservation of freedom" (*Corruption, Conflict, and Power in the Works and Times of Niccolò Machiavelli* [Berkeley: University of California Press, 1973], 126).

2. Hanna Fenichel Pitkin contrasts Machiavelli's view of human autonomy with the medieval view of social relations that posits a hierarchy culminating in God. Although she finds human autonomy to be a central concern in his thought, she also discerns a critical ambiguity on the subject. She regards Machiavelli's thought as revealing that masculine independence or *virtù* is always threatened by the woman capable of rendering men dependent and weak (*Fortune Is a Woman: Gender*

and Politics in the Thought of Niccolò Machiavelli [Berkeley: University of California Press, 1984]).

3. Cf. Hans Baron, "Machiavelli: The Republican Citizen and the Author of 'The Prince,'" *English Historical Review* 76 (1961): 217–53. Baron maintains: "one may take it for certain that as a rule (Machiavelli is never wholly consistent) *il vivere politico*—almost identical with *una republica*—means what we call a republic, while *il vivere libero, il vivere civile, la vita civile* may be found in monarchies as well as republics" (226, n. 1; see also 224–25, n. 2). See also Maurizio Viroli's discussion of *il vivero politico* in "Machiavelli and the Republican Idea of Politics," in *Machiavelli and Republicanism,* ed. Gisela Bock, Quentin Skinner, Maurizio Viroli (Cambridge: Cambridge University Press, 1990), 161; cf. Maurizio Viroli, *From Politics to Reason of State: The Acquisition and Transformation of the Language of Politics, 1250–1600* (Cambridge: Cambridge University Press, 1992), 155, 157–58, 131. Of course, my positing of Machiavelli's view of the Christian god's antagonism toward human liberty has ramifications for an understanding of the relation between *The Prince* and the *Discourses;* I treat that subject below.

4. Sebastian de Grazia, *Machiavelli in Hell* (Princeton: Princeton University Press, 1989), 58, 89. See also Dante Germino's comments on de Grazia's work in "Blasphemy and Leo Strauss's Machiavelli," *Review of Politics* 53 (winter 1991): 151–53.

5. Much recent literature on Machiavelli has endeavored to understand his thought by viewing it in a context of a classical republican or civic humanist tradition. Although an understanding of Machiavelli's context is essential, I believe that the scholar's determination of this context, without careful consideration of Machiavelli's own indications of his particular concerns, is ill advised. See my article, "Machiavelli's Momentary 'Machiavellian Moment': A Reconsideration of Pocock's Treatment of the *Discourses,*" *Political Theory* 20 (1992): 309–18. Victoria Kahn has challenged the hegemony of the classical republican interpretation of Machiavelli by arguing that the view of him as a proponent of force and fraud, which the interpretation of him as a dedicated republican has depreciated and muted, is not fundamentally mistaken. Instead she argues that the view of Machiavelli as dangerously deceptive arises from his rhetorical strategies in *The Prince* and the *Discourses.* See her *Machiavellian Rhetoric: From the Counter-Reformation to Milton* (Princeton: Princeton University Press, 1994).

6. *The Discourses of Niccolò Machiavelli,* trans. Leslie J. Walker, 2 vols. (New Haven: Yale University Press, 1950), 1:114.

7. Leo Strauss, *Thoughts on Machiavelli* (Chicago: University of Chicago Press, 1958), 230–31.

8. Strauss, *Thoughts,* 230.

9. In this, Machiavelli's irreligious state must be distinguished from Marx's interest in liberating the masses from religious belief.

10. Cf. Leo Strauss, "Niccolò Machiavelli," in *History of Political Thought,* ed. Leo Strauss and Joseph Cropsey, 3d ed. (Chicago: University of Chicago Press, 1987), 314–15.

11. Machiavelli appears to anticipate many features of the process by which the claims of Christianity became secularized, a process that Karl Löwith delineates in *Meaning in History* (Chicago: University of Chicago Press, 1949).

12. Strauss maintains, in contrast, that Machiavelli had very little recourse to Christian understanding. Although Machiavelli appeals to future generations through his writings (what Strauss calls propaganda), Strauss insists that this idea "is the only link between [Machiavelli's] thought and Christianity" (Leo Strauss, "What Is Political Philosophy?" in *What Is Political Philosophy? and Other Studies* [1959; reprint, Chicago: University of Chicago Press, 1988], 45). See also Strauss's reaction in "Restatement on Xenophon's *Hiero*" (*On Tyranny,* rev. ed., ed. Victor Gourevitch and Michael S. Roth [New York: Free Press, 1991], 183–85) to Eric Voegelin's suggestion that Machiavelli's new ruler is "Western Christian as opposed to Hellenic Pagan" (review of *On Tyranny* by Leo Strauss, *Review of Politics* 11 [April 1949]: 243).

13. Baron states: "The closer the comparison of the two works, the more absurd seems the idea that these should be two harmonious parts of one and the same philosophy" ("Republican Citizen," 228). Conversely, John Plamenatz maintains that the "arguments of *The Prince* are perfectly consistent with the arguments of the much longer *Discourses,* in which Machiavelli expresses his strong preference for popular government. As has often been noticed, there is scarcely a maxim in *The Prince* whose equivalent is not to be found in the *Discourses*" (*Man and Society: A Critical Examination of Some Important Social and Political Theories from Machiavelli to Marx,* 2 vols. [London: Longman, Green, 1963], 1:13).

14. Mark Hulliung, *Citizen Machiavelli* (Princeton: Princeton University Press, 1983).

15. Early in his life Machiavelli transcribed a portion of Lucretius's *De rerum natura.* See Felix Gilbert, "Machiavelli in Modern Historical Scholarship," *Italian Quarterly* 14 (1970): 14–15; John H. Geerken, "Machiavelli Studies since 1969," *Journal of the History of Ideas* 37 (1976): 352.

16. Strauss, for example, begins his essay on Machiavelli with a discussion of Aristotle's *Ethics* and declares that "Machiavelli appears to have broken with all preceding political philosophers" ("Machiavelli,"

296–300.) See also Clifford Orwin's treatment of Machiavelli's repudiation of the Aristotelian virtue of liberality in "Machiavelli's Unchristian Charity," *American Political Science Review* 72 (1978): 1220–22; and Paul Rahe, *Republics Ancient and Modern: Classical Republicanism and the American Revolution* (Chapel Hill: University of North Carolina Press, 1992), 261–67. In contrast, Anthony J. Parel views Machiavelli as a premodern based on what he finds to be the Florentine's embrace of astrology. See *The Machiavellian Cosmos* (New Haven: Yale University Press, 1992). Parel maintains that "[r]eligion for Machiavelli is also the product of the motions of the heavens" (7). In addition to offering a view of human autonomy in Machiavelli's thought that is very different from Parel's interpretation, I argue that Machiavelli was keenly aware of the defects of paganism.

17. Cf. Friedrich Nietzsche's declaration that "Christianity is Platonism for 'the people'" in *Beyond Good and Evil: Prelude to a Philosophy of the Future,* trans. Walter Kaufmann (New York: Vintage Books, 1966), 3.

18. In treating the controversy over Machiavelli's knowledge of Greek, Mansfield writes: "It is possible to believe, with the great majority of scholars, that he did not know Greek, but after experiences with the level of Machiavelli's competence, it is easier to believe that he knew it and deliberately suppressed his knowledge, playfully extinguishing the preceding philosophical sect and perverting the memory of antiquity *a suo modo*" (Harvey C. Mansfield, Jr., *Machiavelli's New Modes and Orders: A Study of the "Discourses on Livy"* (Ithaca: Cornell University Press, 1979, 206). Cf. J. H. Hexter's elaborate construction for explaining Machiavelli's having made use of Polybius 6 in writing 1.2 of the *Discourses,* given that he did not know Greek and that no translation was in print at the time ("Seyssel, Machiavelli, and Polybius VI: The Mystery of the Missing Translation," *Studies in the Renaissance* 3 [1956]: 75–96).

19. Machiavelli's letter to Vettori in which he writes of the pleasures of his communion with the ancients will be discussed in chapter 6.

20. See also his statement in *The Prince* that his "intent is to write something useful to whoever understands it" (*P* 15.61).

Chapter 1: The Church and Machiavelli's Depiction of Italy's Historical Situation

1. Scholars agree that all or most of the work was completed in 1513. At this time Machiavelli had intended to address the work to Leo's brother, Giuliano, duke of Nemours (see Machiavelli's letter to Francesco Vettori, 10 December 1513). Giuliano did not particularly

want the role of secular leader of the Medici's political fortunes, a role his brother sought for him. Giuliano died in 1516, and Machiavelli dedicated *The Prince* to Lorenzo instead.

2. Hans Baron and J. H. Whitfield each propound a version of this thesis. See Baron's "The *Principe* and the Puzzle of the Date of Chapter 26," *Journal of Medieval and Renaissance Studies* 21 (spring 1991) and Whitfield's *Discourses on Machiavelli* (Cambridge: W. Heffer, 1969), 87. Baron declares with respect to *The Prince* that "suddenly, the fervent request is made that the *casa Medici* should provide leadership in expelling the alien invaders by founding, in accord with the rules established in the book, a strong new state modeled on the one built a decade earlier by Cesare Borgia as a power nucleus on the borders of north and central Italy—a historic enterprise which only misfortune had prevented from becoming the starting point for Italy's liberation" (*Principe* and the Puzzle," 85). See also Baron, "Republican Citizen," 249. Baron maintains moreover that chapter 26 was a later addition to *The Prince,* written in 1515 when Machiavelli had learned of Leo's plan to found a state for Giuliano in north central Italy composed of Parma, Piacenza, Modena, and Reggio, but before the French victory at Marignano in the autumn of that year. Giuliano died in 1516 after a long illness, and later that year Leo named his nephew, Lorenzo, as duke of Urbino, to whom Machiavelli ultimately dedicates the treatise (91–92). David Wootton embraces Baron's thesis (*Machiavelli: Selected Political Writings,* ed. and trans. David Wootton [Indianapolis: Hackett, 1994], xvii–xx). Whitfield differs from Baron in adhering to the notion that the entire treatise was composed in 1513, and therefore that the last chapter is a general response on Machiavelli's part to the hopes engendered by the creation of a Medicean pontiff. Conversely, Federico Chabod is not "inclined . . . to look overmuch for specific reasons for the writing of *The Prince*" (*Machiavelli and the Renaissance,* trans. David Moore [1958; reprint, New York: Harper & Row, 1965], 39, n. 1).

3. Whitfield claims that Cesare offers to Machiavelli "the only historical parallel, the proof of how much one can build upon the favour of a pope when there is the added backing of the favour of a king" and that Machiavelli, in turn, offers this proof to his readers, particularly his Medicean readers, eager to replicate Cesare's example (Whitfield, *Discourses,* 28).

4. Jacob Burckhardt provides a chilling portrait of Alexander's reign in *The Civilization of the Renaissance in Italy,* trans. S. G. C. Middlemore, (New York: Harper Torchbooks, 1958), 120–33.

5. Machiavelli comments in *Florentine Histories* 8.18 that "as Ludovico remained sole governor of the dukedom of Milan, he was, as will be shown, the cause of the ruin of Italy" (339). Machiavelli does not actually narrate these events in this work.

6. See, e.g., Francesco Guicciardini, *The History of Italy*, trans. Sidney Alexander (New York: Macmillan, 1969), 46–48. Ferdinand Schevill discusses the impact of this earlier invasion on Italy in *History of Florence from the Founding of the City through the Renaissance* (New York: Harcourt, Brace, 1936), 433–34.

7. "Candia's death and defeat" here is a reference to Alexander's elder son, Giovanni Borgia, duke of Candia. Burckhardt claims that Cesare murdered this brother, a murder to which the father acquiesced because of his fear of Cesare (Burckhardt, *Civilization of the Renaissance*, 129; cf. Guicciardini, *History of Italy*, 124).

8. See also Machiavelli's "A Description of the Method Used by Duke Valentino in Killing Vitellozzo Vitelli, Oliverotto da Fermo, and Others" (*CW* 1:163–69).

9. I treat the importance of Machiavelli's repudiation of forgiveness in chapter 7.

10. The Italian communes were triumphant by the end of the twelfth century. After the death of Emperor Henry III the papacy gained the initiative during the long minority of Henry IV, and Pope Gregory VII for a time was effective in asserting the claims of the papacy during the Investiture Controversy. See Geoffrey Barraclough, *Origins of Modern Germany* (Oxford: Blackwell, 1947), 120–27. Subsequently, the Hohenstaufen emperors as well as Henry VII attempted to reassert imperial control of Italy (Schevill, *History of Florence*, 77, 80–86, 93–96, 179–93).

11. Cesare actually did the dirty work, of course. In chapter 7 of *The Prince* Machiavelli furnishes a memorable description of Cesare's technique in the Romagna.

12. For a discussion of Machiavelli's intimations about what Cesare should have done to solidify his rule, see John T. Scott and Vickie B. Sullivan, "Patricide and the Plot of *The Prince*: Cesare Borgia and Machiavelli's Italy," *American Political Science Review* 88 (December 1994): 887–99. To maintain power Cesare would have had to end the rule of the papacy.

13. See also *FH* 8.17, where Machiavelli describes the deliberation among Florentines over forming an alliance with the pope. Machiavelli reports that they rejected this course because they deemed it unreliable: "for the shortness of life of popes, the change through succession, the slight fear that the Church has of princes, and the few scruples it has in adopting courses require that a secular prince cannot have entire confidence in a pontiff or safely share his fortune with him. For in wars and dangers, whoever is friend of the pope will be accompanied in victories and be alone in defeats, since the pontiff is sustained and defended by spiritual power and reputation" (*FH* 8.17.338).

14. The reign of Hadrian VI intervened. Pope Leo commissioned the *Florentine Histories* in 1520, and the work was presented to Clement VII in 1525.

15. Baron responds to the general challenge to his thesis of this analysis of the papacy's role in Italian disunity by declaring that "this Italian perspective of the twelfth chapter [of the *Discourses*], I am sure, can be shown to be a later insertion, probably not made until the role of the papacy in preventing the unification of the peninsula had been discovered in detail during Machiavelli's historical studies for his *Istorie fiorentine*" ("*Principe* and the Puzzle," 102). Baron's response is inadequate in my view because both the *Discourses* and *The Prince* reveal Machiavelli's deep-seated dissatisfaction with the role the Church played in Italian politics. The dating of the writing and the order of composition of the *Discourses* became an intensely debated topic among prominent scholars of Machiavelli during the mid-twentieth century. Although many divergent views were expressed, no single theory has disposed of the issue, although it is agreed that 1513 is the earliest date at which Machiavelli could have begun the work, and no scholar looks beyond 1519 for its completion. For accounts of the controversy see Eric Cochrane, "Machiavelli: 1940–1960," *Journal of Modern History* 33 (June 1961): 133–36; Gilbert, "Modern Historical Scholarship," 18–22; Harvey C. Mansfield, Jr., "Necessity in the Beginnings of Cities," in *The Political Calculus: Essays on Machiavelli's Philosophy*, ed. Anthony Parel (Toronto: University of Toronto Press, 1972), 101–4.

16. See also Machiavelli's letter to Vettori of 20 December 1514 for a discussion of Julius's accomplishments (*CW* 2:954).

17. In 1520, upon the death of Lorenzo de' Medici, Pope Leo X commissioned Machiavelli to write "A Discourse on Remodeling the Government of Florence." At this time Florence was controlled by the papacy because now the two remaining heirs of the Medicean line were men of the Church (see Schevill, *History of Florence*, 471–82). In this discourse Machiavelli offers advice that would permit a newly constituted Florentine republic to live after the deaths of Pope Leo and Cardinal Giuliano de' Medici.

18. Having seen Italy become host to a multitude of foreign interests and armies, Machiavelli could support Louis's endeavor to reclaim Lombardy in his letter of 10 August 1513 to Francesco Vettori. The republic for which Machiavelli had worked maintained a pro-French position.

19. Machiavelli uses the ancient term for the French here, "*Galli*" (*O* 940). In other writings Machiavelli is partial to the modern term *French* when referring to the ancient people, the Gauls, particularly when speaking of the Gallic invasion of Rome. See, e.g., *Discourses* 1.7,

2.29, and 3.1. Machiavelli seems to think these two invasions of Italy at the hands of the French are interchangeable in some way. On this possibility see 3.36 of the *Discourses:* "The causes why the French have been and are still judged in fights, as more than men at the beginning, and later as less than women." In the case of ancient Rome, Camillus returned from exile to save Rome from the humiliation of making peace with money (*D* 2.30). Also in the *Discourses* (3.1) Machiavelli claims that this near catastrophe reinvigorated Rome. One wonders what event in Machiavelli's view could turn the contemporary disaster into a benefit for modern Rome or Italy.

20. See Edward Gibbon's discussion of these events in *Decline and Fall of the Roman Empire,* 3 vols. (New York: Modern Library, n.d.), 2:447–64.

21. Those who were subjugating Italy in Machiavelli's time were also Christian, of course. He clearly holds the conquerors in contempt despite their victories. In *Discourses* 1.55 he asserts that the Spanish, French, and Italians constitute "the corruption of the world" (*D* 1.55.3). In *Discourses* 2.30 he points out that the king of France "lives as a tributary of the Swiss and the king of England" (*D* 2.30.2). See also *Discourses* 3.15 on the defectiveness of French and Italian armies and 2.16 for a discussion of the weakness of "Christian armies" generally (*D* 2.16.2).

22. In the *Discourses* Machiavelli also refers to *"i peccati de' principi italiani"* who have enslaved Italy to foreigners through their depreciation of infantry, and hence reliance on the cavalry of the *condottieri* (*D* 2.18; *O* 172). See also his statement that Italy "has been sacked, ruined and overrun by foreigners for no other sin [*peccato*] than that she has given little attention to soldiers on foot and put all her soldiers on horseback" (*AW* 2.602; *O* 321). He promotes the benefits of infantry in his discussions of mercenaries also in *The Prince* (e.g., 52, 56).

23. Machiavelli elaborates: "The arms of Italy, therefore, were in the hands of lesser princes or of men without a state; for the lesser princes, unmoved by any glory, wore them so as to live either more rich or more secure, and the others, nurtured in them since childhood and not knowing any other art, sought to be honored for them by having them or by power" (*FH* 1.39.50).

24. See *FH* 1.1 for Machiavelli's treatment of Theodosius's use of the Visigoths as mercenaries. In the *Discourses* Machiavelli also discusses the unhappy result for the Roman Empire of disarming the populace: when Rome "entered under the emperors, and the emperors began to be bad and to love the shade more than the sun, they also began to buy themselves off, now from the Parthians, now from the Germans, now from other peoples round about, which was the beginning of the

ruin of so great an empire" (*D* 2.30.2). Giuseppe Prezzolini links this particular passage to the "'lazy ambition'" of the Christians (*Machiavelli*, trans. Gioconda Savini [New York: Farrar, Straus & Giroux, 1967], 26–27). These payments occurred long before the time of Theodosius. The Romans made such a grant to the Parthians in 227 A.D. See *Discourses*, trans. Walker, 2:142–43. See also Fabrizio's discussion of the preference of the moderns for the shade in contrast to the ancients who did things in the sun (*AW* 1.570).

25. In the *Florentine Histories* Machiavelli links the increasing influence of Christianity and its Roman bishops to the decline of the Roman Empire. "For the first [popes] after Saint Peter had been revered by men for the holiness of their lives and for the miracles, and their examples so extended the Christian religion that princes had necessarily to submit to it so as to dispel the great confusion abroad in the world" (1.9.19).

26. Parel furnishes an excellent exposition of Machiavelli's depiction of the class conflict in Florence (*Machiavellian Cosmos*, 140–52) but does not treat Machiavelli's descriptions of the role that the Church played in these conflicts.

27. Machiavelli claims in the proem of the first book of the *Discourses* that a certain species of leisure [*ozio*] characterizes the Christian era. I examine the character of this Christian leisure in the next chapter.

28. For example, he criticizes those "barons" of Rome, the Orsini and Colonna, and calls them *"oziosi principi"* (*FH* 1.39; *O* 658).

29. See also Prezzolini, *Machiavelli*, 60.

30. See Burckhardt's description of "the great wealth and easy lives" of the Benedictines during this time (*Civilization of the Renaissance*, 448).

31. For the castles of the clergy, see particularly *FH* 5.27. See also Pasquale Villari, *The Life and Times of Niccolò Machiavelli*, trans. Linda Villari, 2 vols. (London: T. Fisher Unwin, n.d.), 1:45.

32. Cesare Borgia had performed for his father the bloody service of minimizing the influence of the barons of Rome, the Orsini and Colonna, and the succeeding popes continued to persecute these families (*P* 7 and 11). Whereas the power of these gentlemen of Rome was greatly diminished, the clerical variety of these gentlemen still flourished in the city. See Burckhardt's comment in *Civilization of the Renaissance*: Cesare "had earned the gratitude of all the following Popes by ridding them of the Orsini and Colonna" (129).

33. Cf. Walker, who terms this statement a "frank recognition . . . that providence watches out not merely over the Church but over the temporal estates of the Pope" (*Discourses* 1:117).

34. De Grazia interprets this discussion as showing only

Machiavelli's intense admiration for these two saints (*Machiavelli in Hell*, 90–92, 111).

35. In chapter 3 of *The Prince* Machiavelli observes that the Turk has a bloodline (18). Thus the Turk is to be distinguished from the Christian pontificate and the state of the Sultan.

36. See Machiavelli's description of *"i principi orientali"* in *Discourses* 2.2 (O 150).

37. In the *Florentine Histories* Machiavelli describes how before the reforms of Francis and Dominick the people of Rome rebelled against the Church's dominion in its city (e.g., 1.14).

38. Baron claims that Machiavelli's great hopes for a invigorated Italy were nurtured in January 1515, after he learned of Leo's plans for a state for Guiliano. Machiavelli, then, gained this knowledge one month after he committed the following speculations to paper (Baron, "*Principe* and the Puzzle," 97–100).

39. Machiavelli adds that a canzone of Petrarch inspired Porcari to aid his homeland in this particular way. (Machiavelli ends *The Prince* with a passage from Petrarch's poetry.)

40. Livy reports that Camillus was hailed "as a Romulus and Father of his Country and a second Founder of the City," when he returned from exile to expel the Gauls from Rome (*Ab urbe condita* 5.49, trans. B. O. Foster [Loeb Classical Library], 167).

41. Machiavelli's comment here seems very much in the spirit of his maxim in *The Prince:* "And truly it is a very natural and ordinary thing to desire to acquire, and always, when men do it who can they will be praised or not blamed; but when they cannot, and want to do it anyway, here lie the error and the blame" (*P* 3.14–15).

42. Hulliung draws the same conclusion: "Machiavelli more than hinted that the time had come for a political takeover of the church. Where Stefano Porcari and Cesare Borgia had failed, others could succeed" (*Citizen Machiavelli*, 217).

43. See Exod. 32:27–28 RSV.

44. Cf. Livy *Ab urbe condita* 1.7 and 14. I treat Machiavelli's exaggeration of Romulus's crimes in chapter 6. Perhaps this exaggeration derives from Machiavelli's recognizing the magnitude of the crime necessary to found a new Rome, a new power in Italy that would become its head, in the modern era.

45. De Grazia writes: "Anticlericalism is nothing to write home about, nor has it been for the last one thousand years." Nevertheless, de Grazia goes on to deny that Machiavelli even ventures into the territory of ordinary anticlericalism: "Niccolò is not a priest-hater. Strictly speaking, his position is not anti-clerical: it is better described as reform clerical" (*Machiavelli in Hell*, 90).

Chapter 2: The Ravages of Christianity

1. *Citizen Machiavelli,* 66, 68. See also Isaiah Berlin on this point: "What the [Church] has done is to lead, on the one hand, to corruption and political division—the fault of the papacy—and on the other, to other-worldliness and meek endurance of suffering on earth for the sake of the eternal life beyond the grave" ("The Originality of Machiavelli," in *Against the Current* [New York: Viking Press, 1980], 48).

2. Hulliung calls the *Discourses* Machiavelli's "most stridently pagan work" (*Citizen Machiavelli,* 246). Compare Hulliung's statement with that of Ridolfi: "through the centuries there was built up layer by layer a mass of prejudices under which the religious and Christian conscience of the Florentine Secretary was deeply buried" (Roberto Ridolfi, *Life of Niccolò Machiavelli,* trans. Cecil Grayson [Chicago: University of Chicago Press, 1963], 253).

3. In 1.11 of the *Discourses* Machiavelli ventures an interpretation of this earlier statement when he asserts that the human order has not changed: "No one, therefore, should be terrified that he cannot carry out what has been carried out by others, for as was said in our preface, men are born, live, and die always in one and the same *ordine*" (D 1.11.5; O 95).

4. *City of God,* 5.16, trans. William M. Green (Loeb Classical Library), 219.

5. In *The Art of War* Christianity also serves as the reason for the lapse from the military virtue of the ancients. In explaining the inability of the moderns to reinstitute the practices of the Romans, Fabrizio asserts: "One reason why is that to resume customs after they have been destroyed takes time; another is that our way of living today, as a result of the Christian religion, does not impose the same necessity for defending ourselves as antiquity did" (*AW* 2.623).

6. Parel, *Machiavellian Cosmos,* 47; cf. *Discourses,* trans. Walker, 2:34.

7. Matt. 5:10, 39 RSV. For a discussion of the early Christian belief in the imminence of God's reign of earth, see Robert M. Grant, *Augustus to Constantine: The Rise and Triumph of Christianity in the Roman World* (San Francisco: Harper & Row, 1970), 40–52. Clearly this immediate expectation minimized early Christianity's concern with things mundane.

8. Machiavelli's only mention of Christ in the *Discourses* appears in 3.1: Dominick and Francis "with poverty and with the example of the life of Christ . . . brought back into the minds of men what had already been eliminated there [that is, Christianity]" (D 3.1.4).

9. Cf. Geerken's statement: "Since earliest Christianity (because of

its eschatology) was almost totally silent regarding politics, Machiavelli cannot legitimately be contraposed to it" ("Machiavelli Studies," 367). In making this judgment Geerken does not acknowledge that Machiavelli, at least at one point, wishes to appeal—no matter how fallaciously—to the political utility of ancient Christianity.

10. Cf. de Grazia, *Machiavelli in Hell,* 89.

11. The leader of the Church, whom Ferdinand most famously dominated, was Pope Sixtus IV. Sixtus became Ferdinand's instrument in religious persecution, when Ferdinand forced the pope to acquiesce to his demand for the establishment of the Spanish Inquisition. In 1478 Sixtus granted to the Spanish king the right to appoint inquisitors to deal with Jews who had converted to Christianity. After opposition arose to the severity of these inquisitors, Sixtus attempted to block the application of the inquisitors' authority to Aragon, but he ultimately succumbed to the demands of Ferdinand to recognize the independence of the Inquisition. In this manner Sixtus allowed King Ferdinand and Queen Isabella to lay the groundwork for the edict of expulsion of the Jews, which they signed in 1492. The expulsion occurred after the death of Sixtus in 1484.

12. In a note to his translation Mansfield suggests that this prince is Ferdinand and points out that Machiavelli names him openly in chapter 21.

13. Pope Alexander VI bestowed on Ferdinand the honorary title of "the Catholic" in 1496.

14. Cf. Strauss's ascription of a more principled basis to Machiavelli's rejection of Ferdinand's example ("What Is Political Philosophy?," 44).

15. Walker declares that Machiavelli "comments scathingly" on Ferdinand in *The Prince* (*Discourses,* 1:106).

16. Machiavelli considers growing population as an indicator of political health and liberty (*D* 2.2 and 3).

17. William H. Prescott reports that Bajazet, the sultan of the Ottomans during this time, commented: "'Do they call this Ferdinand a politic prince, who can thus impoverish his own kingdom and enrich ours!'" (*History of the Reign of Ferdinand and Isabella, the Catholic, of Spain,* 3d ed., 3 vols. [London: Richard Bentley, 1842], 2:137). The next section will treat Machiavelli's injunction "to love" subject people by making them soldiers. Henry Kamen locates the most important cause of the hostility to the Jews in Spain in their prominent role in financial activity, primarily as tax collectors and officials to the court (Kamen, *The Spanish Inquisition* [New York: New American Library, 1965], 15–17).

18. In his chapter on fortresses in the *Discourses,* Machiavelli comments that the mistreatment of subjects coming from the use of fortresses will weaken a prince's rule. For a discussion of the manner in which Machiavelli's criticism of a faith in the use of fortresses resembles

a belief in fixity, see Sheldon Wolin, *Politics and Vision: Continuity and Innovation in Western Political Thought* (Boston: Little, Brown, 1960), 212–13. See also D 3.27. Because Machiavelli explicitly links fortresses with the papacy (*Discourses* 2.24.2), and because the basis for Machiavelli's criticism of fortresses is that they make you more audacious and more violent toward your subjects (D 2.24.1), his criticism of fortresses appears to replicate a criticism of religious persecution. The ultimate basis for his dissatisfaction with the use of fortresses is not that it is hurtful to a prince's subjects, but rather to the prince's own rule.

19. This judgment of Ferdinand conforms to the sentiments that Machiavelli expresses in a letter to Vettori dated 29 April 1513: "I have always thought Spain more crafty and fortunate than wise and prudent" (CW 2:904). As my discussion of Numa in chapter 5 will show, Machiavelli believes leaders who base their rule on a belief in another world depend on fortune. But even in this letter, which offers such strident criticism of the Spanish king, Machiavelli goes on to praise his actions when he casts Ferdinand in a new light, proposing to "abandon my opinion and consider him prudent, and let us discuss his decision as that of a wise man" (906). Machiavelli's subsequent praise in this letter bears a strong resemblance to what he will write in chapter 21 of *The Prince*: "This king from a slight and weak position has come to his present greatness, and has had always to struggle with new states and distrusted subjects. Yet one of the ways with which new states are held, and unsure minds are either made firm or are kept uncertain and unresolved, is to rouse great expectations about oneself, all the time keeping men's minds occupied in considering what is going to be the end of new decisions and new undertakings." After giving Ferdinand's undertakings in Granada, Africa, and Naples as examples of this method of proceeding, Machiavelli claims in this letter that the king "saw the end of none of these; indeed his end is not a particular gain or a particular victory but to give himself reputation among his people and to keep them uncertain among the great number of his affairs. Therefore he is a spirited maker of beginnings [*Et però lui fu sempre animoso datore di principii*], to which he later gives the particular end that is placed before him by chance and that necessity teaches him" (909; O 1139). In this manner, Machiavelli admires Ferdinand's craft as a *datore* of beginnings but cannot wholeheartedly embrace his example because he is not the type of *datore* who envisions the end of an entirely different use of Christianity (cf. D 2.2)— the type of *datore* that Machiavelli himself represents. For an acute alternative reading of this letter and its bearing on Machiavelli's view of himself, which does not address the problem of Christianity, see John M. Najemy, *Between Friends: Discourses of Power and Desire in the Machiavelli–Vettori Letters of 1513–1515* (Princeton: Princeton University

Press, 1993), 126–35. Najemy notes perceptively that the "picture of the Ferdinand who tries one thing and then something else, who never waits for the verdict on a particular action before beginning another, and thus keeps everyone watching him in a state of suspense and wonderment, seems a perfect description of Machiavelli's letter to Vettori." According to Najemy's analysis this picture exemplifies "a recurring and apparently irresistible temptation on Machiavelli's part to . . . transfer himself into his image or representation of political figures who stood for, indeed were exemplars of, power and success." This "was a way of neutralizing, or domesticating, the threat Ferdinand represented, by reducing or subjecting it to Machiavelli's power to understand" (134–35).

20. In linking Christianity to political division here, he mirrors his indictment of the Church for creating division within Italy (*D* 1.12). Also in this chapter Machiavelli claims provocatively that "all these modes and these opinions diverging from the truth arise from the weakness of whoever is lord [*signore*]" (*D* 3.27.4; *O* 234).

21. The chapter titles of *The Prince* are given in Latin.

22. Orwin, "Unchristian Charity," 1217–28. For Orwin's discussion of Machiavelli's repudiation of this Christian virtue, see 1222–26. See also Ernst Troeltsch's characterization of this virtue in *The Social Teaching of the Christian Church*, trans. Olive Wyon, 2 vols. (1931; reprint, Louisville: Westminster/John Knox Press, 1992), 1:54: "Since God is active, creative Love, who maketh His sun to rise upon the evil and upon the good, so men who are consecrated to God ought to manifest their love to friend and foe, to the good and to the bad, overcoming hostility and defiance by a generous love which will break down all barriers and awaken love in return."

23. John 13:34 RSV.

24. In this manner, although the Church ultimately felled Cesare's enterprise when Cesare relied on a belief that another would forgive him, Cesare appears to have escaped from Christianity's shadow at least to the extent that he repudiated Christianity's mistaken notion of mercy in his handling of the Romagna.

25. Wolin, *Politics and Vision*, 220–24

26. Cf. Livy, *Ab urbe condita* 8.13.

27. *Oxford Latin Dictionary* (Oxford: Clarendon Press, 1973), s.v. "humilis."

28. James 4:6 RSV.

29. Aquinas, *Summa contra gentiles*, 4.55, trans. Charles J. O'Neil, (Notre Dame: Notre Dame University, 1975), 243.

30. Commentators are divided on the question of how seriously Machiavelli's statements on the power of fortune are to be taken. Strauss, for example, discerns "a movement from God to Fortuna and

then from Fortune via accidents, and accidents occurring to bodies or accidents of bodies, to chance understood as a non-teleological necessity
which leaves room for choice and prudence and therefore for chance understood as the cause of simply unforeseeable accidents" (*Thoughts*,
213–23). Pitkin agrees with Strauss that Machiavelli links fortune with
external accident but finds it significant that Machiavelli chooses to oppose human design with a figure that is "a large senior female person."
According to Pitkin's analysis, Machiavelli's depiction of this malevolent
force arises from his ambivalence toward manhood and "anxiety about
being sufficiently masculine and concern over what it means to be a
man" (*Fortune Is a Woman*, 164–65, 4). Ernst Cassirer finds Machiavelli's depiction of fortune as indicative of a different type of defect in
Machiavelli's attempt to reduce the world to human control. Machiavelli's attempt to construct a political science was confronted with the
unexpected in human affairs: "His logical and rational method deserted
him at this point." Being so deserted, Machiavelli created a "half-myth-
ical power" (*The Myth of the State*, [New Haven: Yale University Press,
1946], 157). See also Parel's interpretation that claims that the "empires
of heaven and Fortune set a limit to what human autonomy can accomplish" (*Machiavellian Cosmos*, 63–85). For a summary of the views of
commentators as of 1972 on the subject of fortune, see Thomas Flanagan, "The Concept of *Fortuna* in Machiavelli," in Parel, ed., *Political
Calculus*.

    31. Machiavelli ascribes this view to Livy "for it is rare that he
makes any Roman speak where he tells of virtue and does not add fortune to it" (*D* 2.1.1). Cf. Parel's discussion of this chapter in *Machiavellian Cosmos*, 72. In arguing that Machiavelli holds a premodern view of
the universe, which rejects human autonomy because the motions of the
heavens fundamentally determine human action, Parel dismisses much of
Machiavelli's boldness in this chapter. He says for example: "His
polemics against Livy and Plutarch might give the false impression that
he ignores Fortune in favour of *virtù*. He only chastises them for attributing too much to Fortune. He readily concedes that it was due to
Fortune that Rome did not have to fight two major wars simultaneously,
and that she could take on her enemies one by one." In citing this example of Machiavelli's view of fortune's role in the order of Rome's wars
with its neighbors, Parel neglects Machiavelli's later analysis of Rome's
use of fraud in its order of prosecuting them (see particularly *D* 2.13).
By this use of fraud the Romans eschewed fortune as such and utilized
virtue of a decidedly Machiavellian sort.

    32. Near the end of the second book of the *Discourses* Machi-
avelli delivers a somewhat different message on fortune: "I affirm it indeed anew to be very true, according to what is seen through all the

histories, that men can second fortune but not oppose it, that they can weave its warp but not break it. They should indeed never give up for, since they do not know its end and it goes by oblique and unknown ways, they have always to hope and, since they hope, not to give up in whatever fortune and in whatever travail they may find themselves" (*D* 2.29.3). Reflection on the events that lead to the Gallic invasion of Rome produces these melancholic musings; however, two chapters later, in 3.1, with reference to the same Roman event Machiavelli produces a plan to control political life by extending the life of a regime. As that plan mixes Roman history with Machiavelli's own understanding of the strength of modern times, that chapter will be treated later (chapter 7).

33. Cf. Walker's statement that Machiavelli "in his own pagan way admits" that God guides the world (*Discourses,* 1:8).

34. Augustine, *City of God* 5.1, 135.

35. Dante Alighieri, *De monarchia,* 2.1, trans. Herbert W. Schneider (Indianapolis: Library of Liberal Arts, 1957), 24.

36. For Aquinas's comments on the sacrament of penance see particularly *Summa contra gentiles* 4.72.

37. Obviously, Machiavelli is concerned not with theological disputation, but with the general and practical effect of Christian doctrine. Cf. "Free Will and Free Choice," in *The Cambridge History of Later Medieval Philosophy,* ed. Norman Kretzmann, Anthony Kenny, and Jan Pinborg (Cambridge: Cambridge University Press, 1982).

38. As we shall see in chapter 7, Machiavelli adapts the Christian notion of sinfulness to his republic.

39. Augustine, *City of God* 5.12–14.

40. Compare Machiavelli's declaration in the *Discourses:* "princes are always spoken of with a thousand fears and a thousand hesitations" (*D* 1.58.4).

41. He calls Christendom the *republica christiana* in 1.12 of the *Discourses* (*O* 95).

42. 2 Cor. 10: 3–6 RSV.

43. He does add here, however, that anyone who wants further confirmation of his opinion should read Xenophon's work "*Of Tyranny.*"

44. The character of Machiavelli's unconventional republic that eschews the rule of the Christian god will be treated in chapter 7.

Chapter 3: The Foundation for Tyranny in Rome

1. For the significance of Machiavelli's embrace of Rome's class conflict, see Skinner, *Renaissance,* 181–82; Skinner, *Machiavelli,* 65–67;

and Quentin Skinner, "Machiavelli's *Discorsi* and the Pre-Humanist Origins of Republican Ideas," in *Machiavelli and Republicanism,* 135–36.

2. In *Discourses* 1.2 Machiavelli exaggerates Sparta's longevity by claiming that the orders of Lycurgus lasted more than eight hundred years (*D* 1.2; *Discourses,* trans. Walker, 2:6–7; Mansfield, *Modes and Orders,* 39). In a note to their translation Mansfield and Tarcov observe that Machiavelli thus identifies Sparta's downfall as the time when Rome absorbed Sparta under Augustus (n. 2 to *D* 1.2). In *D* 1.6.4, however, Machiavelli places Sparta's downfall much earlier when he says that Sparta was "altogether ruined" when Thebes rebelled. This rebellion occurred in 379 B.C. (see also *D* 2.3). As for the case of Venice, Machiavelli says the Venetians lost at Vailà "what they had acquired with such trouble in eight hundred years" (*P* 12.52). Their loss occurred in 1509. See *Discourses* 2.31 and "Second Decennale," 172–95, for more detailed descriptions of this loss (*CW* 3:1461).

3. See, e.g., Aristotle, *Politics* 1325a1–15, 1333a35–b4, and 1271a42–1271b11; Plato, *Laws* 628d–e.

4. On this basis Hulliung aligns Machiavelli with the Roman historians against Greek philosophy (*Citizen Machiavelli,* esp. pp. 136–37). In contrast Viroli maintains that for Machiavelli the "fundamental obligation of the good ruler must be to seek peace and the security of his subjects: it is for the sake of peace and the protection of his subjects, not for the sake of war and conquest, that he has to know how to make war" (*From Politics,* 164). In support of this reading Viroli looks not to the *Discourses* but to the dialogue *The Art of War.*

5. J. G. A. Pocock claims that Machiavelli rejects Sparta on the basis of its long existence; its case is not interesting to Machiavelli because "a formula for timelessness was written in a single moment by a legislator virtually independent of time" (*The Machiavellian Moment: Florentine Political Thought and the Atlantic Republican Tradition* [Princeton: Princeton University Press, 1975], 190; see also 197). Pocock then reverses himself on the reason for Machiavelli's rejection of Sparta when he mentions Machiavelli's treatment of Sparta's downfall, and thus concedes that Machiavelli discerns a critical fault in Sparta's constitution (198).

6. Plutarch reports that it was during the life of Tiberius Gracchus that blood was first spilled in a sedition in Rome since the expulsion of the kings (*Tiberius and Caius Gracchus* 20).

7. This conclusion agrees with his declaration in *The Prince* that "truly it is a very natural and ordinary thing to desire to acquire" (*P* 3.14).

8. Pocock's interpretation of the *Discourses* does not emphasize Machiavelli's embrace of Rome's class conflict, and when Pocock does navigate close to the subject, he obscures the causes of the conflict. When

treating Machiavelli's observation that for a republic to make use of its people in important enterprises, it must give them an outlet for their ambition, Pocock renders *ambizione* as a more temperate "aspirations" (*Machiavellian Moment*, 196).

9. See also Aristotle, *Politics* 1318b16–17: "for the mass of mankind are more covetous of gain than of honor," trans. H. Rackham (Loeb Classical Library), 499.

10. See also his admonishment to a prince to "abstain from the property of others, because men forget the death of a father more quickly than the loss of a patrimony" (*P* 17.67).

11. Cf. Heb. 11:1 RSV: "Now faith is the assurance of things hoped for, the conviction of things not seen."

12. Cf. Mansfield's discussion of Machiavelli's statement that the law "turned Rome upside down" (*New Modes and Orders*, 122).

13. Livy notes (2.41) that the first agrarian law was proposed during the consulship of Spurius Cassius and Proculus Verginius in 486–85 B.C.

14. Machiavelli notes that liberality played a similar role in Cosimo de' Medici's ascent to power in Florence (*FH* 4.26–27).

15. Rinaldo was the enemy of Cosimo de' Medici and opposed Cosimo's exile, advocating that he be killed instead (*FH* 4.29). Rinaldo's cause was ruined when he followed the advice of Pope Eugene to lay down his arms (*FH* 4.32–33).

16. 16 April 1527. The translation is my own from O 1250. In the *Florentine Histories* he relates that Cosimo de' Medici's enemies charged him with loving this world more than the next (7.6).

17. Machiavelli discusses the siege and capture of Veii in his section on religion, *Discourses* 1.12 and 13.

18. In the text Machiavelli refers to *De monarchia;* the passage is to be found in *Convivio* 1.11.54 (*Discourses*, trans. Walker, 2:83).

19. Cf. Mansfield, *New Modes and Orders*, 158.

20. Again, Augustine's claim that the appeal of the Eternal City is much more alluring than that of any earthly city appears to be relevant to this discussion (*City of God* 5.16). Mansfield discusses the divided city of Rome in a different context in his consideration of *Discourses* 1.57 in *New Modes and Orders*, 167.

21. See 1 Pet. 2:11 RSV: "Beloved, I beseech you as aliens and exiles to abstain from the passions of the flesh that wage war against your soul."

Chapter 4: Corruption, Youth, and Foreign Influences

1. *Machiavellian Moment*, 184. Skinner (*Renaissance*, 164) offers a similar depiction of Machiavelli's view of corruption: "what

[Machiavelli] basically has in mind in speaking of 'corruption' is a failure to devote one's energies to the common good, and a corresponding tendency to place one's own interests above those of the community." See also Skinner's *Machiavelli*, 56–57, and "Machiavelli's *Discorsi*," 138–39.

2. Skinner ultimately concludes that "Machiavelli . . . is a consistent, an almost Hobbesian sceptic about the possibility of inducing men to behave well except by cajolery or force" (*Renaissance*, 185).

3. This conclusion accords with that of Bonadeo on the issue: "the source of corruption is identified by Machiavelli with a narrow social and political group: the rich, the powerful, and the nobles; to this group, furthermore, belongs the responsibility for spreading the disease throughout the commonwealth" (*Corruption*, 34).

4. Mansfield, *New Modes and Orders*, 85.

5. Four chapters later, when discussing the ominous threat that the agrarian law presented to Rome, Machiavelli recommends the same strategy of temporization and, indeed, refers to the earlier chapter: "As was discoursed of above at length, one does nothing but accelerate the evil to which the disorder is leading you; but by temporizing with it, either the evil comes later or it eliminates itself on its own with time, before it reaches its end" (*D* 1.37.3).

6. Machiavelli refrains in this chapter from calling Caesar's Florentine associate a tyrant. See the speech Machiavelli assigns to Niccolò da Uzzano in the *Florentine Histories*, which acknowledges "the suspicion" surrounding Cosimo that "a prince may be established in this city" (*FH* 4.27.175, see also 7.1 and *P* 9).

7. See particularly Mansfield, *Modes and Orders*, 32–41, and Harvey C. Mansfield, Jr., "Machiavelli's Political Science," *American Political Science Review* 75 (1981): 301–2.

8. Polybius, *Histories*, trans. W. R. Paton (Loeb Classical Library, 1923), 6.5.1–2. Translations from the Greek are mine.

9. Ibid., 6.5.4–7.

10. Ibid., 6.5.7.

11. Ibid., 6.5.8 and 6.4.7.

12. Ibid., 6.6.4–5. Polybius uses the word *logismos* for reason, rather than the more common *logos*. The former term carries the additional meaning of a reckoning or calculation, and Polybius utilizes it perhaps because these observers are weighing past benefits received against current conduct, which here results in an unequal accounting. In this manner the conduct that produces this unequal accounting is determined to be unjust.

13. Ibid., 6.6.6–9.

14. Cf. his statement in *Discourses* 1.33.2 that a youth becomes

dangerous when his ambition mixes "with the favor that nature" has given him.

15. Mansfield, *New Modes and Orders*, 35-36.

16. Polybius, *Histories* 6.10.6-11; Mansfield, *New Modes and Orders*, 39.

17. Polybius, *Histories* 6.57.

18. Mansfield, *New Modes and Orders*, 38-39. Skinner cites Machiavelli's use of Polybius's cycle to claim that Machiavelli "accepts the ultimately fatalistic view that, in spite of the best efforts of our statecraft, there is an inexorable cycle of growth and decay through which all commonwealths must pass" (*Renaissance*, 187). In this conclusion Skinner fails to note the way Machiavelli in this very chapter utilizes foreign relations to question the inexorableness of this cycle.

19. This issue will be treated in more detail in chapter 7.

20. Mansfield in *New Modes and Orders*, 34-35, and "Machiavelli's Political Science," 301, and Rahe in *Republics Ancient and Modern*, 410-11, both recognize that Machiavelli does not accept the distinction between the correct and incorrect version of each regime. Nevertheless, Machiavelli is intensely interested in the cause of tyranny in the republic of Rome and how to prevent a reoccurrence of such tyranny.

21. Livy, *Ab urbe condita* 7.38.5.

22. Mansfield equates Capua with Jerusalem (*New Modes and Orders*, 251). Cf. Skinner, *Renaissance*, 163; Pitkin, *Fortune Is a Woman*, 117.

23. Grant, *Augustus to Constantine*, ix.

24. Juvenal, *Satires* 6.292-93. Juvenal devotes this satire to a denunciation of the depravity of Roman women.

25. *Satires* 1.155-57.

26. Livy notes that the practice had been introduced into Italy when a Greek of humble origin arrived in Etruria (*Ab urbe condita* 39.8).

27. Ibid., 39.18.

28. I thus disagree with Hulliung's assertion that "Machiavelli did not explain how the slavish Christians triumphed over the masterful pagans." Hulliung, in claiming that Machiavelli did not apply himself to this question, notes that he was not, after all, the author of *Genealogy of Morals* (*Citizen Machiavelli*, 248).

29. Cf. Machiavelli's discussion of the grave threat posed by Rome's neighbors in *Discourses* 1.33.

Chapter 5: Machiavelli's Ambiguous Praise of Paganism

1. For forceful presentations of this view, see Villari, *Life and Times*, 2:92–93; Berlin, "Originality of Machiavelli," 54–55, 63–64; Hulliung, *Citizen Machiavelli*, 8, 28, 227–28, 245–46; Parel, *Machiavellian Cosmos*, 51–52, 61.

2. *Myth of the State*, 138. See also J. W. Allen, *A History of Political Thought in the Sixteenth Century* (London: Methuen, 1928), 458–59.

3. Skinner, *Machiavelli*, 62–63.

4. Hulliung, *Citizen Machiavelli*, 45. Machiavelli's presentation of the Roman religion differs from Livy's. Whereas Livy maintains that during the early part of the republic the patricians were pious, Machiavelli intimates that the patricians were always so impious that they used the divine to obtain their own results. Compare, for example, Machiavelli's citation of Livy's praise for the piety that reigned during the ancient republic and his own censure of the piety of his own time in *Discourses* 1.13 with the title of 1.14: "The Romans interpreted the auspices according to necessity, and with prudence made a show of observing religion when forced not to observe it; and if anyone rashly disdained it, they punished him" (cf. Livy, *Ab urbe condita* 3.20).

5. Friedrich Meinecke, *Machiavellism: The Doctrine of Raison d'Etat and Its Place in Modern History*, trans. Douglas Scott (New Haven: Yale University Press, 1957), 35.

6. Fabrizio in Machiavelli's dialogue *The Art of War*, who refers to the ancient Romans as "my Romans" (e.g., *AW*, 571), approves of the manner in which the Romans used their religion to inspire their troops (661–62, 691, 699).

7. Machiavelli also brings up Pulcher's case in 3.33, saying that "[i]f any consul or other captain of theirs had come to combat against the auspices, they would have punished him as they punished Claudius Pulcher" (*D* 3.33.1). In 1.14 Machiavelli calls this irreverent commander Appius Pulcher; the full name was Appius Claudius Pulcher (*Discourses*, trans. Walker, 2:198).

8. Cf. *AW* 6.691.

9. Livy, *Ab urbe condita* 3.10.5–6.

10. Ibid., 3.10.6–10.

11. Strauss, *Thoughts*, 228.

12. Livy, *Ab urbe condita* 5.14.

13. Cf. ibid., 4.7.

14. Although Pitkin cites both passages, she does not acknowledge that Machiavelli's presentation of Romulus offers an exception to the

claim that founders require religion (*Fortune Is a Woman*, 89–90).

15. *P* 6. Machiavelli makes clear the reasons for this ultimate judgment later in the *Discourses* when Numa is compared unfavorably to his successor, Tullus. I treat Machiavelli's explicit criticism of Numa below.

16. Livy, *Ab urbe condita* 1.6.4–7.4 and 1.8.1. See also Plutarch, *Romulus* 22.1–2.

17. On this issue Machiavelli seems to be on the side of the nobles, as he insists on the necessity of war (*D* 1.6).

18. Pocock and Skinner find in Machiavelli's praise of Numa and of the ancient Roman religion support for their claim that Machiavelli endorses a republicanism that demands the sacrifice of selfish interests for the sake of the "common good" or "community." Pocock glosses over and Skinner ignores Machiavelli's reappraisal of Numa in the later chapters of the first book. See Pocock, *Machiavellian Moment*, 61–62, 64. Machiavelli's reappraisal of Numa also has consequences for Parel's argument, which maintains that Machiavelli is a neopagan for whom the cosmological ordainment of human affairs is primary (*Machiavellian Cosmos*, 62, 43). For this reason Parel makes much out of Machiavelli's declaration that the heavens inspired the Senate to elect Numa (46). In Machiavelli's revision of his earlier statements on Numa and in his discussion of the problems that arise when one effeminate prince succeeds another, such a weak successor appears to be merely a case of bad luck, particularly in the context of a hereditary monarchy (*D* 1.9). To maintain Parel's thesis, one would have to say that after Machiavelli's reappraisal he implies that the heavens desired to jeopardize the future of fledgling Rome in choosing Numa to be king.

Chapter 6: Old Lands and Machiavelli's New One

1. Skinner too relates corruption to Christianity (*Renaissance*, 167). See also Bonadeo, *Corruption*, 5–6.

2. Machiavelli's alacrity in forgiving Romulus's crimes must be contrasted with his refusal to forgive Cesare Borgia's missteps.

3. Livy, *Ab urbe condita* 2.14; Plutarch, *Romulus* 23.

4. Tarcov argues that Machiavelli appears to display "indifference as to whether these good ends achieved through bad means result from good men willing to use bad means or from bad men willing to seek good ends" ("Machiavelli's *Discourses on the First Decade of Titus Livy*," unpublished lecture delivered at Claremont McKenna College, 14 March 1993, 19).

5. Although the existence of republics in Florence, Siena, and Lucca point to the goodness of the material in Tuscany, Machiavelli suggests that Florence has not had a government that could be called a true republic. See *D* 1.49.

6. As we know, Machiavelli asserts that the Church has been the obstacle to the unification of Italy.

7. Cesare Borgia's deed at Sinigaglia furnishes a model of the way to accomplish such slaughter successfully (P 7).

8. Machiavelli shares with Moses the problem of envy. See 1.pr.1.

9. See also his statement in "A Discourse on Remodeling the Government of Florence": "Besides this, no man is so much exalted by any act of his as are those men who have with laws and with institutions remodeled republics and kingdoms; these are, after those who have been gods, the first to be praised" (CW 1:114).

10. He explains in this chapter that Moses found his people enslaved in Egypt, Romulus was not received in Alba, Cyrus found his people discontented with the rule of the Medes, and Theseus found the Athenians dispersed.

11. Machiavelli reveals the difficulty with such a procedure when discussing Savonarola. Machiavelli claims that Savonarola himself understood the necessity that impelled Moses "to kill infinite men." The friar, however, "was not understood well by those who followed him, who would have had authority for it. Nevertheless it did not obtain for him, and his sermons are full of accusations of the wise of the world, and of invectives against them, for so he called the envious and those who were opposed to his orders" (D 3.30.1).

12. Buondelmonti, to whom Machiavelli dedicates the Discourses, was exiled after an unsuccessful attempt in 1522 on the life of Guilio de' Medici, who was then a cardinal (Skinner, Machiavelli, 49). Guilio became Pope Clement VII the next year.

13. Despite the frustration he expresses here, that military and political leaders do not even think to imitate the ancients, Machiavelli later indicates that modern political leaders do quite consciously imitate the ancients and that their method of imitation results in military disaster: "When these idle [oziosi] princes or effeminate republics send out a captain of theirs, the wisest commission they think they give him is to impose on him that he not come to battle in some mode, indeed that above all he refrain from fighting. Since it appears to them they are imitating in this the prudence of Fabius Maximus who in deferring combat saved the state for the Romans, they do not understand that most often this commission is null or is harmful" (D 3.10.1; O 214). Thus Machiavelli again points to a problem with mere imitation—whether that problem emanates from the type of imitation the modern princes practice or from imitation simply.

14. Machiavelli does not mention here the Greek of the New Testament.

15. Francis Bacon asserts that Machiavelli's account here is too limited in scope: "As for the observation that Machiavel hath, that the

jealousy of sects doth much extinguish the memory of things, traducing Gregory the Great, that he did what in him lay to extinguish all heathen antiquities, I do not find that those zeals do any great effects, nor last long: as it appeared in the succession of Sabinian, who did revive the former antiquities" (essay 58 in *The Essays,* ed. John Pitcher [London: Penguin Books, 1985], 229).

16. One finds accounts of such disasters also in Plato. See *Critias* 111e–12a; *Timaeus* 22a–23c; *Laws* 677a–679e. The knower of antiquity who perverts his knowledge for his own purposes is absent from Plato's accounts. See also Polybius, *Histories* 6.5.4–6.

17. Cf. Gen. 6–9 RSV.

18. Cf. Plato, *Timaeus* 23a–b.

19. See Burckhardt, *Civilization of the Renaissance,* particularly 196–210, for a discussion of the endeavor of the humanists to recover the works of ancient authors.

20. In the preface to the first book he self-depreciatingly refers to his "weak knowledge of ancient things" (*D* 1.pr.1).

21. This perversion of antiquity is immediately evident in the presentation of the work as a commentary on Livy. Later in this chapter I argue that Machiavelli also transforms the Christian understanding to show that a new interpretation of the religion can result in political virtue (cf. *D* 2.2).

22. Burckhardt in particular portrays the humanists as dissatisfied with their own times and endeavoring to recover all aspects of antiquity, even elements of the pagan religion. This disposition brought them into disrepute during the Counter-Reformation. Cf. Giuseppe Toffanin's portrayal of the humanists as pious Christians (*History of Humanism,* trans. Elio Gianturco [New York: Las Americas, 1954]).

23. Fabrizio Colonna appears to represent humanist understanding in Machiavelli's *Art of War.* See Mansfield, "An Introduction to Machiavelli's *Art of War.*"

24. Jesus is, of course, the Greek form of the Hebrew name Joshua.

25. The countries that Machiavelli points to here as having experienced these name changes are the very ones that he cites as constituting the corruption of the world in *Discourses* 1.55.

26. He appears to wish to occupy Rome, however. Although this is an inhabited place, he suggests that his new understanding can insinuate itself quite peacefully there. Nevertheless, given his many bloodthirsty remarks, might he not countenance force as well as fraud in the capture of this land?

27. Cf. Gilbert's statement that the "dominating idea" in both *The Prince* and the *Discourses* "is an appeal to recognize the crucial importance of force in politics" (*Machiavelli and Guicciardini: Politics and*

History in Sixteenth-Century Florence, [1965; reprint, New York: Norton, 1984], 154).

28. Berlin, "Originality of Machiavelli," 64.

29. Mary Dietz makes an argument for reading Machiavelli in this fashion ("Trapping the Prince: Machiavelli and the Politics of Deception," *American Political Science Review* 80 [September 1986]: 777–99). Kahn details Machiavelli's use of "dichotomizing mode of argument, hyperbolic and theatrical style, apparent contradictions and deliberately failed examples" (*Machiavellian Rhetoric*, 26). Neither Dietz nor Kahn relates Machiavelli's rhetorical trickery to his opposition to Christianity.

30. Anthony Parel ("Machiavelli's Method and His Interpreters" in *Political Calculus*) traces the evolution of Machiavelli's reputation. See also Felix Gilbert, "Machiavellism," in *History: Choice and Commitment* (Cambridge, Mass.: Belknap Press, 1977), 155–76, and Cassirer, *Myth of the State*, 117–24. Machiavelli was placed on the Index in the sixteenth century and not removed until the nineteenth. Hulliung terms "revisionist" the contemporary republican scholarship that emphasizes the importance of liberty in Machiavelli's thought to the exclusion of power (*Citizen Machiavelli*, 4–5).

31. 1 Sam. 17:50–51 RSV.

Chapter 7: A Temporal Christianity and the Princes of the Republic

1. For Machiavelli's use of Christian doctrine for a temporal purpose see Harvey C. Mansfield, Jr., *Taming the Prince: The Ambivalence of Modern Executive Power* (New York: Free Press, 1989), 121–49.

2. Machiavelli's view of this Christian virtue was examined in chapter 2 above.

3. This Latin quotation appears to be manufactured. Walker states that the only occurrence of the words *poena* and *obsequiam* in the same sentence in Tacitus draws the opposite conclusion: "'Hence subservience toward a prince and the desire to emulate him counts for more than penalties imposed by laws and fear'" (Tacitus, *Annals* 3.55.5, cited in *Discourses*, trans. Walker, 2:183).

4. Machiavelli seems to be padding Manlius's résumé in order to draw this equivalence between the two consuls. Walker notes that Livy does not credit Manlius with a single triumph, but that Diodorus mentions one such honor (*Discourses*, trans. Walker, 2:187).

5. Machiavelli does not mention the sequel here. Camillus emerged from his exile to redeem Rome (see *D* 3.1).

6. Livy, *Ab urbe condita* 5.23.5–6, 81.

7. Emphasis added. The status of Machiavelli's promise of eternal

life for a republic is considered in chapter 8.

8. Wolin identifies an element of "religious feeling and imagery" in Machiavelli's thought and points to *Discourses* 3.1, in addition to Machiavelli's call for a savior-prince at the conclusion of *The Prince* (*Politics and Vision*, 204–6).

9. Mansfield, *Taming the Prince*, 132. For Mansfield's discussion of Machiavelli's view of executions generally, see 131–35. Cf. Löwith, *Meaning in History*, 88.

10. Livy, *Ab urbe condita* 3.58.

11. Hulliung also points to Machiavelli's evocative use of Christian terms and maintains that Machiavelli uses them in "an attempt to displace and supplant the Christian world-view with an alternative world-view, one reminiscent of ancient paganism" (*Citizen Machiavelli*, 205). Although I do not differ with Hulliung on the issue of Machiavelli's subversive intent with regard to Christianity, I do maintain, in contrast to Hulliung's view, that Machiavelli retains transformed elements of Christianity in his politics in such a way as to suggest that he admires Christianity. Hulliung does not perceive how Machiavelli both acknowledges the power of Christianity and endeavors to replicate this power in a wholly temporal capacity. See also Pitkin, *Fortune Is a Woman*, 43.

12. The quotation is in Latin in Machiavelli's text.

13. Aquinas, *Summa theologica* 1.103.6–8.

14. Luke 1:53 RSV. See Strauss, *Thoughts on Machiavelli*, 49; and Mansfield, *Machiavelli's New Modes and Orders*, 99. Claude Lefort likens these actions to those of Christ (*Le Travail de l'oeuvre Machiavel* [Paris: Gallimard, 1972], 504).

15. Germino opposes the view that this chapter is anti-Christian. He argues that Philip, not David, is the exemplar of very cruel methods in this chapter: "[Machiavelli] does not say that David was the addressee of the precise words of the *Magnificat*. Nor does he say of David that he made everything new with new governments, new names, new authorities and new men. It was Philip of Macedonia, not King David ("Blasphemy," 151). Nevertheless, Machiavelli uses both David and Philip as examples of rulers who utilized the cruel method of making everything anew.

16. Gilbert, who maintains that Machiavelli recognizes that politics demands a morality divergent from Christian morality, neglects this passage when he cites *Discourses* 1.26 as evidence that "men could arrange their lives in such a manner that they could follow Christian morality" (*Machiavelli and Guicciardini*, 196).

17. Machiavelli's recommendation approximates the injunction of The Unjust Speech of Aristophanes' *Clouds*: Do not do as the gods say, do as they do.

18. By referring in *Discourses* 1.26 to God before Christ's birth, Machiavelli draws a distinction between the Father and the Son. In that same chapter he also draws a comparison between God and Philip on the basis of their recourse to similar methods. With this distinction between the Christian god and Christ and comparison of Philip and God, Machiavelli hints at another likeness between Philip and God: each begat a son who conquered the world. When Machiavelli rejects the example of acquisition that Philip and Alexander offer in favor of a republic, Machiavelli suggests also that such a republic could surpass the acquisitive success even of Christianity.

19. It is relevant to recall here Machiavelli's praise of the free life on the basis that one's children can grow up to be "princes" (*D* 2.2.3). I am indebted to Tarcov for alerting me to the importance of princes in Machiavelli's descriptions of Rome.

20. Cf. Machiavelli's discussion of the *"uno tiranno virtuoso"* in *Discourses* 2.2.

21. According to Livy, Appius Claudius—the same Appius whom Machiavelli contrasts unfavorably to Quintius—used this punishment. When the Volsci attacked his army, Appius's troops took flight. After the melee he called an assembly and dispensed harsh punishment: those who had left their ranks were to be beaten and then beheaded, and of those who remained every tenth man was selected for punishment (cf. Livy, *Ab urbe condita* 2.59.11). Thus Machiavelli vindicates Appius not only by embracing Appius's own severity when he embraces that of Manlius, but also by recommending the very methods of Appius.

22. Mansfield associates this practice with the Christian doctrine of original sin (*Taming the Prince*, 133).

23. Tarcov suggested to me the kinship between some of Machiavelli's comments in the section on ingratitude and certain Christian doctrines.

24. There is a striking similarity between this prince and Valerius, the Roman captain who exemplifies the way of love. Just as a prudent prince will assure that all "the glory and the acquisition" redound to him (*D* 1.30.1), Valerius too was able to portray himself as the cause of good: "Valerius was able to make all humanity arise from him, from which he could acquire the soldiers' favor and their contentedness" (*D* 3.22.3). Of course, Machiavelli rejects the example of Valerius's beneficence for a republic.

25. Matt. 16:26 RSV.

26. Augustine expatiates on the corruption of those who appear to be most innocent—infants (*Confessions* 1.7). Although Prezzolini declares Machiavelli to be an atheist, he notes a similarity between Machiavelli and Augustine on what he labels their moral pessimism

("The Christian Roots of Machiavelli's Moral Pessimism," *Review of National Literatures* 1 [1970]: 26–37). Although I concur with Prezzolini's judgment that Machiavelli promulgates the need for republics to regard all as corrupt, I differ with his further conclusion that Machiavelli maintains a pessimistic view of what can be accomplished in political life. Instead, I maintain that in Machiavelli's view when a republic correctly channels the passions, it can become a conquering state that also restrains all of its princes from overturning its civil life.

27. Mansfield, *New Modes and Orders*, 97.

28. In *Discourses* 3.1 Machiavelli lists Capitolinus's death among those executions that reinvigorated Rome.

29. Livy, *Ab urbe condita* 1.26.9–1. Edmund E. Jacobitti, in his unpublished essay "Community, Pre-reflective Virtue, and the Cyclopean Power of the Fathers: Vico's Reflections on Unexpected Consequences," points out that Horatius's killing of his sister was considered treason against the primal fathers who at this time possessed the absolute right to punish crimes with death. Indeed, Livy notes that the father of the hero on trial asserted that his son had acted justly in killing his sister, and maintained further that if the son had acted unjustly, he would have used his authority as father to punish his son himself.

30. Strauss, *Thoughts*, 135.

31. See Augustine, *City of God* 21.12 and 14.1 and 15, for an exposition of the way God's grace saves those tainted by sin from punishment. Cf. my chapter 1, which discusses Machiavelli's refusal to forgive Cesare for believing in forgiveness.

32. Machiavelli indicates that he understands forgiveness to be central to Christianity in his "Exhortation to Penitence." In this sermon of unknown date, probably delivered before a religious society, he declares: "God the gracious creator has showed us the way for raising ourselves up, which is penitence. . . . What sin will God not forgive you, my brothers, if you sincerely resort to penitence, since he forgave these [sins] to [Saint Peter and David]? And not merely did he forgive them, but he honored them among the highest of those chosen in heaven" (CW 1:173–74). Germino has pointed to this work, in which Machiavelli appears as a "fervent and pious believer," to counter the portrait of him as one bent on the destruction of Christianity ("Second Thoughts on Leo Strauss's Machiavelli," *Journal of Politics* 28 [1966]: 794–817; see also his more recent piece, "Blasphemy," 146–56). Although I concur with Germino's assessment of the work's importance, I believe that it should be read in light of his criticism of Rome for its forgiveness of its captains in the *Discourses*. As that criticism shows, Machiavelli rejects forgiveness as bad political policy: Rome's gratitude toward its great men fostered enough arrogance for them to attempt to transcend its civil life.

Even in the sermon he suggests that God's embrace of penitent sinners encourages others in crime. Thus, in promulgating the centrality of forgiveness to Christianity, Machiavelli is also fostering an arrogance that itself could be dangerous to Christianity's reign.

33. Harvey C. Mansfield, Jr., "Machiavelli's New Regime," *Italian Quarterly* 52 (1970): 67–70.

34. In *The Prince* Machiavelli praises Cesare Borgia's execution of his minister who had come to be hated by the people of the Romagna: "to purge the spirits of that people and to gain them entirely to himself, [Cesare] wished to show that if any cruelty had been committed, this had not come from him but from the harsh nature of his minister. And having seized this opportunity, he had him placed one morning in the piazza at Cesena in two pieces, with a piece of wood and a bloody knife beside him. The ferocity of this spectacle left the people at once satisfied and stupefied" (*P* 7.30). Thus, Machiavelli again adopts the ways of lone rule to a republic.

35. Plutarch in *The Life of Caesar* relates that Sulla had contemplated having Caesar put to death as a youth (1.2–3) and that, later, Piso and Catulus blamed Cicero for sparing Caesar's life when, as still a young man, he was elected high priest (7).

Chapter 8: Machiavelli's Rule and Human Liberty

1. Wolin maintains that "to an important degree, the difference between *The Prince* and *The Discourses* consists in a greater appreciation on Machiavelli's part of the political capabilities of the masses and correspondingly greater doubts about the utility of political heroes" (*Politics and Vision*, 229). Although in the *Discourses* Machiavelli praises the ability of the masses to maintain orders, he still expresses doubts about their capabilities.

2. On this issue Pocock argues that according to Machiavelli the "many" of Rome had "moral sagacity enough to elect and defer to their natural superiors in the civic elite" (*Machiavellian Moment*, 202). Cf. Skinner, *Renaissance*, 159–60).

3. This result is in accord with his neglect of Polybius's assertion that the city's justice is founded in nature. See my discussion of *Discourses* 1.2 in chapter 4.

4. Thucydides' discussion of the early history of the Greek cities points to a similar view of the relation between nature and necessity, and helps us understand the process that seems to be at work here. Thucydides finds that those cities founded in fertile places came to grief because nature's gifts allowed some to amass wealth easily, which in turn created domestic turmoil. Because this turmoil attracted the

attention of foreign invaders, these wealthy cities often suffered through changes of population, in addition to the changes of regime that were a consequence of their internal division. In contrast those cities in more forbidding places ultimately prospered because their citizens lacked such opportunity for amassing wealth; the populace was more united, and stable governments were the result. Their stability in turn attracted refugees of war from the other cities who sought a more tranquil environment. A consideration of such evidence suggests that a sterile site is the more worthy of choice (1.2). I am grateful to Tarcov for alerting me to this contrast.

5. Mount Athos has furnished the home for a community of monks since the tenth century.

6. Mansfield relates Deinocrates' plan to the city of Plato's *Republic*, which is modeled upon an individual soul ("Necessity in the Beginnings of Cities," 119).

7. *Discourses*, trans. Walker, 2:173.

8. Aquinas, *De regimine principum*, in *Aquinas: Selected Political Writings*, trans. J. G. Dawson (Oxford: Blackwell, 1948), 2-3.

9. Aristotle, *Politics* 1253a10-11, trans. H. Rackham (Loeb Classical Library), 11.

10. Rahe examines in depth the significance of the moderns' rejection of the Aristotelian conception of *logos*. See, particularly, *Republics, Ancient and Modern*, 34-41 and 249-67.

11. Cf. *D* 1.2 and Polybius, *Histories* 6.5.7.

12. Machiavelli's neglect of fraudulent religious appeals is wholly consistent with *Discourses* 3.33, in which Machiavelli enumerates ways to render an army resolute and then adds that the "Romans used to make their armies pick up this confidence by way of religion" (*D* 3.33.1). Religious fraud was merely the way of the Romans and need not be employed in every instance.

13. Livy, *Ab urbe condita* 4.28.4, 349. See Mansfield, *New Modes and Orders*, 357-58.

14. E.g., Plato, *Laws* 624a.

WORKS CITED

Allen, J. W. *A History of Political Thought in the Sixteenth Century.* London: Methuen, 1928.

Aquinas. *De regimine principum.* In *Aquinas: Selected Political Writings.* Trans. J. G. Dawson. Oxford: Blackwell, 1948.

——. *Summa contra gentiles.* Trans. Charles J. O'Neil. Notre Dame: Notre Dame University, 1975.

——. *Summa Theologiae.* 60 vols. New York: McGraw-Hill, 1963.

Aristotle. *Politics.* Trans. H. Rackham. Loeb Classical Library.

Augustine. *City of God.* Trans. William M. Green. Loeb Classical Library.

Bacon, Francis. *The Essays.* Edited by John Pitcher. London: Penguin Books, 1985.

Baron, Hans. "Machiavelli: The Republican Citizen and the Author of 'The Prince.'" *English Historical Review* 76 (1961): 217–53.

——. "The *Principe* and the Puzzle of the Date of Chapter 26." *Journal of Medieval and Renaissance Studies* 21 (spring 1991): 83–102.

Barraclough, Geoffrey. *Origins of Modern Germany.* Oxford: Basil Blackwell, 1947.

Berlin, Isaiah. "The Originality of Machiavelli." In *Against the Current.* New York: Viking Press, 1980.

Bonadeo, Alfredo. *Corruption, Conflict, and Power in the Works and Times of Niccolò Machiavelli.* Berkeley and Los Angeles: University of California Press, 1973.

Burckhardt, Jacob. *The Civilization of the Renaissance in Italy.* Trans. S. G. C. Middlemore. New York: Harper Torchbooks, 1958.

Cambridge History of Later Medieval Philosophy, The. Edited by Norman Kretzmann, Anthony Kenny, and Jan Pinborg. Cambridge: Cambridge University Press, 1982.

Cassirer, Ernst. *The Myth of the State.* New Haven: Yale University Press, 1946.

Chabod, Federico. *Machiavelli and the Renaissance.* Trans. David Moore. 1958. Reprint, New York: Harper & Row, 1965.

Cochrane, Eric. "Machiavelli: 1940–1960." *The Journal of Modern History* 33 (June 1961): 113–36.

Dante Alighieri. *De monarchia.* Trans. Herbert W. Schneider. Indianapolis: Library of Liberal Arts, 1957.

de Grazia, Sebastian. *Machiavelli in Hell.* Princeton: Princeton University Press, 1989.

Dietz, Mary. "Trapping the Prince: Machiavelli and the Politics of Deception." *American Political Science Review* 80 (September 1986): 777–99.

Flanagan, Thomas. "The Concept of *Fortuna* in Machiavelli." In *The Political Calculus: Essays on Machiavelli's Philosophy,* edited by Anthony Parel. Toronto: University of Toronto Press, 1972.

Geerken, John H. "Machiavelli Studies since 1969." *Journal of the History of Ideas* 37 (1976): 351–68.

Germino, Dante. "Blasphemy and Leo Strauss's Machiavelli." *Review of Politics* 53 (winter 1991): 146–56.

———. "Second Thoughts on Leo Strauss's Machiavelli." *Journal of Politics* 28 (1966): 794–817.

Gibbon, Edward. *Decline and Fall of the Roman Empire.* 3 vols. New York: Modern Library, n.d.

Gilbert, Felix. *Machiavelli and Guicciardini: Politics and History in Sixteenth-Century Florence.* 1965. Reprint, New York: Norton, 1984.

———. "Machiavelli in Modern Historical Scholarship." *Italian Quarterly* 14 (1970): 9–26.

———. "Machiavellism." In *History: Choice and Commitment.* Cambridge, Mass.: Belknap Press, 1977.

Grant, Robert M. *Augustus to Constantine: The Rise and Triumph of Christianity in the Roman World.* San Francisco: Harper & Row, 1970.

Guicciardini, Francesco. *The History of Italy*. Trans. Sidney Alexander. New York: Macmillan, 1969.

Hexter, J. H. "Seyssel, Machiavelli, and Polybius VI: The Mystery of the Missing Translation." *Studies in the Renaissance* 3 (1956): 75–96.

Hulliung, Mark. *Citizen Machiavelli*. Princeton: Princeton University Press, 1983.

Jacobitti, Edmund E. "Community, Pre-reflective Virtue, and the Cyclopean Power of the Fathers: Vico's Reflections on Unexpected Consequences." Unpublished essay.

Juvenal. *Satires*. Trans. G. G. Ramsay. Loeb Classical Library, 1928.

Kahn, Victoria. *Machiavellian Rhetoric: From the Counter-Reformation to Milton*. Princeton: Princeton University Press, 1994.

Kamen, Henry. *The Spanish Inquisition*. New York: New American Library, 1965.

Lefort, Claude. *Le Travail de l'oeuvre Machiavel*. Paris: Gallimard, 1972.

Livy. *Ab urbe condita*. Trans. B. O. Foster. Loeb Classical Library.

Löwith, Karl. *Meaning in History*. Chicago: University of Chicago Press, 1949.

Machiavelli, Niccolò. *The Discourses of Niccolò Machiavelli*. Trans. Leslie J. Walker. 2 vols. New Haven: Yale University Press, 1950.

———. *Discourses on Livy*. Trans. Harvey C. Mansfield and Nathan Tarcov. Chicago: University of Chicago Press, 1996.

———. *Florentine Histories*. Trans. Laura F. Banfield and Harvey C. Mansfield, Jr. Princeton: Princeton University Press, 1988.

———. *Machiavelli: The Chief Works and Others*. Trans. Allan Gilbert. 3 vols. Durham: Duke University Press, 1989.

———. *Machiavelli: Selected Political Writings*. Trans. David Wootton. Indianapolis: Hackett, 1994.

———. *Machiavelli: Tutte le opere*. Edited by Mario Martelli. Florence: Sansoni, 1971.

———. *The Prince*. Trans. Harvey C. Mansfield, Jr. Chicago: University of Chicago Press, 1985.

Mansfield, Harvey C., Jr. "An Introduction to Machiavelli's *Art of War*." Unpublished essay.

———. *Machiavelli's New Modes and Orders: A Study of the "Discourses on Livy."* Ithaca: Cornell University Press, 1979.

———. "Machiavelli's New Regime." *Italian Quarterly* 52 (1970): 63–95.

———. "Machiavelli's Political Science." *American Political Science Review* 75 (1981): 293–305.

————. "Necessity in the Beginnings of Cities." In *The Political Calculus: Essays on Machiavelli's Philosophy*, edited by Anthony Parel. Toronto: University of Toronto Press, 1972.

————. *Taming the Prince: The Ambivalence of Modern Executive Power*. New York: Free Press, 1989.

Meinecke, Friedrich. *Machiavellism: The Doctrine of Raison d'Etat and Its Place in Modern History*. Trans. Douglas Scott. New Haven: Yale University Press, 1957.

Najemy, John M. *Between Friends: Discourses of Power and Desire in the Machiavelli-Vettori Letters of 1513–1515*. Princeton: Princeton University Press, 1993.

Nietzsche, Friedrich. *Beyond Good and Evil: Prelude to a Philosophy of the Future*. Trans. Walter Kaufmann. New York: Vintage Books, 1966.

Orwin. Clifford. "Machiavelli's Unchristian Charity." *American Political Science Review* 72 (1978): 1217–28.

Parel, Anthony J. *The Machiavellian Cosmos*. New Haven: Yale University Press, 1992.

————. "Machiavelli's Method and His Interpreters." In *The Political Calculus: Essays on Machiavelli's Philosophy*, edited by Anthony Parel. Toronto: University of Toronto Press, 1972.

Pitkin, Hanna Fenichel. *Fortune Is a Woman: Gender and Politics in the Thought of Niccolò Machiavelli*. Berkeley: University of California Press, 1984.

Plamenatz, John. *Man and Society: A Critical Examination of Some Important Social and Political Theories from Machiavelli to Marx*. 2 vols. London: Longman, Green, 1963.

Plato. *Critias*. Trans. R. G. Bury. Loeb Classical Library.

————. *Laws*. Trans. R. G. Bury. Loeb Classical Library.

————. *Timaeus*. Trans. R. G. Bury. Loeb Classical Library.

Plutarch. *Lives*. Trans. Bernadotte Perrin. Loeb Classical Library.

Pocock, J. G. A. *The Machiavellian Moment: Florentine Political Thought and the Atlantic Republican Tradition*. Princeton: Princeton University Press, 1975.

Polybius. *Histories*. Trans. W. R. Paton. Loeb Classical Library, 1923.

Prescott, William H. *History of the Reign of Ferdinand and Isabella, the Catholic, of Spain*. 3d ed. 3 vols. London: Richard Bentley, 1842.

Prezzolini, Giuseppe. "The Christian Roots of Machiavelli's Moral Pessimism." *Review of National Literatures* 1 (1970): 26–37.

————. *Machiavelli*. Trans. Gioconda Savini. New York: Farrar, Straus & Giroux, 1967.

Rahe, Paul. *Republics Ancient and Modern: Classical Republicanism and the American Revolution.* Chapel Hill: University of North Carolina Press, 1992.

Ridolfi, Roberto. *Life of Niccolò Machiavelli.* Trans. Cecil Grayson. Chicago: University of Chicago Press, 1963.

Schevill, Ferdinand. *History of Florence from the Founding of the City through the Renaissance.* New York: Harcourt, Brace, 1936.

Scott, John T., and Vickie B. Sullivan. "Patricide and the Plot of *The Prince*: Cesare Borgia and Machiavelli's Italy." *American Political Science Review* 88 (December 1994): 887–99.

Skinner, Quentin. *The Foundations of Modern Political Thought.* 2 vols. Cambridge: Cambridge University Press, 1978.

———. *Machiavelli.* Past Masters Series, edited by Keith Thomas. New York: Hill and Wang, 1981.

———. "Machiavelli's *Discorsi* and the Pre-humanist Origins of Republican Ideas." In *Machiavelli and Republicanism,* edited by Gisela Bock, Quentin Skinner, and Maurizio Viroli. Cambridge: Cambridge University Press, 1990.

Strauss, Leo. "Niccolò Machiavelli." In *History of Political Thought,* edited by Leo Strauss and Joseph Cropsey. 3d ed. Chicago: University of Chicago Press, 1987.

———. "Restatement on Xenophon's *Hiero.*" In *On Tyranny,* edited by Victor Gourevitch and Michael S. Roth. Rev. ed. New York: Free Press, 1991.

———. *Thoughts on Machiavelli.* Chicago: University of Chicago Press, 1958.

———. "What Is Political Philosophy?" In *What Is Political Philosophy? and Other Studies.* 1959. Reprint, Chicago: University of Chicago Press, 1988.

Sullivan, Vickie B. "Machiavelli's Momentary 'Machiavellian Moment': A Reconsideration of Pocock's Treatment of the *Discourses.*" *Political Theory* 20 (1992): 309–18.

Tacitus. *Annals.* Trans. John Jackson. Loeb Classical Library.

Tarcov, Nathan. "Machiavelli's *Discourses on the First Decade of Titus Livy.*" Unpublished lecture delivered at Claremont McKenna College, 14 March 1993.

Thucydides. *Peloponnesian War.* Trans. Charles Forster Smith. Loeb Classical Library.

Toffanin, Giuseppe. *History of Humanism.* Trans. Elio Gianturco. New York: Las Americas, 1954.

Troeltsch, Ernst. *The Social Teaching of the Christian Church.* Trans. Olive Wyon. 2 vols. 1931. Reprint, Louisville: Westminster/John Knox Press, 1992.

Villari, Pasquale. *The Life and Times of Niccolò Machiavelli.* Trans. Linda Villari. 2 vols. London: T. Fisher Unwin, n.d.

Viroli, Maurizio. *From Politics to Reason of State: The Acquisition and Transformation of the Language of Politics, 1250–1600.* Cambridge: Cambridge University Press, 1992.

———. "Machiavelli and the Republican Idea of Politics." In *Machiavelli and Republicanism,* edited by Gisela Bock, Quentin Skinner, and Maurizio Viroli. Cambridge: Cambridge University Press, 1990.

Voegelin, Eric. Review of *On Tyranny,* by Leo Strauss. *Review of Politics* 11 (April 1949): 241–44.

Whitfield, J. H. *Discourses on Machiavelli.* Cambridge: W. Heffer, 1969.

Wolin, Sheldon. *Politics and Vision: Continuity and Innovation in Western Political Thought.* Boston: Little, Brown, 1960.

INDEX

the Church, 30; empire and, 96–101; foreign influence and, 96–101; inequality and, 85–86; leisure and, 12–14; reformation and, 124–31; republicanism and, 166

Cropsey, Joseph, 193n.10

Cruelty, 44–47, 149–53, 158

Cycle of regimes, 90–95, 210n.18

Cyrus, 136, 213n.10

Dante Alighieri, 52, 57, 76, 206n.35

David (biblical), 144–45, 158, 216n.15

de Grazia, Sebastian, 4, 11, 192n.4, 199n.34, 200n.45, 202n.10

Deinocrates, 184, 220n.6

Democracy, 90–95

Dietz, Mary, 215n.29

Diodorus, 215n.4

Discourses on Livy, 4, 6, 8–13, 18, 23, 25–26, 29–30, 32–35, 95, 197n.15, 200n.36; agrarian reform and, 66–72; ambiguity of, 38–41; ancient Rome as inspiration, 57–59, 174–90; Christian piety and, 36–41, 48–55; Christian republic and, 162–71; citation of Jesus Christ, 155–56; corruption and, 124–45; corruption in ancient Rome and, 81–87, 99; empire and, 63–80, 100; fortresses and, 202n.18; human order and, 201n.3; leisure and, 65; paganism and, 104–17; republicanism and, 147–71; Roman captains and, 148–53; Sparta

and, 207n.2; youth and, 87–95

Divination, 109

Dominick (saint), 30, 32, 155, 201n.8

Education, 45–49

Elections, 31–32, 86, 92, 107

Empire, 96–101; republicanism and, 63–80; tumult and, 63–74

England, 198n.21

Epicureanism, 11

Etruscans, 173–74

Eugene (pope), 208n.15

Fabius Maximus Cunctator, 213n.13

Fabius Maximus Rullianus, Quintus, 155, 169

Ferdinand (king of Spain), 28, 42–45, 202n.11–15, 203n.19; cruelty of, 44–45, 48

Flanagan, Thomas, 205n.30

Flood, image of, 133–37

Florence, 11, 13, 29, 46, 197n.17, 212n.5; class conflict and, 199n.26; foreign powers and (*see* Italy); Rome and, 17–18

Florentine Histories, 4, 10, 12, 13, 18, 23–24, 26–27, 35, 130, 175, 195n.5, 197n.14, 198n.23, 199n.25, 200n.37, 208n.16, 209n.6; Christianity and, 141; reputation in a state and, 74–75; sects and, 75

Foreign influence, 24–29, 96–101. *See also specific cities, countries*